DATE DUE

MY 3 0 '96	JE 9 '04		
SE 28 '96	NO 1 2 09		
MAY 2 0 1997			
AG 8 '97			
SE 9 '97			
16 9 7 ON			
NO 6 9			
FE 13 '98			
MR 6 '98			
RENEW			
AP 10			
SE 18 '98			
SE 26 00			
MY 1 8 04			
JE 8 04			

Keeping the Books

Other books by the same authors:

Anatomy of a Business Plan

The Home-Based Entrepreneur

Target Marketing for the Small Business

Steps to Small Business Start Up

The Woman Entrepreneur

Keeping the Books

BASIC RECORDKEEPING AND ACCOUNTING FOR THE SMALL BUSINESS

Linda Pinson

and

Jerry Jinnett

UPSTART PUBLISHING COMPANY, INC.
The Small Business Publishing Company
Dover, New Hampshire

Published by Upstart Publishing Company, Inc.
A Division of Dearborn Publishing Group, Inc.
12 Portland Street
Dover, New Hampshire 03820
(800) 235-8866 or (603) 749-5071

Neither the author nor the publisher of this book is engaged in rendering, by the sale of this book, legal, accounting or other professional services. The reader is encouraged to employ the services of a competent professional in such matters.

First published in 1989 by
Out of Your Mind . . . And Into the Marketplace™

Library of Congress Cataloging-in-Publication Data

Pinson, Linda.
    Keeping the books : basic recordkeeping and accounting for the small business / Linda Pinson and Jerry Jinnett. — 2nd ed.
      p.   cm.
    Includes Index.
    ISBN 0-936894-47-4
    1. Bookkeeping. 2 Small business—United States. I. Jinnett, Jerry. II. Title.
    HF5635.P649   1993
    657' .2—dc20   93-20087
                                                          CIP

Cover design by Phillip Augusta, Portsmouth, NH.

Printed in the United States of America
10 9 8 7 6 5 4 3 2

For a complete catalog of Upstart's small business publications, call (800) 235-8866.

TABLE OF CONTENTS

Dedication

This book is dedicated to Virginia Haverty, a wonderful friend who is now gone, but not forgotten. Her gifts of encouragement and confidence live on in the completion of our books.

Acknowledgment

We would like to take this opportunity to thank two people who have generously given of their time to help us to improve the quality of this book. The first is Marilyn Dauber, C.P.A., who contributed the indispensible last chapter entitled "Analyzing Financial Statements." We would also like to recognize Judee Slack, Enrolled Agent, who spent a great deal of her time going through the entire book to check it for correctness of content and who provided us with all the current tax forms.

We would also like to thank all of our students and readers. Our books are better because of the input we have received from classes and individual users.

Last but not least, we thank our families who have put up with the many inconveniences caused by our single-mindedness while writing all of our books. With their encouragement, understanding and patience, we have found it much easier to reach our goals.

—Linda and Jerry

Recordkeeping Basics

The keeping of accurate records is imperative if you are going to succeed at business. From time to time, we have had students in our small business classes who have wonderful ideas for products or services, but who do not want to be bothered with the details of recordkeeping. Their businesses are already doomed to failure. This book was written with the assumption that you are starting from scratch and know nothing about the recordkeeping process. We have tried to solve the puzzle for you. By the time you have finished applying the principles in the book, we hope that you will understand how all of the pieces fit together to develop a simple, but accurate set of books.

FUNCTIONS OF RECORDKEEPING

The first, and most important, function is to provide you with information that will help you to see the trends that are taking place within your operation. You will see, as you study this book, that a complete and simple set of records will make it possible to tell at a glance what is happening with your business—which areas are productive and cost-effective and which will require the implementation of changes. The second function of recordkeeping is to provide you with income tax information that can be easily retrieved and verified.

WHO SHOULD DO YOUR RECORDKEEPING?

YOU, the business owner, should be personally involved rather than delegating this job to an outsider. Keeping your own books and records will make you doubly aware of what is going on in your business **and** it will also save you money that can be used to benefit your business in other areas. For example, you may now be able to afford a piece of effective advertising that will generate more sales. Even if time will not allow you to keep your own records and you assign the task to someone else, it will be a major benefit to you to make every attempt to understand how your records are organized and to learn how to read and use them to make decisions in your business.

Do You Need an Accountant?

We do not advocate the elimination of an accounting professional. In fact, end-of-the-year tax accounting requires special expertise and will best be handled by an accountant who can maximize your tax benefits. You will have to decide whether to use a C.P.A., Enrolled Agent (Tax Accountant) or non-certified accountant. The first two are empowered to represent you at an IRS audit. The accountant is dependent on the financial information that you provide. To ensure the most profitable results for your business, you will need to set up and maintain general records as the source of financial data. You should also work with the accountant to establish a good line of communication and a smooth flow of that data.

Depending on the size and scope of your business, you will have to decide which of the recordkeeping chores you can handle and which ones should be delegated to an expert. For instance, you may be able to do all of your accounting except for payroll, which is very exacting and will probably be more effectively handled by your accountant. You may also decide that you would like to use an accountant at the end of the month to generate your financial statements. In fact, if the scope of your business becomes very large, it may become necessary to turn over your entire accounting operation to an expert. If so, it will still be imperative that you understand the process, so you will be able to use your financial information to make sound business decisions.

Accounting Software

One of the most frequently asked questions is about which accounting software programs will make the process easy. There are many programs on the market today that will adequately take care of your needs. However, if you do not understand the recordkeeping basics, you will not know how to tailor the program to your business or feed in the proper information. You may best be served by beginning with a manual system. You can always translate it into a computer application as the need arises. At that time, if you are working with an accountant, it will probably be best to use a program that he or she suggests and one that will easily interface with what is currently being used in that office.

Every Business is Unique

The system you use must be tailored to your individual needs. Obviously a service-oriented industry will not use the same records as a retail business. Because no two businesses will have exactly the same concerns, it is imperative that you develop your own system. You will have to consider any information that will be used by your particular venture and set up your records according to those needs.

WHEN DOES RECORDKEEPING BEGIN?

Your business commences as soon as you begin to refine your idea. You do not have to wait until you have a license and are open for business to start with your recordkeeping. In fact, you will do yourself a great disservice if you are not keeping records at this very moment. Many of your initial expenses are deductible if you have begun to actively pursue your business. A good way to begin is as follows:

DEDUCTIBLE EXPENSES: The first thing you should do is familiarize yourself with the expenses that are commonly deductible for a business. When you are doing things that relate to your business, begin to think of the costs involved and record them for future use. (See pp. 4-5.)

DIARY: Buy yourself a hardbound journal at your local stationers. Keep a diary of your thoughts and actions related to your new business. Number the pages, write in pen and initial any corrections you make. Your journal will serve to protect your idea as well as provide you with a record of your contacts and the information you gather for the future. You can also list any expenses incurred and file away your receipts. Be sure to date all entries.

BEGINNING JOURNAL: I like to utilize the last few pages of the journal to keep a record of Income and Expenses during the planning stages of a business. It need not be complicated. You can set it up like the sample provided on page 6.

SIMPLICITY IS THE KEY

Simplicity is the key to small business accounting. Your records must be complete, but not so complicated that they cannot be read and interpreted. It will be the function of this book to not only introduce you to the terminology and forms necessary to set up a recordkeeping system for your business, but to enable you to actually set up records that will give you the information you need to satisfy tax requirements, examine trends and implement changes that will make your business venture more profitable and rewarding.

INFORMATION AND SAMPLE FORM: The next two pages contain information on Common Deductible Expenses. On page 6 there is an example of a Beginning Journal.

COMMON DEDUCTIBLE EXPENSES

The list on the next page will help you to identify many of those items that are normally deductible for income tax purposes. The new business owner should become familiar with those appropriate to the business. DO NOT wait until tax preparation time to look at this list. Knowing ahead of time which expenses are deductible will help you to better utilize them to your advantage while keeping proper records for income tax verification and business analysis. DO keep in mind that this is only a partial list. There may very well be additional deductible expenses relating to your business. Call or visit the IRS. They have free publications that will answer many of your questions. Another source of information is your accountant. Be sure to have documentation for all expenses so you can verify them if you are audited.

FULLY DEDUCTIBLE OR DEPRECIABLE?

Expenses fall into two major categories: 1) Those that are deductible in their entirety in the year in which they are incurred, and 2) Those items that are depreciated and deducted over a fixed number of years.

1. FULLY DEDUCTIBLE EXPENSES: All expenses incurred in the operation of your business are deductible in their entirety in the year in which they occur and reduce your net income by their amount unless they are major expenses that fall in the depreciable assets category. Expenses will have to be itemized for tax purposes and receipts should be easily retrievable for verification.

2. DEPRECIABLE EXPENSES: If you buy business property that has an expected life in excess of one year and that is not intended for resale, it is considered depreciable property. The cost (generally in excess of $100.00) must be spread over more than one year and the depreciation deductions claimed over the useful life or recovery period of the property. They generally include such tangible assets as buildings, vehicles, machinery and equipment and also intangible properties such as copyrights or franchises. Depreciation is taken at a fixed rate. The portion allowed for the current year is deducted as an expense.

Under Code Section 179, you can elect to treat all or part of the cost of certain qualifying property as an expense rather than as a depreciable asset. The total cost you can elect to deduct for a tax year cannot exceed $10,000. This maximum applies to each taxpayer and not to each business operated by a taxpayer.

CAUTION: Be sure that you do not list the same costs of any purchase as both a deductible expense and a depreciable asset. For example, if you have purchased a computer for $3,000 and you are depreciating it, be sure that it is not also listed as a fully deductible expense under office equipment.

HOME OFFICE EXPENSES: In order for your home to qualify as a business expense, that part of your home used for business must be used "exclusively and on a regular basis." For further information on what is and is not allowed, send for free IRS Publication #587, *Business Use of Your Home.*

COMMON DEDUCTIBLE EXPENSES

Note: Please read the text on the previous page for more information on deductions. There may be other expenses that apply to your business. Those listed below are the most common deductions.

DEDUCTIONS TO BE EXPENSED

ADVERTISING - yellow pages, news-paper, radio, direct mail, etc.

BAD DEBTS - from sales or services

BANK CHARGES - checks, etc.

BOOKS & PERIODICALS - bus. related

CAR & TRUCK EXPENSES - gas, repair, license, insurance, maintenance.

COMMISSIONS - to sales reps.

CONTRACT SERVICES - Independent

CONVENTION EXPENSES

DISPLAY & EXHIBIT EXPENSES

DONATIONS

DUES - professional

EDUCATIONAL FEES & MATERIALS

ELECTRIC BILLS

ENTERTAINMENT OF CLIENTS

FREIGHT - UPS, FedEx, Postal, etc.

GAS BILLS

IMPROVEMENTS - under $100.00

INSURANCE - business-related

INTEREST PAID OUT

LAUNDRY/CLEANING - uniforms, etc.

LEGAL & PROFESSIONAL FEES

LICENSE FEES - business license

MAINTENANCE - material & labor

OFFICE EQUIPMENT - under $100

OFFICE FURNITURE - under $100

OFFICE SUPPLIES

PARKING FEES

PENSION & PROFIT-SHARING PLANS

POSTAGE

PRINTING EXPENSES

PROFESSIONAL SERVICES

PROMOTIONAL MATERIALS

PROPERTY TAX

PUBLICATIONS

RENT

REPAIRS

REFUNDS, RETURNS & ALLOWANCES

SALES TAX - sales tax collected is offset by reimbursement to the State Board of Equalization

SALES TAX PAID - purchases

SUBSCRIPTIONS

TELEPHONE

TOOLS - used in trade and with a purchase price under $100

UNIFORMS PURCHASED

UTILITIES - see gas, electric, and telephone

WAGES PAID OUT

TO BE DEPRECIATED*

* *Section 179 Deduction - You may elect to expense rather than depreciate all or part of qualifying fixed assets (up to $10,000 a year). Check with your accountant.*

BUSINESS PROPERTY - not land

OFFICE FURNITURE - over $100

OFFICE EQUIPMENT - over $100

PRODUCTION MACHINERY

TANGIBLE PURCHASES - used for business and costing over $100 (not intended for resale)

TOOLS - purchase price over $100

VEHICLES - percentage used for business purposes only

ABC COMPANY
BEGINNING JOURNAL

Date	1. Check # 2. Cash 3. C/Card	Paid To or Received From	Explanation of Income or Expense	Income		Expense	
1/07/93	Pers. Ck 1476	Coastline Comm. College	Registration Fee "Small Business Start Up"			65	00
1/09/93	CASH	Tam's Stationers	Office Supplies			25	63
1/17/93	CASH	Ace Hardware	Tools			71	80
2/03/93	VISA	A-1 Computer	486-33 Computer			1821	34
2/04/93	P. Check 1493	AT&T	January telephone business calls			52	00

REMEMBER: All expenses relating to your new business endeavors should be recorded. A few examples are as follows:

1. Conference, seminar and workshop fees
2. Mileage to and from business pursuits
3. Meals related to business (see tax rulings)
4. Books, tapes, videos, etc. purchased for business
5. Office supplies (notebooks, journals, pens, etc.)
6. Telephone calls relating to business
7. Professional organizations (dues, fees, etc.)
8. Materials used for developing your product
9. Tools or equipment purchased for your business

There are many other business expenses, including those mentioned under the pages on "Common Deductible Expenses." A good rule-of-thumb is that when a purchase or activity seems to have any possible bearing on your business, journalize it, keep receipts, look up tax rulings and then use the information accordingly.

Income and Expenses

Accounting for small businesses is based on one premise. Every transaction that takes place involves money that is earned, spent, infused into or taken out of the business. All earnings and monies spent as a result of doing business fall under one of two classifications, **Income (or Revenue)** and **Expenses**. Before you set up your records, it is necessary to understand some basic facts about the two terms.

INCOME (OR REVENUE)

Income is all the monies received by your business in any given period of time. It is made up of monies derived from retail sales, wholesale sales, sale of services, interest income and any miscellaneous income.

You will want to be sure that you do not mix income with expenses. Under no circumstance do you use monies received to purchase goods and plan to deposit the remainder. A simple formula for tax accounting requires that your **income equals your deposits**. It is interesting to note that the IRS does not require you to keep copies of your receipt book if you follow this formula. The *income equals deposit equation* is supported by the 1986 Tax Reform.

EXPENSES

Expenses are all monies paid out by your business. They include those paid by check and those paid by cash. All require careful recording. Expenses fall into distinct categories:

1. COST OF GOODS TO BE SOLD (INVENTORY)

a. The cost of the merchandise or inventory sold during an accounting period.

b. Included are material and labor or the purchase price of manufactured goods.

2. VARIABLE EXPENSES (SELLING, DIRECT)

a. Those expenses directly related to your product or service.

b. Includes advertising, production salaries, shipping, vehicle expenses, machinery and equipment and any product or service overhead (also known as controllable).

3. FIXED EXPENSES (ADMINISTRATIVE, INDIRECT)

a. These are costs not directly related to your production or rendering of services. They are the type of expenses that all businesses have in common.

b. Includes normal overhead (fixed expenses) such as office salaries, rents, licenses, office supplies, utilities, insurance, etc. Administrative expenses are those that usually remain constant if your business suddenly ceases production or services for a period of time.

3. OTHER EXPENSES

a. Interest Expense

b. Monies paid out for interest on purchases, loans, etc.

NOTE: Some categories of expense may be divided into both selling and administrative and selling expenses. Examples are:

Utilities - Those used for production as differentiated from utilities consumed in the office, heating, restrooms, etc.

Telephone - Telemarketing and advertising are selling expenses. Monthly charges and office telephone charges are administrative expenses.

Freight and Postage - Shipping of your product is a selling expense. Postage used as office overhead is an administrative expense.

The categories that certain expenses should be placed in can be confusing. The important thing to remember is that all expenses must be recorded somewhere. If you erroneously record a selling expense as an administrative expense, it will not carry any serious consequence. However, if you can properly classify expense information, you will have a good basis for analyzing your business and implementing changes.

Essential Records for Small Business

Every small business will require certain records to keep track of its activities during the fiscal year. The most common are as follows:

1. General Journal
2. General Ledger
3. Revenue & Expense Journal*
4. Petty Cash Record
5. Inventory Records
6. Fixed Assets Log
7. Accounts Receivable
8. Accounts Payable
9. Payroll Records
10. Transportation, Entertainment and Travel Records
11. Customer Records
12. Business Checkbook
13. Filing System

The Revenue & Expense Journal is the Single Entry alternate for the General Journal and General Ledger. This will be explained during this chapter's discussion of General Records.

Again, we would like to emphasize the need to keep your records as simple as possible. You will need to think about all the things that will pertain to your business and then determine the simplest way to have the information at your fingertips. We will discuss each of the above records, try to show you how they may be used, and finally give you an example of the form each can take. You will have to adapt these records to serve your particular business. Eliminate any that are unnecessary. For instance, if you are a repair business and your customers pay you when you perform your service, you will not need an "Accounts Receivable" record. You may also wish to develop new records that will help you to keep track of information that will make your business more effective.

FORMAT

All of your records will be utilized in the development of your financial statements. For this reason, it will be important to use forms that have been developed using an accepted format. The forms discussed in this section will provide you with records that are easy to use and interpret both by you and by anyone else who has occasion to retrieve information pertaining to your business.

SINGLE AND DOUBLE ENTRY SYSTEMS

There are two basic bookkeeping methods: 1) Single Entry and 2) Double Entry. In the past, only double entry accounting was thought to be proper for businesses. However, it is now generally recognized that a single entry system will adequately serve most smaller businesses. As the business grows and becomes more complex, it may then become more effective to move into double entry accounting.

SINGLE ENTRY

This is a term referring to a recordkeeping system that uses only income and expense accounts. Its main requirement is a Revenue & Expense Journal which you maintain on a daily basis for recording receipts and expenditures. You will need to keep General Records in which you record petty cash, fixed assets, accounts payable and receivable, inventory, mileage, travel and entertainment and customer information. (Note: Payroll will be discussed later and should be handled by your accountant.) Single Entry Recordkeeping is the easier of the two systems to understand and maintain and can be extremely effective and 100 percent verifiable.

DOUBLE ENTRY ACCOUNTING

This is a bookkeeping and accounting method by which every transaction is recorded twice. This is based on the premise that every transaction has two sides. A sale, for example, is both a delivery of goods and a receipt of payment. On your Balance Sheet, the delivery of goods would be recorded as a credit (reduction of assets), while the payment would be counted as a debit (increase of assets). You should note that the words debit and credit do not have the usual connotation in this application. The two halves of the double entry always have to be equal. Many small businesses use only the single entry system, while larger businesses, especially partnerships and corporations, will need to set up their accounting by the double entry system. A clear understanding of the double entry system is necessary before using this method. A thorough study may be made from resources in your local library—or you may wish to have your accountant set it up for you.

Be Sure to Read This

In the next nine pages, you will be introduced to some basic information on double entry accounting. Unless your business is larger and more complex, you will not need to set up this type of system. You will only need a single entry system. Talk to your accounting professional if you are in doubt.

SMALLER BUSINESSES REQUIRING SINGLE ENTRY SKIP TO THE REVENUE AND EXPENSE JOURNAL

You will not use a General Journal or General Ledger for single entry recordkeeping. However, you may wish to familiarize yourself with the double entry concept and then skip ahead to the Revenue & Expense Journal where you will begin setting up your own recordkeeping as described in the rest of the chapter.

IF YOUR BUSINESS REQUIRES DOUBLE ENTRY ACCOUNTING

If you are a larger, more complex business and will need double entry accounting, the next few pages will give you a basic understanding and you can work with your accountant to tailor a system for your business.

FLOW OF DATA IN DOUBLE ENTRY ACCOUNTING

After a transaction is completed, the initial record of that transaction, or of a group of similar transactions, is evidenced by a business document such as a sales ticket, a check stub, or a cash register tape. On the basis of the evidence provided by that document, transactions are then entered in chronological order in the General Journal. The amounts of the debits and the credits in the journal are then transferred to the accounts in the ledger. The flow of data from transaction to ledger may be diagrammed as follows:

| Business TRANSACTION Occurs | <———> | Business DOCUMENT Prepared | <———> | Entry Recorded In JOURNAL | <———> | Entry Posted To LEDGER To Individual Accounts |

NUMBERING OF ACCOUNTS

Double Entry Accounting requires the numbering of accounts. These account numbers are used when recording transactions in the General Journal and posting them to Individual General Ledger Accounts. In the next chapter of this book, we will be discussing Financial Statements. Two of these statements, the Balance Sheet and Income Statement are compiled from information derived from the accounts in the General Ledger. If you are using a double entry system, it will be necessary for you to understand how to develop a "Chart of Accounts."

MAJOR DIVISIONS OF A CHART OF ACCOUNTS

All accounts in the General Ledger are divided into the following major divisions:

1. ASSETS

2. LIABILITIES

3. CAPITAL

4. REVENUE

5. EXPENSES

Each division contains its own individual accounts that must be numbered. Although accounts in the ledger may be numbered consecutively as in the pages of a book, the flexible system of indexing as described on the next page is preferable.

Setting Up a Chart of Accounts

To illustrate this concept, the following is a sample chart of accounts for a fictitious business. Each account has three digits. The first digit indicates the major division of the ledger in which the account is placed. Accounts beginning with (1) represent assets; (2) liabilities; (3) capital; (4) revenues; and (5) expenses. The second and third digits indicate the position of the account within its division. For example: In the chart below, Account Number 105 (Prepaid Rent), the 1 indicates that Prepaid Rent is an asset account and the 5 indicates that it is in the fifth position within that division. A numbering system of this type has the advantage of permitting the later insertion of new accounts in their proper sequence without disturbing other account numbers. Using the three-digit system accommodates up to 99 separate accounts under each division. For a large enterprise with a number of departments or branches, it is not unusual for each account number to have four or more digits.

CHART OF ACCOUNTS
FOR A FICTITIOUS BUSINESS

Balance Sheet Accounts

1. ASSETS

101 Cash
102 Accounts Receivable
104 Supplies
105 Prepaid Rent
108 Production Equipment
109 Accumulated Depreciation

2. LIABILITIES

201 Accounts Payable
202 Salaries Payable

3. CAPITAL

301 John Jones, Capital
302 John Jones, Drawing
303 Income Summary

Income Statement Accounts

4. REVENUES

401 Sales
402 Services Income
405 Interest Income

5. EXPENSES

501 Rent Expense
504 Supplies Expense
505 Salary Expense
509 Depreciation Expense
514 Misc. Expense

—*Remember*—

The next two records, General Journal and General Ledger are only for those businesses who are going to set up Double Entry Accounting. Those using Single Entry Accounting, which will probably be most of you, will want to skip two records ahead to the Revenue & Expense Journal and start there with the setting up of your recordkeeping system.

GENERAL JOURNAL

As its name implies, the General Journal is used to record all the types of transactions that a business has. The transactions are listed in chronological order—that is in the order that they occur. Each entry effects two accounts, one in which a debit is entered and one in which its corresponding credit is entered.

Recording transactions in the General Journal requires a clear understanding of the terms "debit" and "credit." In the sample Chart of Accounts we set up five categories. Increases and decreases in each of these accounts are represented by debits or credits as follows:

A. ASSET (100) & EXPENSE (500) ACCOUNTS

1. Increases = debits
2. Decreases = credits

B. LIABILITY (200), CAPITAL (300) & REVENUE (400) ACCOUNTS

1. Increases = credits
2. Decreases = debits

SAMPLE GENERAL JOURNAL: To help you understand how transactions are recorded in the General Journal, the next page is a sample General Journal page with entries for the following five transactions of a fictitious business. Each entry provides a written analysis of one transaction, showing which accounts and what amounts should be debited and credited. It is also very important to include the description for each entry.

On July 31st, ABC Company had five transactions.

1. Received payment for consulting, $1,900 in cash.
2. Sold inventory for $1,200 on credit.
3. Paid $154 to vendor on credit account.
4. Paid rent for August in amount of $725.
5. John Jones took an owner draw of $800.

ABC COMPANY
GENERAL JOURNAL

GENERAL JOURNAL   Page 6

DATE		DESCRIPTION OF ENTRY	POST. REF.	DEBIT		CREDIT	
1993							
Jul.	31	Cash	101	1900	00		
		Services	402			1900	00
		Consulting for J. Smith Co. paid with their check no. 2546. My invoice 4302.					
	31	Accounts Receivable	102	1,200	00		
		Sales	401			1,200	00
		Sold 100 books at 40% discount, on credit, Net 90 to Norman Wholesale Books. Invoice 4303					
	31	Accounts Payable	201	154	00		
		Cash	101			154	00
		Pd. Unique Office Supply, Invoice Nos. 3207 & 3541, Check 1294					
	31	Rent Expense	501	725	00		
		Cash	101			725	00
		Paid Aug. rent to J. R. Properties Check no. 1295					
	31	John Jones, Drawing	302	800	00		
		Cash	101			800	00
		Owner draw. Check 1296					

GENERAL LEDGER

We have just seen how transactions are recorded in the General Journal. The next step in the flow of accounting data for double entry accounting is to transfer or post these same transactions to individual accounts in the General Ledger.

Using the Chart of Accounts developed for your business, each account will be kept on a printed form that has a heading and several columns. The forms used for the accounts are on separate sheets in a book or binder and together are make up what is referred to as the **General Ledger**. This is the master reference file for the accounting system because it provides a permanent, classified record of every financial aspect of the business's operations.

FORMAT

Several different forms are available for general ledger accounts. One of the best is the "balance ledger form" because the balance of an account is always recorded after each entry is posted. This is the format that you see on the sample accounts on page 19.

POSTING ENTRIES FROM THE
GENERAL JOURNAL TO THE GENERAL LEDGER

The transfer of information data from the General Journal to the General Ledger is known as "posting." The procedure used in posting data from a general journal entry is to start with the first account listed in the entry—the account to be debited. Locate the corresponding account in the general ledger and follow these steps:

1. Enter the date of the transaction in the Date column.

2. Record the number of the journal page in the Posting Reference column. For example, "J6" is used for all the entries on page 19 because they all came from page **6** of the Journal.

3. The debit amount is recorded in the Debit column.

4. The balance of the account is computed and recorded in the Balance column.

5. The last column is used to note the type of balance. Enter the abbreviation "**DR.**" for debit or "**CR.**" for credit.

6. The number of the ledger account (Ex: Accts. Receivable is **102**) is recorded in the Posting Reference column of the General Journal.

After the debit has been posted, you will need to post the corresponding credit for the same transaction to its appropriate ledger account. Locate the necessary account (the first transaction for ABC Company requires posting a debit to "Cash" (101) and a credit to "Service Income" (402). To post the credit you will follow the same steps as posting the debit amount. Once this work is done, the posting process for the transaction is complete and the journal entry includes the numbers of the two ledger accounts that were posted.

Writing the journal page number in each ledger account and the ledger account number in the journal indicates that the entry has been posted and ensures against posting the same entry twice or of not posting it at all. This use of referencing journal page numbers in the ledger accounts and ledger accounts numbers in the journal also provides a great cross-reference when you need to trace an entry or verify a transaction.

TRIAL BALANCE

The general ledger accounts are arranged as presented earlier in the sample Chart of Accounts, beginning with Asset accounts and ending with Expense accounts. At the end of an accounting period, you or your accountant will list all of the balances of the general ledger accounts on a "Trial Balance Form." The debit and credit balances are added separately. When the Debit and Credit columns of the trial balance are equal, the accountant knows that the financial records are in balance and that a debit has been recorded for every credit.

INCOME STATEMENT AND BALANCE SHEET

When the trial balance shows that the general ledger is in balance, you or your accountant are ready to prepare the financial statements for the period. The accounts from the trial balance are adjusted for such items as expired prepaid expenses, depreciation, etc. and the balances are transferred to another worksheet, "The Adjusted Trial Balance Form." This form contains separate sections for Adjusted Trial Balance, Income Statement and Balance Sheet with a Debit column and a Credit Column for each. This is the point at which the arrangement of accounts in the proper order will speed the preparation of the Income Statement and Balance Sheet presented in the Financial Section of the book.

PRACTICING THE POSTING PROCESS

The next two pages of the book are devoted to an exercise that will take you through the process of posting ABC Company's five transactions from the General Journal to the General Ledger.

TRACING ABC COMPANY'S TRANSACTIONS
POSTING FROM JOURNAL TO LEDGER ACCOUNTS

To help you better understand the transfer of information from the General Journal to the individual ledger accounts, we will follow the same five transactions that were recorded in the General Journal. Individual ledger accounts needed for posting (numbered the same as in the Chart of Accounts) can be seen on page 19 with all entries already posted from the journal.

The journal with its original entries has been reproduced below so that it will be in close proximity to the individual ledger accounts needed for this exercise. Follow the posting of each of the five transactions through both its debit and credit entries to the corresponding individual accounts on the next page.

Locate the corresponding accounts for each transaction in the general ledger and follow these steps:

1. Enter transaction date in the Date column.

2. Record the number of the journal page in the Posting Reference column. ("J6" is used for all the entries on the next page since all are from page 6 of the Journal.)

3. Record the debit amount in the Debit column.

4. The balance of the account is computed and recorded in the Balance column.

5. In the last column enter the abbreviation "DR." (debit) or "CR." (credit) to indicate the type of balance.

6. Record the number of the ledger account (101 for "Cash") in the Posting Reference column of the General Journal.

After the debit has been posted for a transaction, post the corresponding credit for the same transaction to its appropriate ledger account. Locate the necessary account (the 1st transaction for ABC Company requires posting a debit to "Cash" (101) and a credit to "Service Income" (402). TO POST THE CREDIT, FOLLOW THE SAME STEPS AS POSTING THE DEBIT AMOUNT.

ABC COMPANY
GENERAL JOURNAL

GENERAL JOURNAL				Page 6	
DATE	DESCRIPTION OF ENTRY	POST. REF.	DEBIT	CREDIT	
1993					
Jul. 31	Cash	101	1900 00		
	Services Income	402		1900 00	
	Consulting for J. Smith Co. paid with their check no. 2546. My Invoice 4302.				
31	Accounts Receivable	102	1,200 00		
	Sales	401		1,200 00	
	Sold 100 books at 40% discount, on credit, Net 90 to Norman Wholesale Books. Invoice 4303				
31	Accounts Payable	201	154 00		
	Cash	101		154 00	
	Pd. Unique Office Supply, Invoice Nos. 3207 & 3541, Check 1294				
31	Rent Expense	501	725 00		
	Cash	101		725 00	
	Paid Aug. rent to J. R. Properties Check no. 1295				
31	John Jones, Drawing	302	800 00		
	Cash	101		800 00	
	Owner draw. Check 1296				

FOR YOUR USE: A blank General Ledger form is provided in the Appendix.

POSTING
GENERAL JOURNAL ➡ GENERAL LEDGER
Sample for ABC COMPANY

This page shows how ABC Company's July 31st transactions would be posted from the General Journal to individual accounts in the General Ledger.

ACCOUNT CASH   **ACCOUNT NO. 101**

DATE		DESCRIPTION OF ENTRY	POST. REF.	DEBIT		CREDIT		BALANCE		DR. CR.
1993										
Jul.	31	(1. Consulted for cash)	J 6	1900	00			1900	00	DR
	31	(3. Paid vendor on credit account)	J 6			154	00	1746	00	DR
	31	(4. Paid August rent)	J 6			725	00	1021	00	DR
	31	(5. John Jones/Owner Draw)	J 6			800	00	221	00	DR

ACCOUNT JOHN JONES DRAWING   **ACCOUNT NO. 302**

DATE		DESCRIPTION OF ENTRY	POST. REF.	DEBIT		CREDIT		BALANCE		DR. CR.
1993										
Jul.	31	5. John Jones/owner draw)	J 6	800	00			800	00	DR

ACCOUNT ACCOUNTS RECEIVABLE   **ACCOUNT NO. 102**

DATE		DESCRIPTION OF ENTRY	POST. REF.	DEBIT		CREDIT		BALANCE		DR. CR.
1993										
Jul.	31	(2. Sold inventory on credit)	J 6	1200	00			1200	00	DR

ACCOUNT SALES   **ACCOUNT NO. 401**

DATE		DESCRIPTION OF ENTRY	POST. REF.	DEBIT		CREDIT		BALANCE		DR. CR.
1993										
Jul.	31	(2. Sold inventory for credit)	J 6			1200	00	1200	00	CR

ACCOUNT SERVICES INCOME   **ACCOUNT NO. 402**

DATE		DESCRIPTION OF ENTRY	POST. REF.	DEBIT		CREDIT		BALANCE		DR. CR.
1993										
Jul.	31	(1. Consulted for cash)	J 6			1900	00	1900	00	CR

ACCOUNT ACCOUNTS PAYABLE   **ACCOUNT NO. 201**

DATE		DESCRIPTION OF ENTRY	POST. REF.	DEBIT		CREDIT		BALANCE		DR. CR.
1993										
Jul.	31	(3. Pd to vendor on account)	J 6	154	00			154	00	DR

ACCOUNT RENT EXPENSE   **ACCOUNT NO. 501**

DATE		DESCRIPTION OF ENTRY	POST. REF.	DEBIT		CREDIT		BALANCE		DR. CR.
1993										
Jul.	31	(4. Paid August rent)	J 6	725	00			725	00	DR

NOTE: *Descriptions are left blank on routine entries. The column is for special notations. We have used them to reference the transactions of ABC Company in order to help you see see the flow of information from the transactions to the General Journal to the Ledger Accounts. If your entries are posted correctly, the total debit and credit balances will always be equal.*

GENERAL LEDGER ACCOUNT
SAMPLE FORM

ACCOUNT _____   ACCOUNT NO. _____

DATE	DESCRIPTION OF ENTRY	POST. REF.	DEBIT	CREDIT	BALANCE	DR. CR.
19__						

SETTING UP THE "GENERAL LEDGER"

1. Develop a Chart of Accounts as previously described in this section.

2. Set up an individual general ledger page for each account in the Chart of Accounts.

3. Position the accounts in the general ledger book in numerical order.

4. Transfer information from the general journal to ledger accounts just as we did for ABC Company on the two preceding pages.

SINGLE ENTRY ACCOUNTING

This is where you will begin if you are going to maintain your records by the single entry method. At this point you will begin to set up your General Records as presented in the remainder of the chapter, beginning with the Revenue & Expense Journal.

FLOW OF ACCOUNTING DATA

If you read the information on double entry accounting, you learned that a business transaction occurs accompanied by some sort of document. Then the transaction is recorded in the General Journal and the journal entry is posted to an individual General Ledger account. This requires a thorough understanding of the concept of posting debits and credits, which is confusing at best to most business owners. You will not need to develop a numbered Chart of Accounts. However, you should remember that there are five major divisions (Assets, Liabilities, Capital, Revenues and Expenses). You will develop a better understanding of these divisions as you progress through the General Records. They should become even more clear by the time you complete the Financial Statement section of the book.

The beauty of single entry recordkeeping is that it reduces the posting process to simply entering revenues and expenses on a single form and requires no formal accounting education. You are still required to keep those general records pertinent to your business (such as Petty Cash, Accounts Receivable and Payable, Fixed Assets, Travel and Entertainment, Inventory, etc.), but in a very simple and logical way that will still provide for perfect retrieval of needed tax and business analysis information.

With this method the flow of accounting data will be as follows:

		Entry
Business	Business	Recorded in
TRANSACTION <———>	DOCUMENT <———>	REVENUE & EXPENSE
		JOURNAL

Now you are ready to set up your recordkeeping system. We will take you a step at a time through the entire process. Begin by setting up a Revenue & Expense Journal.

REVENUE & EXPENSE JOURNAL

A Revenue & Expense Journal is used to record the transactions of a business. They are recorded as revenues (income) and expenses.

1. **Revenues (income)** are the transactions for which monies are received. Equity deposits and loan funds are not revenues.

2. **Expenses** are all transactions for which monies are paid out. Owner draws and principal payments on loans are not included.

To make your accounting more effective, you will need to have enough columns in the Revenue & Expense Journal to cover major categories of income and expenses (or create two separate forms, *ie.*, one for revenues and one for expenses). If you have done your homework and figured out the areas of direct and indirect expenses, these divisions will serve as headings in your journal. Usually, a 12-column journal will suffice for most small businesses, but feel free to use more or less, as long as your report is clear and easy to interpret.

AVOIDING ERRORS

The use of a Revenue & Expense Journal is part of single entry recordkeeping. However, **each entry is recorded twice** (not to be confused with posting debits and credits). If you will look on the sample form, the first two columns are headed "Revenue" and "Expense." Every transaction is entered in one of these two columns. The next groups of three and five columns are breakdowns of revenues and expenses. The entry is first recorded as a revenue or expense and then entered in its corresponding breakdown column. For example, an advertising expense of $100 would be entered under the heading, "Expense" and also under the expense breakdown heading, "Advertising." When the columns are totaled, the amount under "Expense" will equal the sum of all expense breakdown columns. The "Revenue" total will equal the sum of all revenue breakdown columns. This serves as a check for accuracy and will save hours of searching your records for errors when attempting to balance your books.

HEADINGS IN THE REVENUE & EXPENSE JOURNAL

The column headings in the Revenue & Expense journal for any business will follow the same format. The first five columns headings are:

1. Check No.
2. Date
3. Transaction
4. Revenue
5. Expense

Remaining columns are used for individual categories of revenue and expense for which you most frequently write checks or receive income.

1. The **revenue breakdown columns** will be divided by source (ex: as publishers and teachers, we have "book sales," "software sales," "sales tax" and "seminar fees").

2. The **expense breakdown columns** reflect the categories for which you most frequently write a check. (Ex: "inventory purchases," "freight," "advertising," "office supplies," "vehicle expenses," etc.)

The headings for the individual revenue and expense columns will vary from business to business. Every business is different and it may take some time to determine the categories that will best reflect the transactions of your particular venture. If you are coordinating your recordkeeping with a tax accountant, you might ask that person to help you develop your headings. The best rule of thumb is to devote a column to each type of expense for which you frequently write a check.

MISCELLANEOUS COLUMN

The last column in any Revenue & Expense Journal should be Miscellaneous. This column serves as a catchall for any expense that does not fall under a main heading. For example, insurance may be paid only once a year and, therefore, a heading under that title would not be justified. Record that transaction first under Expense and secondly under Miscellaneous with an explanation either under the Transaction Column or in parentheses next to the amount in the Miscellaneous Column. For example, you write only one check every six months, in the amount of $500, for insurance. You put "$500 (insurance)." The explanation is a must. This will allow you to group infrequent expenses under one column and still be able to allocate them to the proper expense categories at the end of the month when you do a Profit & Loss (or Income) Statement.

TOTALS

Each column should be totaled at the bottom of each journal page. (Remember to check accuracy. The sum of all revenue breakdown columns = the sum of the column headed "Revenue" and the sum of all expense breakdown columns = sum of the column headed "Expense.") All totals are then transferred to the top of the next page and added in until you have completed a month. At the end of the month, the last page is totaled and checked. The breakdown Revenue & Expense totals are transferred to your Profit and Loss Statement and a new month begins with a clean page and all zero balances.

SAMPLE REVENUE & EXPENSE JOURNAL: In order for you to better understand how to develop and make entries in your own Revenue & Expense Journal, we will: 1) create headings for a fictitious company, 2) enter six transactions and 3) total the page.

1. **The Headings Are Determined**

    a. The first five columns and the last column are standard: Check No., Date, Transaction, Revenue, Expense and Miscellaneous.

    b. The individual revenue headings are determined. (Our company sells and services computers. We want to know how much of our revenue comes from sales and how much comes from service. We also want to know how much sales tax is collected. The column headings are: Sales, Sales Tax and Service.)

    c. The individual expense columns are determined. (Checks are most frequently written to purchase inventory, advertise, ship orders and purchase office supplies. The column headings are: Inventory Purchases, Advertising, Freight and Office Supplies.)

2. **The Transactions Are As Follows**

    a. This is the second journal page used for the month of July. The totals from the first page are brought forward and entered on the line entitled "Balance forward."

    b. The new transactions to be entered are as follows:

    (1) Check 234 dated July 13th was written to J. J. Advertising to pay for an advertising promotion ($450.00).

    (2) Check 235 dated July 13th was written to T & E Products to buy a computer to resell to a customer ($380.00).

    (3) Check 236 dated July 16th was written to Regal Stationers for office supplies ($92.50).

    (4) $1,232.00 was deposited in the bank. ($400.00 + $32.00 sales tax came from taxable sales, $165.00 in sales were sold to an out-of-state customer, $370.00 was for a sale to another reseller and $265.00 was received for repairing a customer's computer.)

    (5) The bank statement was reconciled on July 19th. (The bank charged $23.40 for new checks.)

    (6) Check 237 dated July 19th was written to Petty Cash. ($100.00 was deposited to the Petty Cash Account.)

3. **The Journal Page Is Full (Total and Check Columns)**

    a. Add individual revenue columns and check to see that the sum of their totals equals the total of the Revenue column ($3,058.00).

    b. Add individual expense columns and check to see that the sum of their totals equals the total of the Expense column ($1,880.90).

ABC COMPANY

REVENUE & EXPENSE JOURNAL

July 199__, page 2

(handwritten note: Bring a Bal. Forward. from previous mo.)
(handwritten note: = R + R + R)
(handwritten note: = 3058.00)

CHECK NO.	DATE	TRANSACTION	REVENUE	EXPENSE	SALES	SALES TAX	SERV-ICES	INV. PURCH	ADVERT.	FREIGHT	OFF. SUPP.	MISC.
		Balance forward---	1,826 00	835 00	1,218 00	98 00	510 00	295 00	245 00	150 00	83 50	61 50
234	7/13	J. J. Advertising		450 00					450 00			
235	7/13	T & E Products		380 00				380 00				
236	7/16	Regal Stationers		92 50							92 50	
***	7/17	Deposit:	1,232 00									
		1. Sales (Taxable)			400 00	32 00						
		2. Sales (O.S.)			165 00	O.S.						
		3. Sales (Resale)			370 00	Resale						
		4. Services					265 00					
O.K. BANK	7/19	Bank Charges		23 40								(bank chg) 23 40
237	7/19	Petty Cash Deposit		100 00								(p/cash) 100 00
		TOTALS	3,058 00	1,880 90	2,153 00	130 00	775 00	675 00	695 00	150 00	176 00	184 90

PETTY CASH RECORD

Petty cash refers to all the small business purchases made with cash or personal funds instead of with a business check. These purchases may account for several thousand dollars by the end of the year. Failure to account for them can result in a false picture of your business and additional cost in income taxes. It is imperative that you keep an accurate record of all Petty Cash Expenditures, that you have receipts on file, and that you record them in a manner that will enable you to categorize these expenses at the end of an accounting period.

WHERE DO PETTY CASH FUNDS COME FROM?

In order to transfer cash into the Petty Cash Fund, you must first draw a check and expense it to Petty Cash in the Revenue & Expense Journal (see entry in Revenue & Expense Journal). That same amount is entered in the Petty Cash Record as a deposit. When cash purchases are made, they are entered in the Petty Cash Record as Expenses. When the balance gets low, another check is drawn to rebuild the fund. At the end of the tax year, you can let the balance run as a negative, write a final check in that amount and deposit it to Petty Cash to zero out the fund. The end result will be that you will have deposited an amount that is exactly equal to your petty cash expenditures for the year.

PETTY CASH FORMAT

The two purposes of Petty Cash Accounting are: 1) To account for personal expenditures relating to business; and 2) To provide information that will classify those expenses for income tax retrieval and for business analysis. Any accountant will warn you that a large miscellaneous deduction will be suspect and may very well single your return out for an IRS audit. Dividing your Petty Cash Record into the following categories will provide for individual purchases to be summarized, combined with expenses on the Revenue & Expense Journal and entered on the Profit & Loss Statement.

1. Date of Transaction
2. Paid to Whom
3. Expense Account Debited
4. Deposit
5. Amount of Expense
6. Balance

SAMPLE PETTY CASH RECORD: On the next page you will see how deposits and expenses are recorded. If a cash expense also needs to be entered in another record (Inventory, Fixed Assets, etc.), do so at the same time to keep the record current and eliminate omissions.

ABC COMPANY
PETTY CASH RECORD

PETTY CASH - 19___					Page 6	
DATE	PAID TO WHOM	EXPENSE ACCOUNT DEBITED	DEPOSIT	AMOUNT OF EXPENSE	BALANCE	
	BALANCE FORWARD ————			————	10	00
Jul. 19	✳✳ Deposit (Ck. 237)		100 00		110	00
20	ACE Hardware	Maintenance		12 36	97	64
23	Regal Stationers	Office Supplies		20 00	77	64
23	U.S. Postmaster	Postage		19 80	57	84
31	The Steak House	Meals		63 75	(5	91)
Aug 1	✳✳ Deposit (Ck.267)		100 00		94	09

Toward the end of the year, you can let the Petty Cash run a minus balance. On December 31st, a check is written for the balance and the account is zeroed out.

The amount of cash spent during the year will be exactly equal to the amount deposited into the Petty Cash Account from your checking account.

NOTE: 1. Save all receipts for cash purchases.
2. Exchange receipt for cash from Petty Cash Drawer.
3. Use receipts to record expenses on Petty Cash Form
4. File receipts. You may need them for verification.
5. Be sure to record Petty Cash deposits.

INVENTORY RECORD

The term inventory is used to designate: 1) Merchandise held for sale in the normal course of business; and 2) Materials in the process of production or held for such use. The recording of inventories is used both as an internal control and as a means of retrieval of information required for the computation of income tax.

THE GREAT INVENTORY MYTH

Before proceeding with the mechanics of keeping your inventory, we would like to clear up a misconception about the pros and cons of the relationship of inventory size and income tax due. Any business that has had to deal with inventory will almost certainly have heard the statement, "Put your cash into inventory. The larger it is, the few taxes you will have to pay." Conversely, you may also hear that if your inventory is reduced, your taxes will also be reduced. Both are nonsense statements, and we will prove it to you mathematically. The fact is that your net profit remains the same regardless of the amount reinvested in inventory. Ten thousand dollars is $10,000 in your checking account or on the shelves as saleable goods. This can be proved as follows:

Companies A & B: 1) both had beginning inventories of $25,000.

2) both had gross sales of $30,000.

3) both sold their product at 100% markup and reduced their beginning inventory by $15,000.

Company A: Reinvested $20,000 in inventory and deposited $10,000. This gave them an ending inventory of $30,000.

Company B: Reinvested $5,000 in inventory and deposited $25,000.

The result was an ending inventory of $15,000.

Net Profit is arrived at by subtracting deductible expenses from your Gross Profit. The following computation will prove that Companies A and B will in fact have the same Gross Profit (and will not have their Net Profit affected by the amount of reinvestment in inventory):

	Co. A	Co. B
1. Beginning Inventory	$25,000	$25,000
2. Purchase	$20,000	$ 5,000
3. Add lines 1 & 2	$45,000	$30,000
4. Less Ending Inventory	$30,000	$15,000
5. Cost of Goods Sold (sub 4 from 3)	$15,000	$15,000
6. Gross Receipts or Sales	$30,000	$30,000
7. Less Cost of Goods Sold (line 5)	$15,000	$15,000
8. **GROSS PROFIT** (line 6 minus 7)	**$15,000**	**$15,000**

THE GROSS PROFITS ARE EXACTLY THE SAME!

It is very important that you understand the above concept. Inventory only affects your net profit as a vehicle to greater sales potential. How much or how little you stock at tax time will neither increase nor decrease your taxes. Companies A and B will both have a gross profit of $15,000 and will be taxed the same. Some states, however, may have inventory taxes and this could enter in as a factor.

INVENTORY CONTROL

Keeping records for the IRS is actually the lesser reason for keeping track of inventory. We personally know of two companies that nearly failed due to a lack of inventory control. One was a restaurant whose employees were carrying groceries out the back door at closing time. Although the restaurant enjoyed a good clientele and followed sound business practices for the food industry, their year-end profit did not justify their existence. A careful examination of their records showed a failure to properly inventory their stock. By instituting strict inventory control, pilferage was ended and the next years increase in profit saved the business. Inventory control in a retail business can help you to see such things as turnover time, high and low selling periods, changes in buying trends. Periodic examinations of your inventory and its general flow may be the meat of your existence.

FORMAT FOR INVENTORY RECORDS

Basic inventory records must contain the following information in order to be effective.

1. Date Purchased
2. Item Purchased (include stock no.)
3. Purchase Price (cost)
4. Date Sold ⎤ This information is especially helpful for determining
5. Sale Price ⎦ shelf life and trends in market value of your product

If your inventory is at all sizeable, you will want some sort of Point-of-Sale (P.O.S.) inventory system. However, it is possible to keep it in handwritten form based on two premises: 1) You begin immediately; and 2) You keep it current and do it regularly. I have a clock shop with approximately two thousand items for sale. On any given day, I know how long I have had each item, which items are selling repeatedly and what time periods require the stocking of more inventory. Keep in mind that all businesses differ. Compile your inventory according to your specific needs. Be sure that it is divided in such a way as to provide quick reference. I sort mine out by using separate pages for each company from which I make my purchases. Another method might be to separate pages by type of item. The important thing is to make your inventory work for you.

COMMON KINDS OF INVENTORY

1. Merchandise or stock in trade
2. Raw materials
3. Work in process
4. Finished products
5. Supplies (that become a part of a product intended for sale)

To arrive at a dollar amount for your inventory, you will need a method for identifying and a basis for valuing the items in your inventory. Inventory valuation must clearly show income and, for that reason, you must use this same inventory practice from year to year.

COST IDENTIFICATION METHODS

There are three methods that can be used to identify items in inventory. They are as follows:

1. Specific Identification Method: In some businesses it is possible to keep track of inventory and to identify the cost of each inventoried item by matching the item with its cost of acquisition. In other words, there is specific identification of merchandise and you can determine the exact cost of what is sold. There is no question as to which items remain in the inventory. Merchants who deal with items having a large unit cost or with one-of-a-kind items may choose to keep track of inventory by this method.

For those businesses dealing with a large quantity of like items, there must be a method for deciding which items were sold and which remain in inventory.

2. FIFO (first-in-first-out): assumes that the items you purchased or produced first are the first sold. This method most closely parallels the actual flow of inventory. Most merchants will attempt to sell their oldest inventory items first and hopefully will have the last items bought in current inventory.

3. LIFO (last-in-first-out): assumes that the items of inventory that you purchased or produced last are sold first. You must check tax rules to qualify before electing this method.

The FIFO and LIFO methods produce different results in income depending on the trend of price levels of inventory items. In a period of rising prices, valuing your inventory by the LIFO method will result in a higher reported cost of goods sold and a lower reported net income. This is because it is assumed that you sold goods purchased at the higher price. Conversely, in a period of falling prices, the LIFO method would result in a lower reported cost of goods sold and a higher reported net income than the FIFO method.

VALUING INVENTORY

The two common ways to value your inventory if you use the FIFO method are the specific cost identification method and the lower of cost or market method. If at the end of your tax year the market price of items in your inventory decline, you may elect to use the following method of evaluation:

> **Cost or Market, Whichever is Lower:** At inventory time, if your merchandise cannot be sold through usual trade channels for a price that is above its original cost, the current market price is determined and compared to your accepted costing method (FIFO, LIFO, or Specific Identification). The lower figure, "cost" or "market" is selected. This is especially useful for outdated inventory. If you use this method you must value each item in the inventory.

> **You must be consistent.** As a new business using FIFO, you may use either the cost method or the lower of cost or market method to value your inventory. However, you must use the same method consistently and, again, you must use it to value your entire inventory. You may not change to another method without permission of the IRS.

PHYSICAL INVENTORIES

You must take physical inventories at reasonable intervals and the book figure for inventory must be adjusted to agree with the actual inventory. The IRS requires a beginning and ending inventory for your tax year.

SAMPLE INVENTORY RECORDS: The sample inventory record on the next page is for the "Specific Identification Method" of taking inventory. Remember, it is for inventory of those products that differ from each other and can be individually accounted for as to purchase date, description and cost.

The sample inventory record on p. 33 is for "Non-Identifiable Inventory." An example would be the purchase or production of 2,000 units of a like item— the first thousand being produced at a unit cost of $5.00 and the second at a unit cost of $6.00. It would be impossible to determine which remain in inventory. They must be identified by the FIFO or LIFO method and valued accordingly to figure taxable income.

For further information on inventory rules, please read Chapter 8 in the IRS Publication 334, *Tax Guide for Small Business.*

ABC COMPANY INVENTORY RECORD
IDENTIFIABLE STOCK

WHOLESALER: ALL TIME CLOCK CO.						Page 1	

PURCH. DATE	INVENTORY PURCHASED		PURCH. PRICE		DATE SOLD	SALE PRICE		NAME OF BUYER (Optional)
	Stock #	Description						
1/23/93	25-72 D	Oak Gallery (25")	352	00				
2/19/93	24-37 A	Desk Alarm (1)	18	00	4/08/93	28	50	N/A
		(2)	18	00				
		(3)	18	00				
2/21/93	26-18 C	"The Shelby" GF	1420	00	4/20/93	1865	00	J. Kirkland
3/19/93	25-67 D	Mahog. Regulator	247	00				
5/04/93	26-18 C	"The Shelby" GF	1420	00				

NOTE: 1. Use this record for keeping track of identifiable goods purchased for resale. If your inventory is very large, it may be necessary to use some sort of **Point-of-Sale** inventory system.

2. Each page should deal with either (1) purchases in one category or (2) goods purchased from one wholesaler.

3. Use the name of the wholesaler or the category of the purchase as the heading.

ABC COMPANY INVENTORY RECORD
NON-IDENTIFIABLE STOCK

DEPARTMENT/CATEGORY: _Ski Hats / Headwear_

PRODUCTION OR PURCHASE DATE	INVENTORY PURCHASED OR MANUFACTURED		NUMBER OF UNITS	UNIT COST		VALUE ON DATE OF INVENTORY (Unit Cost X Units on Hand)	
	Stock #	Description				Value	Date
2/05/91	07-43	Knitted Headbands	5,000	2	50	Ø	1/93
3/25/91	19-12	Face - Masks	3,000	5	12	450.80	1/93
9/14/91	19-10	Hat / Mask Combo	1,200	7	00	3,514.00	1/93
4/18/92	19-09	Hats - Multi Col.	10,500	4	00	5,440.00	1/93
8/31/92	19-07	Gortex w/ Bill	10,000	8	41	50,460.00	1/93
8/31/92	07-43	Knitted Headbands	5,000	2	35	3,057.35	1/93
BEGIN 1993							
2/01/93	19-12	Face Masks	2,500	4	80		
2/28/93	19-09	Hats, Multi-Col.	10,300	4	00		

NOTE: 1. This record is used for inventory of like items that are purchased or manufactured in bulk. It is a good idea to divide your records by department, category or by manufacturer.

2. Inventory these items by a physical count or by computer records. A physical inventory is required at the close of your tax year.

3. Inventory is valued according to rules that apply for **FIFO** or **LIFO**. Read the information in your tax guide carefully before determining inventory value. The selected method must be used consistently.

FIXED ASSETS LOG

At the end of each tax year you will have to provide your accountant with a list of all assets for which depreciation is allowed. Many different kinds of property can be depreciated, such as machinery, buildings, vehicles, furniture, equipment and proprietary rights such as copyrights and patents. These are items purchased for use in your business usually at a cost in excess of $100.

WHAT CAN BE DEPRECIATED?

In general, property is depreciable if it meets these requirements:

1. It must be used in business or held for the production of income.

2. It must have a determinable life and that life must be longer than one year.

3. It must be something that wears out, decays, gets used up, becomes obsolete or loses value from natural causes.

You can never depreciate land, rented property or the cost of repairs that do not increase the value of your property. You cannot depreciate your inventory or any item that you intend for resale.

SECTION 179 DEDUCTION

You can elect to treat all or part of the cost of certain depreciable property as an expense rather than as a capital expenditure. The total cost you can elect to deduct for a tax year cannot exceed $10,000. In lay terms, instead of depreciating assets placed in service during the current year, you may be allowed to directly expense them up to a $10,000 limit. There are some restrictions that apply and you will need the help of your accountant to make the final decision for tax purposes.

KEEPING TRACK OF FIXED ASSETS

You will need to keep an inventory of depreciable purchases made during the current tax year. You will also have to be able to tell your accountant if any of these purchases were entered in your Revenue & Expense Journal to avoid double-expensing. Be aware that you are also accountable for disposition of these items. If you have depreciated an automobile down to $2,000 and then sell it for $3,500, you will have to report a profit of $1,500. Depreciation can be very tricky and the laws change. Your job is to be able to provide your accountant with basic information. Your accountant must then apply the law to maximize your benefits.

SAMPLE FIXED ASSETS LOG: The form that follows will help you to do your part and have a general overview of what assets you have that fall in this category.

ABC COMPANY
FIXED ASSETS LOG

COMPANY NAME: ABC Company

ASSET PURCHASED	DATE PLACED IN SERVICE	COST OF ASSET	% USED FOR BUSINESS	RECOVERY PERIOD	METHOD OF DEPRECIATION	DEPRECIATION PREVIOUSLY ALLOWED	DATE SOLD	SALE PRICE
1987 Dodge Van	1/08/88	18,700 00	80%	5 yr.	200% DB	15,469 00	9/12/92	8,500 00
IBM Computer	7/15/89	6,450 00	100%	5 yr.	200% DB	3,620 00		
Ricoh Copier	12/29/89	3,000 00	100%	5 yr.	S/L-DB	1,469 00		
Fence	6/17/92	4,500 00	100%	15 yr.	150% DB	—		
1992 Dodge Van	8/05/92	21,000 00	80%	5 yr.	200% DB	—		
Desk	8/15/92	1,500 00	100%	7 yr.	200% DB	—		

NOTE: See IRS Publication 334 (Rev. Nov. 92), *Tax Guide for Small Business*, (Chapter 13) for more detailed information on depreciation. Also see Publication 534, *Depreciation*.

ACCOUNTS RECEIVABLE

An accounts receivable record is used to keep track of money owed to your business as a result of extending credit to a customer who purchases your products or services. Some businesses deal in cash transactions only. In other words, the product or service is paid for at the time of the sale. If this is the case in your business, you will not need "Accounts Receivable" records. However, if you do extend credit, the amount owed to you by your credit customers will have to be collected in a timely manner to provide you with the cash needed for day-to-day operations. It will be essential to have detailed information about your transactions and to always know the balance owed to you for each invoice. This can be accomplished by setting up a separate Accounts Receivable record for each customer.

FORMAT

In order to ensure that you have all the information needed to verify that customers are paying balances on time and that they are within credit limits, the form used will need to include these categories:

1. **Invoice Date:** This will tell you the date the transaction took place and enable you to age the invoice.
2. **Invoice Number:** Invoices are numbered and can be filed in order. If you need to refer to the invoice, the number makes it easy to retrieve.
3. **Invoice Amount:** Tells how much the customer owes for each invoice.
4. **Terms:** Tells the time period allowed until invoice is due and also if a discount applies. (Ex: Net30/2%Net10 means the invoice is due in 30 days, but a 2% discount will be allowed if payment is made in 10 days.)
5. **Date Paid:** Shows when the invoice was paid.
6. **Amount Paid:** Shows whether the customer made a partial payment or paid the invoice in full.
7. **Invoice Balance:** Tells what portion of the invoice is not paid.
8. **Header Information:** The customer's name, address and phone number will tell you where to send statements and how to make contact.

At the end of a predetermined billing period, each open account will be sent a statement showing their invoice number and amounts, balance due and preferably age of balances (over 30, 60 and 90 days). The statement should also include terms of payment. When the payment is received, it is recorded on the accounts receivable record. The total of all the outstanding balances in Accounts Receivable is transferred to Current Assets when preparing a Balance Sheet for your business.

SAMPLE ACCOUNTS RECEIVABLE RECORD: The form on the next page contains a sample form to show you how it should be filled out. There is a blank form in the Appendix for you to copy and use.

ABC COMPANY
ACCOUNTS RECEIVABLE
ACCOUNT RECORD

CUSTOMER: T & E Movers

ADDRESS: 222 E. Handy Rd.
WINNEMUCCA, NV 89502

TEL. NO: (702) 843-2222   **ACCOUNT NO.** 1016

INVOICE DATE	INVOICE NO.	INVOICE AMOUNT		TERMS	DATE PAID	AMOUNT PAID		INVOICE BALANCE	
6/04/92	3528	247	00	Net 30	7/2/92	247	00	—	—
7/14/92	4126	340	00	Net 30	8/15/92	340	00	—	—
9/26/92	5476	192	00	N30/2%10	10/02/92	188	16	—	—
10/03/92	5783	211	00	30/2%10	11/01/92	109	00	102	00
10/12/92	6074	386	00	30/2%10				386	00

ACCOUNTS PAYABLE

Those debts owed by your company to your creditors for goods purchased or services rendered fall into accounts payable. Having open account credit will allow your company to conduct more extensive operations and use your financial resources more effectively. If you are going to have a good credit record, the payment of these invoices must be timely and you will need an efficient system for keeping track of what you owe and when it should be paid. When your accounts payable are not numerous and you do not accumulate unpaid invoices by partial payments, you may wish to eliminate accounts payable records and use an accordion file divided into the days of the month. Invoices Payable may be directly filed under the date on which they should be paid, taking into account discounts available for early payment.

FORMAT

If your Accounts Payable are stretched over a longer period, you will need to keep separate records for the creditors with whom you do business. The form used will need to include these categories:

1. **Invoice Date:** This will tell you when the transaction took place.

2. **Invoice Number:** If you need to refer to the actual invoice, the number makes it easy to retrieve. File unpaid invoices behind the record.

3. **Invoice Amount:** Tells the amount of the transaction.

4. **Terms:** Tells the time period allowed until invoice is due and also if a discount applies. (Ex: Net 30/2% Net10 means the invoice is due in 30 days, but a 2% discount will be allowed if payment is made in 10 days.)

5. **Date Paid:** Shows when you paid the invoice.

6. **Amount Paid:** Shows whether the you made a partial payment or paid the invoice in full.

7. **Invoice Balance:** Tells what portion of the invoice is not paid.

8. **Header Information:** The creditor's name, address and phone number will tell you where to send payments and how to make contact.

You will be billed regularly for the balance of your account, but the individual records will help you to know at a glance where you stand at any given time. They should be reviewed monthly and an attempt should be made to satisfy all your creditors. After the invoice is paid in full and the payment is recorded, mark the invoice paid and file with the rest of your receipts. At the end of your accounting period, the total for Accounts Payable should be transferred to the Current Liabilities portion of the Balance Sheet.

SAMPLE ACCOUNTS PAYABLE RECORD: The next page contains a sample form showing how it should be filled out. A blank form is located in the Appendix for you to copy and use.

ABC COMPANY
ACCOUNTS PAYABLE
ACCOUNT RECORD

CREDITOR: CHARLES MFG.

ADDRESS: 1111 E. TRENTON RD.

TARINGTON, NH 03928

TEL NO: (603) 827-5001

ACCOUNT NO. 2072

INVOICE DATE	INVOICE NO.	INVOICE AMOUNT		TERMS	DATE PAID	AMOUNT PAID		INVOICE BALANCE	
2/16/92	10562	1500	00	Net 15	2/24/92	1500	00	Ø	
2/25/92	11473	870	00	Net 30	2/18/92	870	00	Ø	
3/17/92	12231	3200	00	N30/2%10	3/25/92	3136	00	Ø	
7/02/92	18420	2400	00	N30/2%10	8/01/92	1800	00	600	00
8/15/92	19534	2600	00	N30/2%10				2600	00

PAYROLL RECORDS

The decision to add employees should not be taken lightly. In addition to having a responsibility to the employees you hire, you also acquire the responsibility to withhold, report and pay taxes to the federal, state and sometimes your local government. The next few pages will be devoted to taking you through the necessary steps of putting employees on your payroll, paying them, making payroll tax deposits, completing quarterly payroll tax returns and making year end reports.

At the end of this section, we will make a suggestion that you work with an accounting professional to make sure that everything is done according to requirements.

FEIN, W-4, FORM I-9, OFFICIAL NOTICE

If you decide to hire employees, you will have to do the following:

1. FEIN: When you decide you will hire employees, you must file for a Federal Employer Identification Number (FEIN). This is done by completing Form SS-4 and sending it to the Internal Revenue Service. You will receive a packet that includes Circular E, Employer's Tax Guide. This publication contains the charts you will use to determine the amount of Federal Income Tax to be withheld from your employees' paychecks. (In addition to registering as an employer with the IRS, you will need to determine your state and local government requirements.

2. W-4's: Your new employees MUST complete a Form W-4, furnishing their full names, addresses, social security numbers, marital status and number of withholding allowances to be claimed, all of which you must have in order to compute your employees' first and succeeding paychecks.

3. Forms I-9: Employers are required to verify employment eligibility for all of their employees. This is accomplished by completing Form I-9, Employment Eligibility Verification. When you register as an employer, the *Handbook for Employers*, (containing complete instructions), will be sent to you.

4. Official Notice: As an employer, you will be required to adhere to regulations regarding minimum wage, hours and working conditions. Again, as part of your "registration," you will receive the "Official Notice" describing these regulations. The notice must be posted for all employees to read. Now is the time for you to familiarize yourself with these regulations.

PAYING YOUR EMPLOYEES

You can determine how often you want to pay your employees: weekly, biweekly, semimonthly or monthly. Your employees can be paid by the hour, job or commission.

1. Determine Gross Wage: Since taxes to be withheld will be based on the employee's gross wage, your first step is to determine that amount. For example, if your employee is hired to work 40 hours and the agreed upon hourly rate is $6.00, that employee's gross wage is $240.00.

2. FICA (Social Security): FICA is calculated as a percent of the employee's gross wages. The percentage (7.65% in 1992) is a combination of old-age, survivors, and disability insurance (OASDI at 6.2%) and hospital insurance (medicare at 1.45%). This tax is also imposed in an equal amount on the employer and applies to the wage base of $55,500 for OASDI and $130,200 for medicare for the year 1992.

3. Federal Income Tax: Based upon the employee's marital status and the number of withholding allowances claimed on Form W-4, Federal Income Tax must be withheld from each employee's paycheck. Circular E, Employer Tax Guide contains the charts used to calculate the amount of withholding. Separate charts are used according to frequency of payment (weekly, biweekly, semimonthly or monthly) and marital status of the employee. **Note: State and local taxes may also apply.** It is your responsibility to determine these requirements.

PAYROLL TAX DEPOSITS

The taxes that are withheld from employees' paychecks must be turned over to the IRS.

1. Open a Separate Account: To avoid "accidentally" spending these funds, you should open a separate bank account for withheld taxes. When you write your employees' paychecks, calculate your tax liability (FICA and Federal Income Tax withheld and the employer's matching share of FICA) and immediately deposit that amount into that account.

2. When Tax Liability Exceeds $500: If, at the end of each month, your total tax liability exceeds $500 you must make a tax deposit within fifteen days.

To do this you will have to complete a Federal Tax Deposit Coupon (Form 8109), write a check payable to your bank for your tax liability and take it to the bank. Since the check is payable to the bank, it is important to get a receipt for your payment in case the IRS questions the amount of your deposits.

QUARTERLY PAYROLL TAX RETURNS

At the end of each quarter (March, June, September and December), you must send quarterly payroll tax returns to the IRS.

1. Social Security and the Withholding of Income Taxes: You will have to report to the IRS the total amount of wages you paid throughout the quarter, as well as the amount of taxes you withheld from your employees. This reporting is done on Form 941. Any monthly deposits you made will be reported on this form and will be applied to your tax liability. Any balance due (less than $500) must be paid with your return.

2. FUTA (Unemployment Tax) Deposits: If, at the end of any calendar quarter, you owe but have not yet deposited, more than $100 in Federal Unemployment (FUTA) Tax for the year, you must make a deposit by the end of the next month. Most states have reporting requirements that are similar to the IRS and that also include unemployment insurance payments. Contrary to popular belief, unemployment insurance is not deducted from your employees' paychecks. It is an expense of the employer.

YEAR END REPORTS

The end of the year is a busy time for payroll reporting. Since it is also the end of a quarter, all of the quarterly tax returns described above are also due at the same time.

1. ANNUAL FUTA RETURN: Form 940 Employer's Annual Federal Unemployment (FUTA) Tax Return must be completed. This return reports each employees' wages that are subject to unemployment tax. Any quarterly deposits will be applied to the total tax liability.

2. FORM W-2: This form must be prepared for each employee. Form W-2 reports the total wages paid for the year and itemizes the total of each type of tax withheld from his or her paychecks. Multiple copies of these forms must be prepared. A packet of 3 to 4 are sent to the employee to be attached to his or her personal return. You must send a copy to the Social Security Administration and additional copies to your state and local government agencies.

ACCURACY IN REPORTING

It is vitally important that information reported on the Form W-2's, Form 941 Employer's Quarterly Federal Tax Return and Form 940 Employer's Annual Federal Unemployment (FUTA) Tax Return agrees. The Internal Revenue Service and Social Security Administration regularly compare information and will send notices to employers that have submitted conflicting information.

CAN YOU TAKE THE RESPONSIBILITY?

The IRS, Social Security, state and local agencies require that all of your reporting be exact. This can be a very heavy burden. The amount of paperwork alone requires many hours of work. The fact that you cannot afford to make a mistake makes it even more frightening.

Many small business owners buy a computer program, which supposedly makes the job easy. However, we have spoken with several people who still find themselves not knowing what they are doing. Some hire an in-house employee to do the job. This too can be costly. My suggestion is this:

Hire A Professional!

You can have your payroll done by an accounting professional or by a payroll service for a very nominal fee. You will pay your employees and report wages paid to your payroll service. They will work with you, take the responsibility for collecting the proper information from you on wages paid and see that all of the required reports are prepared and filed in a timely manner.

FOR YOUR INFORMATION

The Tax Section of the book, (Chapter 5), will give you more information on tax reporting requirements for employees. There are also examples of Forms W-2, W-3, W-4, FUTA and FICA returns. Read over the information and familiarize yourself with the requirements. Then you can make a decision as to whether you wish to do your own or hire a professional.

TRANSPORTATION, ENTERTAINMENT AND TRAVEL EXPENSES

You will have to prove your deductions for transportation, entertainment and travel business expenses with adequate records or by sufficient evidence that will support your claim. Records required should be kept in an account book, diary, statement of expense or similar record. In the following paragraphs, we will discuss general information pertaining to transportation expenses, meal and entertainment expenses and travel expenses. It is important that these expenses be recorded as they occur. It is difficult to remember them accurately after the fact.

TRANSPORTATION EXPENSES

These are the ordinary and necessary expenses of getting from one work place to another in the course of your business (when you are not traveling away from home). They **do** include the cost of transportation by air, rail, bus, taxi, etc., and the cost of driving and maintaining your car. They **do not** include transportation expenses between your home and your main or regular place of work, parking fees at your place of business or expenses for personal use of your car.

CAR EXPENSES: If you use your car for business purposes, you may be able to deduct car expenses. You generally can use one of these two methods to figure these expenses:

   a. **Actual Expense** - Gas, oil, tolls, parking, lease or rental fees, depreciation, repairs, licenses, insurance, etc.

   b. **Standard Mileage Rate** - Instead of figuring actual expenses, you may choose to use the standard mileage rate, which means that you will receive a deduction of a specific amount of money per mile (28 cents in 1992) of business use of your car. Standard Mileage Rate is not allowed if you do not own the car, use the car for hire, operate two or more cars at the same time or have claimed depreciation in previous years using any method but straight line.

MILEAGE LOG: You are required to record business miles traveled during the year. A filled-out form is provided on the next page, and a blank one is available in the Appendix for your use. The first year, it may be helpful to compare the results of both methods before making your decision. Also, be aware that if the use of the car is for both business and personal use, you must divide your expenses and deduct only the percentage used in business pursuit. For more detailed information get IRS Publication 917, *Business Uses of a Car* and IRS Publication 334, Chapter 16, *Tax Guide for Small Business.*

ABC COMPANY
MILEAGE LOG

NAME: _ABC Co. (John Higgins)_

DATED: From _Nov. 1st_ To _Nov. 30, 1992_

DATE	CITY OF DESTINATION	NAME OR OTHER DESIGNATION	BUSINESS PURPOSE	NO. OF MILES
11·01	Orange, CA	ExCal, Inc.	Present Proposal	67 mi
11·03	Cypress, CA	The Print Co.	P/U Brochures	23 mi.
11·04	Long Beach	Wm Long	Consultation	53 mi.
11·07	Fullerton, CA	B. of A.	Loan Meeting	17 mi.
11·23	Los Angeles	Moore Corp.	Consulting	143 mi.
11·30	Los Angeles	Moore Corp.	Consulting	140 mi.
			TOTAL MILES THIS SHEET	443

NOTE: 1. A Mileage record is required by the IRS to claim a mileage deduction. It is also used to determine the percentage of business use of a car.

2. Keep your mileage log in your vehicle and record your mileage as it occurs. It is very difficult to recall after the fact.

MEALS AND ENTERTAINMENT EXPENSES

You may be able to deduct business-related entertainment expenses you have to entertain a client, customer or employee. The expense must be ordinary (common and accepted in your field of business) and necessary (helpful and appropriate for your business, but not necessarily indispensable). In addition, you must be able to show that they are 1) directly related to the active conduct of your trade or business, or 2) associated with the active conduct of your trade or business.

ENTERTAINMENT INCLUDES: Any activity generally considered to provide entertainment, amusement, or recreation. For example, entertaining guests at night clubs, social, athletic and sporting clubs, theaters, sporting events, on yachts, on hunting, fishing, vacation and similar trips. Entertainment also may include satisfying personal, living or family needs of individuals, such as providing food, a hotel suite or a car to business customers or their families.

ENTERTAINMENT DOES NOT INCLUDE: Supper money you give your employees, a hotel room you keep for your employees while on business travel or a car used in your business. However, if you provide the use of a hotel suite or a car to your employee who is on vacation, this is entertainment of the employee.

MEALS AS ENTERTAINMENT: Entertainment includes the cost of a meal you provide to a customer or client. It does not matter whether the meal is a part of other entertainment. Generally, to deduct an entertainment-related meal, you or your employee must be present when the food or beverages are provided.

80 PERCENT LIMIT: Beginning in 1987, you may deduct only 80 percent of business-related meals and entertainment expenses. You must record these expenses with date, place of entertainment, business purpose, the name of the person entertained and the amount spent.

SAMPLE ENTERTAINMENT EXPENSE RECORD: The form provided on the next page will help you to record all information required to justify entertainment expenses. Be sure to fill in all categories. Keep all receipts for verification and file for easy retrieval. For more information see IRS Publication 463, Chapter 2, *Travel, Entertainment and Gift Expenses* and Publication 334, Chapter 16, *Tax Guide for Small Business.*

ABC COMPANY
ENTERTAINMENT EXPENSE RECORD

NAME: _John Higgins_

DATED: From _11·01·92_ To _11·30·92_

DATE	PLACE OF ENTERTAINMENT	BUSINESS PURPOSE	NAME OF PERSON ENTERTAINED	AMOUNT SPENT	
11·04	The 410 Club	Consulting	Wm Long	27	32
11·23	Seafood Chef	Consulting	Thomas Moore	23	50
11·27	The Cannon Club	Staff Dinner	Company Employees	384	00

NOTE: For more information on Meals and Entertainment, please refer to IRS Publication 463, *Travel, Entertainment and Gift Expenses.*

TRAVEL EXPENSES

Deductible travel expenses include those ordinary and necessary expenses you incur while traveling away from your home on business. The lists that follow provide general guidelines:

EXPENSE THAT CAN BE DEDUCTED

1. Transportation fares: between home and business destination.
2. Taxi, commuter bus, and limousine fares - between the airport and your hotel or temporary work site.
3. Baggage and shipping - actual costs.
4. Car expenses - includes leasing expenses, actual expenses or the standard mileage rate (28 cents in 1992).
5. Lodging.
6. Meals - actual or standard meal allowance.
7. Cleaning and laundry expenses.
8. Telephone expenses.
9. Tips related to any of the above services.
10. Other business-related expenses - connected with your travel.

YOU CANNOT DEDUCT

1. That portion of travel, meals and lodging for your spouse - unless there is a real business purpose for your spouse's presence.
2. Investment travel - such as investment seminars or stockholders' meetings.
3. Amounts you spend for travel - to conduct a general search for, or preliminary investigation of, a new business.

SPECIAL RULINGS: You will need to study special rulings. For instance, when your trip is not entirely for business purposes, you will have to properly allocate the expenses. Treatment of expenses depends on how much of your trip was business-related and what portion occurred within the United States. Also, if you are not traveling for the entire 24-hour day, you must prorate the standard meal allowance and claim only one-fourth of the allowance for each six-hour quarter of the day during any part of which you are traveling away from home.

TRAVEL RECORD: When you travel away from home on business, you need to keep records of all the expenses you incur. Use the Travel Record on the next page to keep track of the the information that you will be required to keep. A blank form is located in the Appendix. You will also need to keep documentation such as receipts, canceled checks or bills to support your expense. For more information, see IRS Publication 463, Chapter 1, *Travel, Entertainment and Gift Expenses* and Publication 334, Chapter 16, *Tax Guide for Small Business.*

ABC COMPANY TRAVEL RECORD

TRIP TO: _Dallas, Texas_

Business Purpose: _Technology Expo (Show Exhibits)_

Dated From: _6·15·93_ To: _6·18·93_

No. Days Spent on Business _5_

DATE	LOCATION	EXPENSE PAID TO	MEALS				HOTEL	TAXIS, ETC.	AUTOMOBILE			MISC. EXP.
			Breakfast	Lunch	Dinner	Miscell.			Gas	Parking	Tolls	
6·15	Phoenix, AZ	Mobil Gas				6 40			21 00			
6·15	Phoenix, AZ	Greentree Inn		12 50								
6·15	Chola, NM	Exxon							23 50			
6·15	Las Cruces, NM	Holiday Inn			27 00		49 00					
6·16	Las Cruces, NM	Exxon							19 00			
6·16	Taft, Tx	Molly's Cafe		16 25								
6·16	Dallas, Tx	Holiday Inn			18 75		54 00					
6·17	Dallas, Tx	Expo Center								8 00		
6·17	Dallas, Tx	Honey's Eatry		21 00								
6·17	Dallas, Tx	Holiday Inn			24 50		54 00					
6·18	Dallas, Tx	Holiday Inn	9 50									
6·18	Dallas, Tx	Expo Center		14 00						8 00		9 00
6·18	Dallas, Tx	Holiday Inn			16 20		54 00					(Fax)
6·19	Pokie, Tx	Texaco							21 00			
6·19	Pokie, Tx	Denny's		18 50								
6·19	Chola, NM	Holiday Inn			27 00		48 00					
6·20	Chola, NM	Holiday Inn	12 75									
6·20	Flagstaff, AZ	Texaco							22 00			
		TOTALS →	22 25	83 25	113 45	6 40	259 00		106 50	16 00		9 00

Attach all receipts for Meals, Hotel, Fares, Auto, Entertainment, etc. Details of your expenses can be noted on the receipts. File your travel record and your receipts in the same envelope. Label the envelope as to trip. File all trip records together. When expenses are allocated, be sure not to double expense anything. (Ex: Gas cannot be used if you elect to use "mileage" for your car.)

CUSTOMER INFORMATION RECORDS

To help a business deal more effectively with its customers, it can be very beneficial to develop a system to keep track of customer information. Without technology to enable them to reach out through data bases and information services, many businesses have no way to keep specialized information on customers due to volume or change in clientele. Small businesses in the service industry and in specialty retail sales are finding that if they can incorporate specialized customer records into their operations, they have a better chance of retaining customers. Service businesses strive for repeat and referral business plus new customers who come to them through commercial advertising. Specialty retail sales shops also look for repeats and referrals as their primary source of business.

By keeping a data base that can selectively draw out information, the customer can be better served. For those without the electronic advantage, a file of 3"x 5" index cards—one for each customer—a business owner can also have ready information at his fingertips. In our clock shop, we have effectively used a manual system of this type to service a customer list of approximately 6,000. The types of things that can be recorded and some uses of that information are as follows:

SERVICE INDUSTRY

Includes: Name, address, telephone numbers (work and home), service performed, charges, special advice to customer, guarantees given and any other information that you feel may be helpful.

Some uses of information: Protection of the business from customers' claims that services were performed that were not recorded, information as proof of dates of warranty service (benefitting both customer and business owner), information to help business owners remember customers and give them specialized attention.

SPECIALTY RETAIL SALES BUSINESS

Includes: Name, address, telephone numbers (work and home), sales information, special interests of customer.

Some uses of information: Use as a mailing list for special sales; when customer calls, use card to jog your memory as to his interests, what he has already purchased and what he might like. These customers like to be remembered and have personalized information.

SAMPLE CUSTOMER FILES: See the next page for examples of customer files for: 1) The Service Industry, and 2) Specialty Retail Sales.

SAMPLE
CUSTOMER DATA FILES

1. SERVICE INDUSTRY

Jones, John W.
123 W. 1st Street
Anywhere, CA 97134

(H) (714) 555-2489
(W) (714) 555-1234

1. *Ridgeway G/F Clock (IHS)*   a. *Repaired pendulum, rep.*
     $55.00   8/19/86   *susp. sprg., serviced.*

2. *S/Thomas O.G.*   a. *Cleaned, bushed movement, balanced.*
     $155.00   6/07/91   Guarantee: 1 year

3. *Waltham L/W?W (antique)*   a. *Stem, clean, repair hspg.*
     $45.00   7/11/92

2. SPECIALTY RETAIL SALES

Smith, Henry L. (D.D.S)
76 Main Street, Suite X
Somewhere, CA 96072

(W) (201) 555-1304

Birthday: May 3rd
Anniversary: Oct. 21st

*Buys for wife's (Ann) collection:

1. *08 CM M/Box w/'Lara's Theme' 1/18 (Rosewood burl)*
     $55.00 + Tax   4/28/92

2. *789 BMP 3/72 w/'Phantom of the Opera'*
     $675.00 + Tax   10/17/92

3. *Novelty M/B - Bear w/Heart $32.00 + Tax 2/13/93*

BUSINESS CHECKBOOK

Your business checkbook is not just a package preprinted forms that represent your business bankroll. It is also the initial accounting record showing when, where and what amount of money was dispersed and when, from what sources and how much money was received by your company. This information is all kept on the recording space provided in your checkbook.

WHAT TYPE OF CHECKBOOK IS MOST EFFECTIVE?

Don't get a pocket-size checkbook. This type of checkbook is small so it does not provide enough space for entry of information (and it is also easily misplaced). Some points to consider when selecting your business checkbook are:

1. Size: A business-sized checkbook is best. There is a personal desk type with three standard size checks on each right-hand page and a register (recording) page of equal size on the left. Instead of one line of check register for each transaction, you will have room to record such things as invoice numbers and descriptions of purchases. You can divide amounts paid with one check into separate expenses. For instance, the payment of an invoice to an office supply store may involve $15.00 for office supplies and $45.00 for exhibit materials. Deposits can be divided into types of revenues received. These and other notations will be invaluable when you do your weekly bookkeeping because you will not have to look for paperwork to supply missing information.

2. Duplicate Feature: Many business owners number among the ranks of those people who do not automatically record information when they write checks. To eliminate the frustration created by this unfortunate habit, banks can provide checkbooks made with carbonless copies underneath each check. If you fail to record a check at the time you write it, a copy will remain in your checkbook. We don't use one, but a lot of people swear by them.

3. Pre-Printing and Numbering of Checks: Your checks should be pre-printed with your business name, address and telephone number. They should also be numbered. Some businesses will not even deal with you if you try to use personal checks or ones without pre-printed information. Some vendors with which you wish to do business perceive them as a possible danger signal and indicator of a lack of your credibility.

4. Deposit Record: There is one last feature that we like when it comes to banking supplies. Instead of deposit slips that can get lost, we like to use a Deposit Record Book. It is a bound book of deposit slips arranged in sets of two. The original goes to the bank and the duplicate stays in your book and is dated, stamped and initialed by the teller. The book can be kept in your bank bag and is ready to use for the next deposit. It ensures that you have a permanent record of all of your deposits.

BALANCING YOUR CHECKBOOK

Once a month your bank will send you a statement of your account, showing a summary of your activity since the last statement date. It will list all deposits, check withdrawals, ATM activity, bank charges and interest earned. You will need to reconcile it with your checkbook on a timely basis. This is one of those chores that is frequently ignored. "I will catch it up later when I have more time." This is the kind of attitude results in undiscovered errors and overdrawn accounts. It is not difficult to balance your checkbook if you follow the steps outlined below.

1. UPDATE YOUR CHECKBOOK
Add: Interest earned.
           Deposits not recorded.
           Automatic credits unrecorded.
Subtract: Service Charges
           Checks not recorded.
           Automatic debits unrecorded.
           Payments not recorded.
Mark Off: Amount of all checks
             paid against statement.
           Amount of all deposits shown.
           All ATM & electronic transactions that are recorded.

2. LIST AND TOTAL
All deposits made and other credits not shown on the statement.
All outstanding checks not shown on current or previous statements.

3. BALANCE
Enter statement balance as indicated.
Add the total deposits and other credits not shown on current or previous statements.
Subtract items outstanding.

Total should agree with checkbook balance.

BALANCE FORM			
Statement Balance			
Add	Deposits made and not shown on this statement		
Total		$	
Subtract	Outstanding Items		
Total	Should agree with your checkbook balance	$	
OUTSTANDING ITEMS			
Check No. or Date	Amount	Check No. or Date	Amount
Total	**$**	**Total**	**$**

IF YOU ARE NOT IN BALANCE: Recheck your addition and subtraction in your checkbook. Check amounts in checkbook against those in statement. Look for uncashed checks from previous statements and be sure they are not still outstanding. Check amount you are off and see if it matches amount on any of your checks. Be sure that you did not add a check when you should have subtracted. Be sure that you recorded and subtracted all ATM withdrawals in your checkbook.

RECORDING STATEMENT INFORMATION

When you are doing your regular recordkeeping, you must remember that you will have to record all bank charges (service charges, check orders, returned check charges, returned checks, etc.) in your Revenue & Expense Journal. If you do not, your expenses will be understated and you will pay more taxes. Also be sure to record interest earnings.

RECEIPT FILES

It is required by the IRS that you be able to verify deductions. For that reason alone, you must have a filing system that ensures that your receipts are easy to retrieve. This is also very important for your own benefit. There will be many times that you will need to find information on a transaction for any one of innumerable reasons. If your filing system is a mess, you are lost.

WHERE DO YOU KEEP RECEIPTS?

For most businesses, an accordion file divided into alphabet pockets will be the most efficient way of filing your receipts. These files also come with pockets divided into months, but we think it becomes cumbersome for retrieval. Picking out all of your utility bills, for example, would require that you pick from 12 different pockets. With the alphabet file, it would require only one. You will probably also need one or more two-drawer file cabinets for systematic filing of other paperwork.

One of the most frequent questions we get asked is how to determine what letter of the alphabet you file the receipt under. The easiest way is to use the first letter entered in a record. If you record a meal in Petty Cash as paid to cash because you don't know the name of a seller, file the receipt under "C." We do keep all the meal receipts in one envelope marked "Meals" and file it under "M" because that is an item frequently audited and we can pull all of the receipts quickly. We also keep all the records for a trip in a single envelope and mark it with the occasion and date. Then we file all travel records under "T" for the same reason. You may wish to keep a separate file for Petty Cash Receipts. We use the same one for those paid by check and by cash.

AT THE END OF THE YEAR

When the tax year is closed, you can add your bank statements, Revenue & Expense Journal, a copy of your tax return, and any other pertinent information for that year. All are put away in the one accordion file and labeled with the year. If, at a later date, you need information for a tax audit or for another purpose, everything is in one place.

■ ■ ■ ■ ■

You have now completed the General Records Section of the book and your day-to-day recordkeeping should be set up. In the next section of this book you will learn about Financial Statements and how they are developed from the records with which we have just been concerned.

Financial Statements

In the three previous chapters of this book, we have introduced you to the functions and types of recordkeeping and some simple accounting terminology. We have discussed double and single-entry accounting and worked through the process of setting up essential general records for your business.

Now it is time to see how financial statements are developed from your general records and how the use of those financial statements can help you to see the financial condition of your business and to identify its relative strengths and weaknesses. The business owner who takes the time to understand and evaluate his operation through financial statements over the life of the business will be far ahead of the entrepreneur who concerns himself only with his product or service.

WHAT ARE FINANCIAL STATEMENTS?

Financial statements show past and projected finances. These statements are both the source of your tax information (Chapter 5) and the means by which you analyze your business (Chapter 8). They are developed from your General Records and fall into two main categories: **Actual Performance Statements**—and—**Pro Forma Statements**. Before you proceed further, it is best to understand what they are and which ones you will use for your business.

ACTUAL PERFORMANCE STATEMENTS

These are the historical financial statements reflecting the past performance of your business. If you are planning a new business, you have no history. However, as soon as you have been in business for even one accounting period, you will begin to generate these two financial statements, both of which will prove to be invaluable to you in making decisions about your business. They are as follows:

1. Balance Sheet
2. Profit & Loss Statement (Income Statement)

We will also introduce you to a **Business Financial History**, which is a composite of the Balance Sheet, Profit & Loss Statement and legal structure information. It is used frequently as a loan application.

PRO FORMA STATEMENTS

The word "pro forma" in accounting means "projected." These are the financial statements that are used for you to predict the future profitability of your business. Your projections will be based on realistic research and reasonable assumptions, trying not to overstate your revenues or understate your expenses. The pro forma statements are:

1. Pro Forma Cash Flow Statement (or Budget)
2. Quarterly Budget Analysis (means of evaluating projections with actual performance within budget)
3. Three-Year Projection (Pro Forma Income Statement)
4. Break-Even Analysis

HOW TO PROCEED

Each of the above financial documents will be discussed as to:

1. definition and use,
2. how to develop the statement; and
3. sources of needed information.

Every business owner will need to understand and use Profit & Loss (Income) Statements, Balance Sheets and Pro Forma Cash Flow Statements with Quarterly Budget Analysis on a regular basis. The others will be required on a business plan and are useful tools in financial planning. The following are some guidelines for different situations:

1. **If you are a new business and you are going to seek a lender or investor** - You will be required to write a business plan. You will need to create all Pro Forma Statements included in this chapter. You have no financial history and cannot include Actual Performance Statements.

2. **If you are a new business and you are not going to seek a lender or investor** - You should still think about writing a business plan. You will include all Pro Forma Statements. Even if you decide not to write one, it is especially important to plan your cash flow (budget).

3. **If you are an existing business and you are going to seek a lender or investor** - You will be required to write a business plan. You will include all financial documents discussed in this chapter plus other elements. (See our book, *Anatomy of a Business Plan*, Chicago: Dearborn Financial Publishing, 1993.)

4. **If you are an existing business and you are not seeking a lender or investor** - All financial statements are beneficial. The Profit & Loss, Balance Sheet and Pro Forma Cash Flow Statement are a must.

*Now You Are Ready to Learn to
Develop Actual Performance Statements*

BALANCE SHEET

WHAT IS A BALANCE SHEET?

The Balance Sheet is a financial statement that shows the financial position of the business as of a fixed date. It is usually done at the close of an accounting period. The Balance Sheet can be compared to a photograph. It is a picture of what your business owns and owes at a particular given moment and will show you whether your financial position is strong or weak. By regularly preparing this statement, you will be able to identify and analyze trends in the financial strength of your business and thus implement timely modifications.

FORMAT

The Balance Sheet must follow an accepted format and contain the following three categories so anyone reading it can readily interpret it. The three are related in that at any given time, a business's assets equal the total contributions by its creditors and owners.

ASSETS = Anything your business owns that has monetary value.

LIABILITIES = Debts owed by the business to any of its creditors.

NET WORTH (CAPITAL) = An amount equal to the owner's equity.

The relationship between these three terms is simply illustrated in a mathematical formula. It reads as follows:

ASSETS - LIABILITIES = NET WORTH

Examined as such, it becomes apparent that if a business possesses more assets than it owes to creditors, its net worth will be a positive. Conversely, if the business owes more money to creditors than it possesses in assets, the net worth will be a negative.

SOURCES OF INFORMATION

If you (or your accountant) have a computerized recordkeeping system, it should automatically generate a Balance Sheet on command, drawing information from your general ledger accounts. If you are using single-entry accounting, the figures come from your general records. Look for the sources given at the end of the category explanations on the next page.

EXPLANATION OF CATEGORIES
BALANCE SHEET

I. ASSETS: Everything owned by or owed to your business that has cash value.

   A. **Current Assets** - Assets that can be converted into cash within one year of the date on the Balance Sheet.

   1. **Cash** - Money you have on hand. Include monies not yet deposited.

   2. **Petty Cash** - Money deposited to Petty Cash and not yet expended.

   3. **Accounts Receivable** - Money owed to you for sale of goods and/or services.

   4. **Inventory** - Raw materials, work in process and goods manufactured or purchased for resale.

   5. **Short-Term Investments** - (Expected to be converted to cash within one year) Stocks, bonds, C. D.'s, List at lesser of cost or market value.

   6. **Prepaid Expenses** - Goods or services purchased or rented prior to use. (ex: rent, insurance, prepaid inventory purchases, etc.)

   B. **Long-Term Investments** - Stocks, bonds, and special savings accounts to be kept for at least one year.

   C. **Fixed Assets** - Resources a business owns and does not intend for resale.

   1. **Land** - List at original purchase price.

   2. **Buildings** - List at cost less any depreciation previously taken.

   3. **Equipment**, Furniture, Autos/Vehicles - List at cost less depreciation. Kelley Blue Book can be used to determine value of vehicles.

II. LIABILITIES: What your business owes; claims by creditors on your assets.

   A. **Current Liabilities** - Those obligations payable within one operating cycle.

   1. **Accounts Payable** - Obligations payable within one operating cycle.

   2. **Notes Payable** - Short-term notes; list the balance of principal due. Separately list the current portion of long-term debts.

   3. **Interest Payable** - Interest accrued on loans and credit.

   4. **Taxes Payable** - Amounts estimated to have been incurred during the accounting period.

   5. **Payroll Accrual** - Current liabilities on salaries and wages.

   B. **Long-Term Liabilities** - Outstanding balance less the current portion due (ex.: mortgage, vehicle).

III. NET WORTH: Also called "Owner Equity"; the claims of the owner or owners on the assets of the business (document according to the legal structure of your business).

   A. **Proprietorship or Partnership** - Each owner's original investment plus earnings after withdrawals.

   B. **Corporation** - The sum of contributions by owners or stockholders plus earnings retained after paying dividends.

ABC COMPANY
BALANCE SHEET

COMPANY NAME: _ABC Company_

Date: _December_ _31_, 19_93_

ASSETS

Current Assets

Cash $ _8,742_

Petty Cash $ _167_

Accounts Receivable $ _5,400_

Inventory $ _101,800_

Short-Term Investments $ _Ø_

Prepaid Expenses $ _1,967_

Long-Term Investments $ _Ø_

Fixed Assets

Land (valued at cost) $ _185,000_

Buildings $ _143,000_
1. Cost _171,600_
2. Less Acc. Depr. _28,600_

Improvements $ _Ø_
1. Cost _____
2. Less Acc. Depr. _____

Equipment $ _5,760_
1. Cost _7,200_
2. Less Acc. Depr. _1,440_

Furniture $ _2,150_
1. Cost _____
2. Less Acc. Depr. _____

Autos/Vehicles $ _16,432_
1. Cost _19,700_
2. Less Acc. Depr. _3,268_

Other Assets
1. $ _____
2. $ _____

TOTAL ASSETS $ _470,418_

LIABILITIES

Current Liabilities

Accounts Payable $ _2,893_

Notes Payable $ _Ø_

Interest Payable $ _1,842_

Taxes Payable
Fed. Inc. Tax $ _5,200_
State Inc. Tax $ _1,025_
Self-Emp. Tax $ _800_
Sales Tax Accrual $ _2,130_
Property Tax $ _Ø_

Payroll Accrual $ _4,700_

Long-Term Liabilities
Notes Payable $ _196,700_

TOTAL LIABILITIES $ _215,290_

NET WORTH

Proprietorship $ _____
or
Partnership
John Smith, 60% Equity $ _153,077_
Mary Blake, 40% Equity $ _102,051_
or
Corporation
Capital Stock $ _____
Surplus Paid In $ _____
Retained Earnings $ _____

TOTAL NET WORTH $ _255,128_

Assets - Liabilities = Net Worth

Total Liabilities and Equity will always be equal to Total Assets

PROFIT & LOSS STATEMENT OR INCOME STATEMENT

WHAT IS A PROFIT & LOSS (INCOME) STATEMENT?

This statement shows your business financial activity over a period of time, usually your tax year. In contrast to the Balance Sheet, which shows a picture of your business at a given moment, the Profit & Loss Statement can be likened to a moving picture—showing what has happened in your business over a period of time. It is an excellent tool for assessing your business. You will be able to pick out weaknesses in your operation and plan ways to run your business more effectively, thereby increasing your profits. For example, you may find that some heavy advertising that you did in March did not effectively increase your sales. In following years, you may decide to utilize your advertising funds more effectively by using them at a time when there is increased customer spending taking place. In the same way, you might examine your Profit & Loss Statement to see what months have the heaviest sales volume and plan your inventory accordingly. Comparison of your P & L's from several years will give you an even better picture of the trends in your business. Do not underestimate the value of this particular tool when planning your tactics.

HOW TO DEVELOP A PROFIT & LOSS STATEMENT

The Profit & Loss Statement (Income Statement) is compiled from actual business transactions, in contrast to pro forma statements, which are projections for future business periods. The Profit & Loss shows where your money has come from and where it was spent over a specific period of time. It should be prepared not only at the end of the fiscal year, but at the close of each business month. It is one of the two principal financial statements prepared from the ledgers and the records of a business. **Income and Expense Account Balances** are used in the Profit & Loss Statement. The remaining Asset, Liability and Capital information provides the figures for the Balance Sheet described on p.57.

In double-entry accounting, the accounts in the General Ledger are balanced and closed at the end of each month. Balances from the Revenue Accounts (numbered 400-499) and the Expense Accounts (numbered 500-599) are transferred to your Profit & Loss Statement. If you use an accountant or have a software program, either should generate a Profit & Loss Statement at the end of every month as well as at the end of your tax year. If you set up a manual bookkeeping system (single-entry) with General Records from Chapter 3, the Profit & Loss Statement is generated by a simple transfer of the end-of-month totals from your Revenue & Expense Journal.

FORMAT AND SOURCES OF INFORMATION

The Profit & Loss (or Income) Statement must also follow an accepted accounting format and contain certain categories. The following is the correct format and a brief explanation of the items to be included or computations to be made in each category in order to arrive at "The Bottom Line" or owner's share of the profit for the period:

INCOME

1. **Net Sales (Gross sales less returns and allowances):** What were your cash receipts for the period? If your accounting is on an accrual basis, what amount did you invoice out during the period?

2. **Cost of Goods Sold:** See the form on p. 63 for computation.

3. **Gross Profit:** Subtract Cost of Goods from Net Sales.

EXPENSES

1. **Selling Expenses (Direct, Controllable, Variable):** What amounts did you actually spend on items directly related to your product or service? (Marketing, commissions, freight, etc.)

2. **Administrative Expenses (Indirect, Fixed):** What amounts were spent during the period on office overhead? (Rent, insurance, accounting, office salaries, etc.)

NET INCOME FROM OPERATIONS: Gross Profit minus Selling and Administrative Expenses.

    OTHER INCOME: Interest received during the period.

    OTHER EXPENSE: Interest paid out during the period.

NET PROFIT (LOSS) BEFORE INCOME TAXES: The Net Income from Operations + Interest Received = Interest Paid Out.

INCOME TAXES: List income taxes paid out during the period (Federal, State, Self-Employment).

NET PROFIT (LOSS) AFTER INCOME TAXES: Subtract all Income Taxes paid out from the Net Profit (or Loss) Before Income Taxes. This is what is known as "The Bottom Line."

SAMPLE FORMS: The next two pages contain two Profit & Loss forms. The first is divided into 12 months. At the end of the year, if filled-in monthly, this form will provide an accurate picture of the year's financial activity. There is a blank form in the Appendix for your use. The form on p. 63 (filled-in) is to be used for either a monthly or an annual Profit & Loss Statement.

PROFIT & LOSS STATEMENT (INCOME STATEMENT)

Company Name: _____

FOR THE YEAR 19___.	JAN	FEB	MAR	APR	MAY	JUN	JUL	AUG	SEP	OCT	NOV	DEC	YEAR TOTAL
INCOME													
1. NET SALES (Gross less ret. & allow.)													
2. COST OF GOODS SOLD (c. - d.)													
a. Beginning Inventory													
b. Purchases													
c. C.O.G. Available for Sale (a+b)													
d. Less End. Inv. (Dec. 31st)													
3. GROSS PROFIT ON SALES (1. minus 2.)													
EXPENSES													
1. VARIABLE (Selling/Direct Exp.) (a. thru h.)													
a. Advertising/Marketing													
b. Freight													
c. Fulfillment													
d. Packaging Costs													
e. Salaries/Wages/Commissions													
f. Travel													
g. Miscellaneous Selling Exp.													
h. Depreciation (Product/Service Assets)													
2. FIXED (Administrative/Indirect) (a. thru h.)													
a. Insurance													
b. Licenses & Permits													
c. Office Salaries													
d. Rent Expense													
e. Financial Admin.													
f. Utilities													
g. Other Overhead													
h. Depreciation (Office Equipment)													
TOTAL OPERATING EXPENSE (Variable+Fixed)													
NET INCOME FROM OPERATIONS (Gross Profit less Operating Expense)													
OTHER INCOME (INTEREST)													
OTHER EXPENSE (INTEREST)													
NET PROFIT (LOSS) BEFORE INCOME TAXES													
TAXES (Federal, Self-Employment, State)													
NET PROFIT (LOSS) AFTER TAXES													

Fill out this form at the end of each month when you have closed and balanced your books. At the end of the year this twelve-month profit & loss statement will provide an accurate financial picture of what has taken place during the year. A blank form is located in the Appendix for your use.

ABC COMPANY
PROFIT & LOSS (INCOME) STATEMENT

For the period beginning _____ and ending _____

INCOME		
1. NET SALES (Gross less ret. & allow.)		$500,000
2. COST OF GOODS SOLD (c. minus d.)		312,000
a. Beginning Inventory	147,000	
b. Purchases	320,000	
c. C.O.G. Available for Sale (a+b)	467,000	
d. Less End. Inv. (Dec. 31st)	155,000	
3. GROSS PROFIT ON SALES (1 minus 2)		$188,000
EXPENSES		
1. VARIABLE (Direct/Selling) (a. thru h.)		67,000
a. Advertising/Marketing	9,000	
b. Freight	19,000	
c. Fulfillment	2,000	
d. Packaging Costs	3,000	
e. Salaries/Wages/Commissions	27,200	
f. Travel	1,800	
g. Miscellaneous Selling Exp.		
h. Depreciation (Product/Services Assets)	5,000	
2. FIXED (Indirect/Administrative) (a. thru h.)		53,000
a. Insurance	19,000	
b. Licenses & Permits	4,000	
c. Office Salaries	6,000	
d. Rent Expense	4,000	
e. Financial Admin.	14,700	
f. Utilities	3,000	
g. Other Overhead		
h. Depreciation (Office Equipment)	2,300	
TOTAL OPERATING EXPENSE (1 + 2)		120,000
NET INCOME FROM OPERATIONS (Gross Profit less Total Op.Exp.)		68,000
OTHER INCOME (INTEREST)		+ 5,000
OTHER EXPENSE (INTEREST)		- 6,000
NET PROFIT (LOSS) BEFORE INCOME TAXES		$67,000
TAXES (Federal, Self-Employment, State)		- 23,000
NET PROFIT (LOSS) AFTER TAXES		**$44,000**

BUSINESS FINANCIAL HISTORY

Your financial history is a financial statement that would be required if you are writing a business plan to go to a lender or investor. It is a summary of financial information about your company from its start to the present. The form will generally be provided by the lender.

IF YOU ARE A NEW BUSINESS

You will have only projections for your business. If you are applying for a loan, the lender will require a **Personal Financial History**. This will be of benefit in that it will show him the manner in which you have conducted your personal business, an indicator of the probability of your succeeding in your business.

IF YOU ARE AN ESTABLISHED BUSINESS

The Loan Application and your Business Financial History are the same. When you indicate that you are interested in obtaining a business loan, the institution considering the loan will supply you with an application. The format may vary slightly. When you receive your loan application, be sure to review it and think about how you are going to answer each item. Answer all questions and, by all means, be certain that your information is accurate and that it can be easily verified.

INFORMATION NEEDED AND SOURCES

As you fill out your Business Financial History (Loan Application), it should become immediately apparent why this is the last financial document to be completed. All of the information needed will have been compiled previously in earlier parts of your plan. To help you with your financial history, the following is a list of information usually included and the source you will refer to for that information:

1. ASSETS, LIABILITIES, NET WORTH - You should recognize these three as Balance Sheet terms. You have already completed a Balance Sheet for your company and need only to go back to that record and bring the dollar amounts forward.

2. CONTINGENT LIABILITIES - These are debts you may come to owe in the future (for example: default on a co-signed note or settlement of a pending lawsuit).

3. INVENTORY DETAILS - Information is derived from your Inventory Record. Also, in the Organizational section of your plan you should already have a summary of your current policies and methods of evaluation.

4. PROFIT & LOSS STATEMENT - This is revenue and expense information. You will transfer the information from your Annual Profit & Loss (last statement completed) or from a compilation of several if required by the lender.

5. REAL ESTATE HOLDINGS, STOCKS AND BONDS - Refer back to the Business portion of your plan. You may also have to go through your investment records for more comprehensive information.

6. SOLE PROPRIETORSHIP, PARTNERSHIP, OR CORPORATION INFORMATION - There are generally three separate schedules on the financial history, one for each form of legal structure. You will be required to fill out the one that is appropriate to your business. In the Organizational section, you will have covered two areas that will serve as the source of this information— Legal Structure and Management. Supporting Documents may also contain some of the information that you will need.

7. AUDIT INFORMATION - Refer back to the Organizational section under Recordkeeping. You may also be asked questions about other prospective lenders, whether you are seeking credit, who audits your books and when they were last audited.

8. INSURANCE COVERAGE - You will be asked to provide detailed information on the amounts of different types coverage (*i.e.* - merchandise, equipment, public liability, earthquake, auto, etc.). The Organizational section contains information on coverage that can be brought forth to the financial history.

SAMPLE FORMS

BUSINESS FINANCIAL HISTORY FORM: On the following pages you will find an example of a Business Financial History that might be required by a potential lender or investor.

PERSONAL FINANCIAL STATEMENT FORM: Following the sample business financial statement, you will find a sample of a personal financial statement form. If you are a new business and need a personal financial statement for your business plan, you can get one from a lender, stationery store or other supplier of office forms.

BUSINESS
FINANCIAL HISTORY

FINANCIAL STATEMENT
INDIVIDUAL, PARTNERSHIP, OR CORPORATION

FINANCIAL STATEMENT OF

NAME_____

ADDRESS_____

RECEIVED AT_____ BRANCH____

BUSINESS_____

AT CLOSE OF BUSINESS_____ 19___

To

The undersigned, for the purpose of procuring and establishing credit from time to time with you and to induce you to permit the undersigned to become indebted to you on notes, endorsements, guarantees, overdrafts or otherwise, furnishes the following (or in lieu thereof the attached, which is the most recent statement prepared by or for the undersigned) as being a full, true and correct statement of the financial condition of the undersigned on the date indicated, and agrees to notify you immediately of the extent and character of any material change in said financial condition, and also agrees that if the undersigned, or any endorser or guarantor of any of the obligations of the undersigned, at any time fails in business or becomes insolvent, or commits an act of bankruptcy, or if any deposit account of the undersigned with you, or any other property of the undersigned held by you, be attempted to be obtained or held by writ of execution, garnishment, attachment or other legal process, or if any of the representations made below prove to be untrue, or if the undersigned fails to notify you of any material change as above agreed, or if the business, or any interest therein, of the undersigned is sold, then and in such case, at your option, all of the obligations of the undersigned to you, or held by you, shall immediately become due and payable, without demand or notice. This statement shall be construed by you to be a continuing statement of the condition of the undersigned, and a new and original statement of all assets and liabilities upon each and every transaction in and by which the undersigned hereafter becomes indebted to you, until the undersigned advises in writing to the contrary.

ASSETS	DOLLARS	CENTS	LIABILITIES	DOLLARS	CENTS
Cash In_____ (NAME OF BANK)			Notes Payable to Banks_____		
Cash on Hand_____			Notes Payable and Trade Acceptances for Merchandise_____		
Notes Receivable and Trade Acceptance (Includes $_____ Past Due)			Notes Payable to Others_____		
Accounts Receivable—$_____ Less Reserves $_____			Accounts Payable (Includes $_____ Past Due)_____		
Customer's . . . (Includes $_____ Past Due)			Due to Partners, Employes, Relatives, Officers, Stockholders or Allied Companies_____		
Merchandise—Finished—How Valued_____			Chattel Mortgages and Contracts Payable (Describe Monthly Payments) . . . . . $		
Merchandise—Unfinished—How Valued_____			Federal and State Income Tax_____		
Merchandise—Raw Material—How Valued_____			Accrued Liabilities (Interest, Wages, Taxes, Etc.)_____		
Supplies on Hand_____			Portion of Long Term Debt Due Within One Year_____		
Stocks and Bonds—Listed (See Schedule B)_____					
TOTAL CURRENT ASSETS			**TOTAL CURRENT LIABILITIES**		
Real Estate—Less Depreciation of: $_____ Net (See Schedule A)			Liens on Real Estate (See Schedule A) $_____		
Machinery and Fixtures— Less Depreciation of: $_____ Net			Less Current Portion Included Above $_____ Net		
Automobiles and Trucks— Less Depreciation of: $_____ Net					
Stocks and Bonds—Unlisted (See Schedule B)_____			Capital Stock—Preferred_____		
Due from Partners, Employes, Relatives, Officers, Stockholders or Allied Companies_____			Capital Stock—Common_____		
Cash Value Life Insurance_____			Surplus—Paid In_____		
			Surplus—Earned and Undivided Profits_____		
Other Assets (Describe)_____			Net Worth (If Not Incorporated)_____		
TOTAL			**TOTAL**		

PROFIT AND LOSS STATEMENT FOR THE PERIOD FROM_____ TO_____

			CONTINGENT LIABILITIES (NOT INCLUDED ABOVE)		
Net Sales (After Returned Sales and Allowances)_____			As Guarantor or Endorser_____		
Cost of Sales:			Accounts, Notes, or Trade Acceptances Discounted or Pledged_____		
Beginning Inventory			Surety On Bonds or Other Continent Liability_____		
Purchases (or cost of goods mfd.)			Letters of Credit_____		
TOTAL			Judgments Unsatisfied or Suits Pending_____		
Less: Closing Inventory			Merchandise Commitments and Unfinished Contracts_____		
Gross Profit on Sales			Merchandise Held On Consignment From Others_____		
			Unsatisfied Tax Liens or Notices From the Federal or State Governments of Intention to Assess Such Liens_____		

RECONCILEMENT OF NET WORTH OR EARNED SURPLUS

Operating Expenses:					
Salaries—Officers or Partners			Net Worth or Earned Surplus at Beginning of Period_____		
Salaries and Wages—Other			Add Net Profit or Deduct Net Loss_____		
Rent				Total_____	
Depreciation			Other Additions (Describe)_____		
Bad Debts				Total_____	
Advertising			Less: Withdrawals or Dividends_____		
Interest			Other Deductions (Explain)_____		
Taxes—Other Than Income					
Insurance				Total Deductions_____	
Other Expenses			Net Worth or Capital Funds on This Financial Statement_____		
Net Profit from Operations					

DETAIL OF INVENTORY

Other Income		
Less Other Expense	Is Inventory Figure Actual or Estimated?_____
Net Profit Before Income Tax	By Whom Taken or Estimated_____ When?_____
Federal and State Income Tax	Buy Principally From_____
Net Profit or Loss	Average Terms of Purchase_____ Sale_____
(To Net Worth or Earned Surplus)	Time of Year Inventory Maximum_____ Minimum_____

FINANCIAL STATEMENT—FIRM OR CORPORATION—WOLCOTTS FORM 2001 (price class 6-2)

BUSINESS FINANCIAL HISTORY
(page 2)

SCHEDULE A   LIST OF REAL ESTATE AND IMPROVEMENTS WITH ENCUMBRANCES THEREON

DESCRIPTION, STREET NUMBER, LOCATION	TITLE IN NAMES OF	BOOK VALUE		MORTGAGES OR LIENS		TERMS OF PAYMENT	HOLDER OF LIEN
		LAND	IMPROVEMENTS	MATURITY	AMOUNT		
		$	$		$	$	
TOTALS		$	$		$	$	

SCHEDULE B   STOCKS & BONDS: Describe Fully. Use Supplemental Sheet if Necessary. Indicate if Stocks Are Common or Preferred. Give Interest Rate and Maturity of Bonds.

NO. OF SHARES AMT. OF BONDS	NAME AND ISSUE (DESCRIBE FULLY)	BOOK VALUE		MARKET VALUE	
		LISTED	UNLISTED	PRICE	VALUE
		$	$		$
TOTALS		$	$		$

SCHEDULE C   Complete if Statement is for an Individual or Sole Proprietorship

Age   Number of Years in Present Business   Date of Filing Fictitious Trade Style

What Property Listed in This Statement is in Joint Tenancy?   Name of Other Party

What Property Listed in This Statement is Community Property?   Name of Other Party

With What Other Business Are You Connected?   Have You Filed Homestead?

Do You Deal With or Carry Accounts With Stockbrokers?   Amount $ Name of Firm

SCHEDULE D   Complete if Statement is of a Partnership

NAME OF PARTNERS (INDICATE SPECIAL PARTNERS)	AGE	AMOUNT CONTRIBUTED	OUTSIDE NET WORTH	OTHER BUSINESS CONNECTIONS
		$	$	

Date of Organization   Limited or General?   Terminates

If Operating Under Fictitious Trade Style, Give Date of Filing

SCHEDULE E   Complete if Statement is of a Corporation

	AUTHORIZED	PAR VALUE	OUTSTANDING		CASH	ISSUED FOR
			SHARES	AMOUNT		OTHER (DESCRIBE)
Common Stock	$	$		$	$	
Preferred Stock	$	$		$	$	

Bonds—Total Issue $ Outstanding $ Due   Interest Rate

Date Incorporated   Under Laws of State of

OFFICERS	AGE	SHARES OWNED		DIRECTORS AND PRINCIPAL STOCKHOLDERS	SHARES OWNED	
		COMMON	PREFERRED		COMMON	PREFERRED
President				Director		
Vice President				Director		
Secretary				Director		
Treasurer						

SCHEDULE F   Complete in ALL Cases   INSURANCE

Are Your Books Audited by Outside Accountants? Name

Date of Last Audit   To What Date Has the U.S. Internal Revenue Department Examined Your Books?

Are You Borrowing From Any Other Branch of This Bank? Which?

Are You Applying for Credit At Any Other Source? Where?

Have You Ever Failed in Business?   If So, Attach a Complete Explanation and State Basis of Settlement With Creditors

Lease Has_____ Years to Run, With Monthly Rental of $____

Merchandise_____ $_____

Machinery & Fixtures_____ $_____

Buildings_____ $_____

Earthquake_____ $_____
Is Extended Coverage Endorsement Included?_____
Do You Carry Workmen's Compensation Insurance?_____

Automobiles and Trucks:

Public Liability $_____ M/$_____ M

Collision_____ $_____

Property Damage_____ $_____

Life Insurance_____ $_____
Name of Beneficiary_____

STATEMENT OF BANK OFFICER:
Insofar as our records reveal, this Financial Statement is accurate and true. The foregoing statement is (a copy of) the original signed by the maker, in the credit files of this Bank.

_____
ASSISTANT CASHIER-MANAGER

The undersigned solemnly declares and certifies that the above statement (or in lieu thereof, the attached statement, as the case may be) and supporting schedules, both printed and written, give a full, true, and correct statement of the financial condition of the undersigned as of the date indicated.

Signature_____

By_____
(TITLE, IF CORPORATION)

PERSONAL
FINANCIAL STATEMENT

PERSONAL FINANCIAL STATEMENT

(DO NOT USE FOR BUSINESS)

As of _____ _____ 19 _____

Received at _____ Branch

Name _____

Employed by _____ Years _____

Address _____

Position _____ Age _____ Name of Spouse _____

If Employed Less Than
1 Year, Previous Employer _____

The undersigned, for the purpose of procuring and establishing credit from time to time with you and to induce you to permit the undersigned to become indebted to you on notes, endorsements, guarantees, overdrafts or otherwise, furnishes the following (or in lieu thereof the attached) which is the most recent statement prepared by or for the undersigned as being a full, true and correct statement of the financial condition of the undersigned on the date indicated, and agrees to notify you immediately of the extent and character of any material change in said financial condition, and also agrees that if the undersigned, or any endorser or guarantor of any of the obligations of the undersigned, at any time fails in business or becomes insolvent, or commits an act of bankruptcy, or dies, or if a writ of attachment, garnishment, execution or other legal process be issued against property of the undersigned or if any assessment for taxes against the undersigned, other than taxes on real property, is made by the federal or state government or any department thereof, or if any of the representations made below prove to be untrue, or if the undersigned fails to notify you of any material change as above agreed, or if such change occurs, or if the business, or any interest therein, of the undersigned is sold, then and in such case, all of the obligations of the undersigned to you or held by you shall immediately be due and payable, without demand or notice. This statement shall be construed by you to be a continuing statement of the condition of the undersigned, and a new and original statement of all assets and liabilities upon each and every transaction in and by which the undersigned hereafter becomes indebted to you, until the undersigned advises in writing to the contrary.

ASSETS	DOLLARS	cents	LIABILITIES	DOLLARS	cents
Cash in B of _____ (Branch)			Notes payable B of _____ (Branch)		
Cash in _____ (Other - give name)			Notes payable _____ (Other)		
Accounts Receivable-Good _____			Accounts payable _____		
Stocks and Bonds (Schedule B) _____			Taxes payable _____		
Notes Receivable-Good _____			Contracts payable _____ (To whom)		
Cash Surrender Value Life Insurance _____			Contracts payable _____ (To whom)		
Autos _____ (Year-Make) _____ (Year-Make)			Real Estate indebtedness (Schedule A) _____		
Real Estate (Schedule A) _____			Other Liabilities (describe)		
Other Assets (describe)			1. _____		
1. _____			2. _____		
2. _____			3. _____		
3. _____			4. _____		
4. _____			TOTAL LIABILITIES		
5. _____			NET WORTH		
TOTAL ASSETS			TOTAL		

ANNUAL INCOME			and ANNUAL EXPENDITURES (Excluding Ordinary living expenses)		
Salary _____			Real Estate payment (s) _____		
Salary (wife or husband) _____			Rent _____		
Securities Income _____			Income Taxes _____		
Rentals _____			Insurance Premiums _____		
Other (describe)			Property Taxes _____		
1. _____			Other (describe-include instalment payments other than real estate)		
2. _____			1. _____		
3. _____			2. _____		
4. _____			3. _____		
5. _____					
TOTAL INCOME			TOTAL EXPENDITURES		

LESS-TOTAL EXPENDITURES

NET CASH INCOME
(exclusive of ordinary living expenses) _____

PERSONAL
FINANCIAL STATEMENT
(page 2)

What assets in this statement are in joint tenancy?_____ Name of other Party_____

Have you filed homestead? _____

Are you a guarantor on anyone's debt?_____ If so, give details _____

Are any encumbered assets or debts secured except as indicated? _____ If so, please itemize by debt and security_____

_____

Do you have any other business connections?_____ If so, give details_____

Are there any suits or judgments against you?_____ Any pending?_____

Have you gone through bankruptcy or compromised a debt?_____

Have you made a will?_____ Number of dependents_____

SCHEDULE A—REAL ESTATE

Location and type of Improvement	Title in Name of	Estimated Value	Amount Owing	To Whom Payable
		$	$	

SCHEDULE B—STOCKS AND BONDS

Number of Shares Amount of Bonds	Description	Current Market on Listed	Estimated Value on Unlisted
		$	$

If additional space is needed for Schedule A and/or Schedule B, list on separate sheet and attach.

INSURANCE

Life Insurance $_____ Name of Company_____ Beneficiary_____

Automobile Insurance:
Public Liability — yes ☐   no ☐   Property Damage — yes ☐   no ☐
Comprehensive personal Liability—yes ☐   no ☐

STATEMENT OF BANK OFFICER:
Insofar as our records reveal, this Financial Statement is accurate and true. The foregoing statement is (a copy of) the original signed by the maker, in the credit files of this bank.

The undersigned certifies that the above statement (or in lieu thereof, the attached statement, as the case may be) and supporting schedules, both printed and written, give a full, true, and correct statement of the financial condition of the undersigned as of the date indicated.

_____ Assistant Cashier Manager

Date signed   Signature

This is the Beginning of the Section on
Pro Forma Financial Statements

Pro Forma
Cash Flow Statement or Budget

What is a Cash Flow Statement?

A third or more of today's businesses fail due to a lack of cash flow. You can avoid this trap with careful planning of cash expenditures. The cash flow statement (or budget) **projects** what your business needs in terms dollars for a specific period of time. It is a pro forma (or projected) statement used for internal planning and estimates how much money will flow into and out of a business during a designated period of time, usually the coming tax year. Your profit at the end of the year will depend on the proper balance between cash inflow and outflow.

The Cash Flow Statement identifies when cash is expected to be received and when it must be spent to pay bills and debts. It also allows the manager to identify where the necessary cash will come from. **This statement deals only with actual cash transactions and not with depreciation and amortization of goodwill or other noncash expense items.** Expenses are paid from cash on hand, sale of assets, revenues from sales and services, interest earned on investments, money borrowed from a lender and influx of capital in exchange for equity in the company. If your business will require $100,000 to pay its expenses and $50,000 to support the owners, you will need at least an equal amount of money flowing into the business just to remain at a status quo. Anything less will eventually lead to an inability to pay your creditors or yourself.

The availability or nonavailability of cash **when** it is needed for expenditures gets to the heart of the matter. By careful planning, you must try to project not only **how much** cash will have to flow into and out of your business, but also **when** it will need to flow in and out. A business may be able to plan for gross receipts that will cover its needs. However, if those sales do not take place in time to pay the expenses, a business will soon be past history unless you plan ahead for other sources of cash to tide the business over until the revenues are realized.

TIME PERIOD: The Cash Flow Statement should be prepared on a monthly basis for the next tax year. To be effective, it must be analyzed and revised quarterly to reflect your actual performance.

PREPARING YOUR CASH FLOW STATEMENT

Before preparing your budget, it might be useful to compile individual projections and budgets. They might be as follows:

1. Revenue Projections (product and service)
2. Inventory Purchases
3. Variable (Selling, Direct) Expense Budget (with Marketing Budget)
4. Fixed (Administrative, Indirect) Expense Budget

PRE-PLANNING WORKSHEETS

Because the cash flow statement deals with cash inflow and cash outflow, the first step in planning can be best accomplished by preparing two worksheets.

1. Cash To Be Paid Out Worksheet: Cash flowing out of your business; identifies categories of expenses and obligations and the projected amount of cash needed in each category. Use the information from your individual budgets (inventory purchases, variable expenses, fixed expenses, owner draws, etc.). These expenditures are not always easy to estimate. If you are a new business, it will be necessary for you to research your market. If you are an existing business, you will be able to combine information from your past financial statements (such as your Profit & Loss) with trends in your particular industry.

2. Sources of Cash Worksheet: Cash flowing into your business; used to estimate how much cash will be available from what sources. To complete this worksheet, you will have to look at cash on hand, projected revenues, assets that can be liquidated, possible lenders or investors and owner equity to be contributed. This worksheet will force you to take a look at any existing possibilities for increasing available cash.

SAMPLE WORKSHEETS: On the next few pages, you will find examples of the two worksheets (filled in for our fictitious company, ABC Company) with explanatory material to help you better understand how they are developed. (Blank forms for your use are located in the Appendix.) Note that the Cash to be Paid Out Worksheet shows a need for $131,000. It is necessary in projecting Sources of Cash to account for $131,000 without the projected sales because payment is not expected to be received until November or December (too late for cash needs January through October). Next year, those revenues will be reflected in cash on hand or other saleable assets.

Note: Be sure to figure all estimates on both your worksheets for the same period of time (annually, quarterly, monthly).

EXPLANATION OF CATEGORIES
CASH TO BE PAID OUT WORKSHEET

1. START-UP COSTS
These are the costs incurred by you to get your business underway. They are generally one-time expenses and are capitalized for tax purposes.

2. INVENTORY PURCHASES
Cash to be spent during the period on items intended for resale. If you purchase manufactured products, this includes the cash outlay for those purchases. If you are the manufacturer, include labor and materials on units to be produced.

3. VARIABLE EXPENSES (Selling/Direct Expenses)
These are the costs of all expenses that will relate directly to your product or service (other than manufacturing costs or purchase price of inventory.)

4. FIXED EXPENSE (Administrative/Indirect Expenses)
Include all expected costs of office overhead. If certain bills must be paid ahead, include total cash outlay even if covered period extends into the next year.

5. ASSETS (Long-Term Purchases)
These are the capital assets that will be depreciated over a period of years (land, buildings, vehicles, equipment). Determine how you intend to pay for them and include all cash to be paid out in the current period.

6. LIABILITIES
What are the payments you expect to have to make to retire any debts or loans? Do you have any Accounts Payable as you begin the new year? You will need to determine the amount of cash outlay that needs to be paid in the current year. If you have a car loan for $20,000 and you pay $500 per month for 12 months, you will have a cash outlay of $6,000 for the coming year.

7. OWNER EQUITY
This item is frequently overlooked in planning cash flow. If you, as the business owner, will need a draw of $2,000 per month to live on, you must plan for $24,000 cash flowing out of your business. Failure to plan for it will result in a cash flow shortage and may cause your business to fail.

Note: Be sure to use the same time period throughout your worksheet.

ABC COMPANY
CASH TO BE PAID OUT WORKSHEET
(Cash Flowing Out Of The Business)

1. START-UP COSTS

Business License	$ 30.00
Corporation Filing	500.00
Legal Fees	920.00
Other start-up costs:	

2. INVENTORY PURCHASES

Cash out for goods intended for resale	32,000.00

3. VARIABLE EXPENSES (SELLING/DIRECT)

Advertising/Marketing	8,000.00
Freight	2,500.00
Fulfillment	800.00
Packaging Costs	Ø
Sales Salaries/Commissions	14,000.00
Travel	1,550.00
Miscellaneous	300.00
TOTAL SELLING EXPENSES	27,150.00

4. FIXED EXPENSES (ADMINISTRATIVE/INDIRECT)

Financial Administration	1,800.00
Insurance	900.00
Licenses and Permits	100.00
Office Salaries	16,300.00
Rent Expense	8,600.00
Utilities	2,400.00
Miscell. Fixed Expense	400.00
TOTAL OPERATING EXPENSE	30,500.00

5. ASSETS (LONG-TERM PURCHASES)

Cash to be paid out in current period	6,000.00

6. LIABILITIES

Cash outlay for retiring debts, loans and/or accounts payable	9,900.00

7. OWNER EQUITY

Cash to be withdrawn by owner	24,000.00

TOTAL CASH TO BE PAID OUT $ 131,000.00

Explanation of Categories
Sources of Cash Worksheet

1. CASH ON HAND
Money that you have on hand. Be sure to include petty cash and monies not yet deposited.

2. SALES (REVENUES)
This includes projected revenues from the sale of your product and/or service. If payment is not expected during the time period covered by this worksheet, do not include that portion of your sales. Think about the projected timing of sales. If receipts will be delayed beyond the time when a large amount of cash is needed, make a notation to that effect and take it into consideration when determining the need for temporary financing. Include deposits you require on expected sales or services. When figuring collections on Accounts Receivable, you will have to project the percentage of invoices that will be lost to bad debts and subtract it from your Accounts Receivable total.

3. MISCELLANEOUS INCOME
Do you, or will you have, any monies out on loan or deposited in accounts that will yield interest income during the period in question?

4. SALE OF LONG-TERM ASSETS
If you are expecting to sell any of your fixed assets such as land, buildings, vehicles, machinery, equipment, etc., be sure to include only the cash you will receive during the current period.

IMPORTANT: At this point in your worksheet, add up all sources of cash. If you do not have an amount equal to your projected needs, you will have to plan sources of cash covered under numbers five and six below.

5. LIABILITIES
This figure represents the amount you will be able to borrow from lending institutions such as banks, finance companies, the S.B.A., etc. Be reasonable about what you think you can borrow. If you have no collateral, have no business plan, or you have a poor financial history, you will find it difficult, if not impossible, to find a lender. This source of cash requires **pre-planning**.

6. EQUITY
Sources of equity come from owner investments, contributed capital, sale of stock, or venture capital. Do you anticipate availability of personal funds? Does your business have potential for growth that might interest a venture capitalist? Be sure to be realistic. You cannot sell stock (or equity) to a nonexistent investor.

ABC COMPANY
SOURCES OF CASH WORKSHEET
(Cash Flowing Into The Business)

1. CASH ON HAND $ __20,000.00__

2. SALES (REVENUES)

Sales Income* *Most of this sales revenue will not be received until November or December.* __90,000.00__

Services Income __22,000.00__

Deposits on Sales or Services __Ø__

Collections on Accounts Receivable __3,000.00__

3. MISCELLANEOUS INCOME

Interest Income __1,000.00__

Payments to be Received on Loans __Ø__

4. SALE OF LONG-TERM ASSETS __Ø__

5. LIABILITIES __40,000.00__

Loan Funds (To be received during period
from banks, SBA and other lending institutions)

6. EQUITY

Owner Investments (Sole Prop/Partners) *(from C.D.)* __10,000.00__

Contributed Capital (Corporation) _____

Sale of Stock (Corporation) _____

Venture Capital __35,000.00__

TOTAL CASH AVAILABLE: **A.** *Without Sales* $ __131,000.00__

B. *With Sales* $ __221,000.00__

USING THE WORKSHEETS

When you have completed the worksheets, you will have estimated how much cash will be needed for the year. You also know what sources are available. Now you will break each one-year projection into monthly segments, predicting when the cash will be needed to make the financial year flow smoothly.

Project sales on a monthly basis based on payment of invoices, demand for your particular product or service and ability to fill that demand. Figure the cost-of-goods, fixed and variable expenses in monthly increments. Most will vary. When do you plan to purchase the most inventory? What months will require the most advertising? Are you expecting a rent or insurance increase? When will commissions be due on expected sales. Determine your depreciable assets needs. How much will the payments be and when will they begin? Fill in as much of the cash flow statement as you can using any projections that you can comfortably determine.

EXAMPLE: We will follow "ABC Company" through January and February.

January Projections
1. ABC projects a beginning cash balance of $20,000.
2. Cash Receipts - Product manufacturing will not be completed until February, so there will be no sales. However, service income of $4,000 is projected.
3. Interest on the $20,000 will amount to about $100.00 at current rate.
4. There are no long-term assets to sell. Enter a zero.
5. Adding 1, 2, 3, and 4 the Total Cash Available will be $24,100.
6. Cash Payments - Product will be available from manufacturer in February and payment will not be due until pickup. However, there will be prototype costs of $5,000.
7. Variable Expenses - Estimated at $1,140.00.
8. Fixed Expenses - Estimated at $1,215.00.
9. Interest Expense - No outstanding debts or loans. Enter zero.
10. Taxes - No profit previous quarter. No estimated taxes would be due.
11. Payments on Long-Term Assets - ABC plans to purchase office equipment to be paid in full at the time of purchase $1,139.00.
12. Loan Repayments - No loans have been received. Enter zero.
13. Owner Draws - Owner will need $2,000 for living expenses.
14. Total Cash Paid Out - Add 6 through 13. Total $10,494.00.
15. Cash Balance - Subtract Cash Paid Out from Total Cash Available ($13,606.00)
16. Loans to be Received - Being aware of the $30,000.00 to be paid to the manufacturer in February, a loan of $40,000.00 is anticipated to increase Cash Available. (This requires advance planning.)
17. Equity Deposit - Owner plans to add $5,000.00 from personal C.D.
18. Ending Cash Balance - Adding 15, 16, and 17 the result is $58,606.00.

February Projections
1. February Beginning Cash Balance - January Ending Cash Balance ($58,606.00).
2. Cash Receipts - Still no sales, but service income is $2,000.00.
3. Interest Income - Projected at about $120.00.
4. Sale of Long-Term Assets - None. Enter zero.
5. Total Cash Available - Add 1,2,3 and 4. The result is $60,726.00.
6. Cash Payments - $30,000 due to manufacturer, $400 due on packaging design.
7. Continue as in January. Don't forget to include payments on your loan.

ABC COMPANY
Partial Cash Flow Statement

	JAN	FEB
BEGINNING CASH BALANCE	$ 20,000	$ 58,606
CASH RECEIPTS		
a. Sales revenues (Cash sales)	4,000	2,000
b. Receivables to be collected	Ø	Ø
c. Interest income	100	120
d. Sale of long-term assets	Ø	Ø
TOTAL CASH AVAILABLE	24,100	60,726
CASH PAYMENTS		
a. Cost of goods to be sold		
1. Purchases	Ø	30,000
2. Material	Ø	Ø
3. Labor	5,000	400
b. Variable expenses (Direct)		
1. Advertising/Marketing	300	
2. Freight	120	
3. Fulfillment	Ø	
4. Packaging Costs	270	
5. Sales Salaries/Commissions	Ø	
6. Travel	285	
7. Miscellaneous	165	CONT. as in JAN.
c. Fixed expenses (Indirect/Administrative)		
1. Financial Admin.	80	
2. Insurance	125	
3. Licenses and permits	200	
4. Office salaries	500	
5. Rent expenses	110	
6. Utilities	200	
7. Miscellaneous fixed expenses	Ø	
d. Interest expense	Ø	
e. Federal income tax	Ø	
f. Other uses	Ø	
g. Payments on long-term assets	1,139	
h. Loan Payment	Ø	
i. Owner draws	2,000	
TOTAL CASH PAID OUT	10,494	
CASH BALANCE/DEFICIENCY	13,606	
LOANS TO BE RECEIVED	40,000	
EQUITY DEPOSITS	5,000	
ENDING CASH BALANCE	$ 58,606	

COMPLETING YOUR CASH FLOW STATEMENT

This page contains instructions for completing the cash flow statement on the next page. The form can be used for your own projections.

    1. VERTICAL COLUMNS are divided into the twelve months and preceded by a "Total Column."

    2. HORIZONTAL POSITIONS on the statement contain all the sources of cash and cash to be paid out. These figures are retrieved from the two previous worksheets and from individual budgets.

PROJECT FIGURES FOR EACH MONTH

Reflect the projected flow of cash in and out of your business for a one-year period. Begin with the first month of your business cycle (January in this example) and proceed as follows:

1. Project the beginning Cash Balance. Enter under "January."

2. Project the Cash Receipts for January.

3. Add Beginning Cash Balance and Cash Receipts to determine Total Cash Available.

4. Project the Variable, Fixed and Interest Expenses for January.

5. Project monies due on Taxes, Long-Term Assets and Loan Repayments. Also project any amounts to be drawn by owners.

6. Total all Expenses and Draws. This is Total Cash Paid Out.

7. Subtract Total Cash Paid Out from Total Cash Available. The result is entered under "Cash Balance/Deficiency." Be sure to bracket this figure if the result is a negative to avoid errors.

8. Project Loans to be received and Equity Deposits to be made. Add to Cash Balance/ Deficiency to get Ending Cash Balance.

9. The Ending Cash Balance for January is carried forward and becomes February's Beginning Cash Balance.

10. The process is repeated until December is completed.

COMPLETE THE "TOTAL COLUMN"

1. The Beginning Cash Balance for January is entered in the first space of the "Total Column."

2. The monthly figures for each category are added horizontally and the result entered in the corresponding Total category.

3. The Total Column is computed in the same manner as individual months. If your computations are accurate, the December Ending Cash Balance will be exactly the same as the Total Ending Cash Balance.

Note: If your business is new, you will have to base your projections solely on market research and industry trends. If you have an established business, you will also use your financial statements from previous years.

PRO FORMA CASH FLOW STATEMENT

Company Name: _____

FOR THE YEAR 19___	TOTAL	JAN	FEB	MAR	APR	MAY	JUN	JUL	AUG	SEP	OCT	NOV	DEC
BEGINNING CASH BALANCE													
CASH RECEIPTS													
a. Sales revenues (Cash sales)													
b. Receivables to be collected													
c. Interest income													
d. Sale of long-term assets													
TOTAL CASH AVAILABLE													
CASH PAYMENTS													
a. Cost of goods to be sold													
1. Purchases													
2. Material													
3. Labor													
b. Variable expenses (Selling, Direct)													
1. Advertising/Marketing													
2. Freight													
3. Fulfillment													
4. Packaging costs													
5. Sales Salaries/Commissions													
6. Travel													
7. Miscellaneous Variable Expenses													
c. Fixed expenses (Administrative, Indirect)													
1. Financial Admin.													
2. Insurance													
3. Licenses and permits													
4. Office salaries													
5. Rent expenses													
6. Utilities													
7. Miscellaneous Fixed Expenses													
d. Interest expense													
e. Federal income tax													
f. Other uses													
g. Payments on long-term assets													
h. Loan payments													
i. Owner draws													
TOTAL CASH PAID OUT													
CASH BALANCE/DEFICIENCY													
LOANS TO BE RECEIVED													
EQUITY DEPOSITS													
ENDING CASH BALANCE													

This is the extension of the form found on page 77. A blank form is located in the Appendix for your use.

QUARTERLY BUDGET ANALYSIS

WHAT IS A QUARTERLY BUDGET ANALYSIS?

Your cash flow statement is of no value to you as a business owner unless there is some means to evaluate the actual performance of your company and measure it against your projections. A Quarterly Budget Analysis is used to compare projected cash flow (or budget) with your business's actual performance. Its purpose is to show you whether or not you are operating within your projections and to help you maintain control of all phases of your business operations. When your analysis shows that you are over or under budget in any area, it will be necessary to determine the reason for the deviation and implement changes that will enable you to get back on track.

FOR EXAMPLE: If you budgeted $1,000.00 in advertising funds for the first quarter and you spent $1,600, the first thing you should do is look to see if the increased advertising resulted in increased sales. If sales were over projections by an amount equal to or more than the $600.00, your budget will still be in good shape. If not, you will have to find expenses in your budget that can be revised to make up the deficit. You might be able to take a smaller draw for yourself or spend less on travel. You might even be able to increase your profits by adding a new product or service.

FORMAT AND SOURCES OF INFORMATION

The Quarterly Budget Analysis needs the following seven columns. Information sources are listed for each column of entries. A blank form is located in the Appendix for your use.

1. **Budget Item**: The list of budget items is taken from headings on the Pro Forma Cash Flow Statement. If you prefer, you can use a separate sheet for "cash in" and "cash out."
2. **Budgeted This Quarter**: Fill in the amount budgeted for current quarter from your Pro Forma Cash Flow Statement.
3. **Actual This Quarter**: Fill in your actual income and expenditures for the quarter.
4. **Variation This Quarter**: Amount spent or received over or under budget. These amounts are found in your Profit & Loss Statements, Fixed Assets Log, Owner Draw and Deposit Record and Loan Repayment Records. Subtract from budgeted amounts to arrive at variation.
5. **Year-To-Date Budget**: Amount budgeted from beginning of year through and including current quarter (from Cash Flow Statement).
6. **Actual Year-To-Date**: Actual amount spent or received from beginning of year through current quarter. Again, go to your General Records.
7. **Variation Year-To-Date**: Subtract amount spent or received year-to-date from the amount budgeted year-to-date and enter the difference.

NOTE: To keep from running out of operating capital early in the year, make your projections, analyze quarterly and revise your budget accordingly.

ABC COMPANY
QUARTERLY BUDGET ANALYSIS

All items contained in the Budget are listed on this form. The second column is the amount budgeted for the current quarter. By subtracting the amount actually spent, you will arrive at the Variation for the Quarter. The last three columns are for year-to-date figures. If you analyze at the end of the 3rd Quarter, figures will represent the first nine months of the tax year.

Making Calculations: When you calculate variations, the amounts are preceded by either a plus (+) or a minus (-), depending on whether the category is a revenue (income) or an expense. If the actual amount is greater than the amount budgeted, (1) Revenue categories will represent the variation as a positive (+); (2) Expense categories will represent the variation as a negative (-).

For the Quarter Ending _Sept. 30_, 19 _92_.   **YTD = year-to-date**

BUDGET ITEM	BUDGET THIS QUARTER	ACTUAL THIS QUARTER	VARIATION THIS QUARTER	YTD BUDGET	ACTUAL YTD	VARIATION YTD
SALES REVENUES	145,000	150,000	+5,000	400,000	410,000	+10,000
Less Cost of Goods	80,000	82,500	-2,500	240,000	243,000	-3,000
GROSS PROFIT	65,000	67,500	+2,500	160,000	167,000	+7,000
VARIABLE EXPENSES						
1. Advert/Mktg	3,000	3,400	-400	6,000	6,200	-200
2. Freight	6,500	5,750	+750	16,500	16,350	+150
3. Fulfillment	1,400	950	+450	3,800	4,100	-300
4. Packaging	750	990	-240	2,200	2,300	-100
5. Salaries/Commissions	6,250	6,250	Ø	18,750	18,750	Ø
6. Travel	500	160	+340	1,500	1,230	+270
7. Miscell.	Ø	475	-475	Ø	675	-675
FIXED EXPENSES						
1. Financial Admin.	1,500	1,500	Ø	4,500	4,700	-200
2. Insurance	2,250	2,250	Ø	6,750	6,750	Ø
3. Licenses & Permits	1,000	600	+400	3,500	3,400	+100
4. Office Salaries	1,500	1,500	Ø	4,500	4,500	Ø
5. Rent	3,500	3,500	Ø	10,500	10,500	Ø
6. Utilities	750	990	-240	2,250	2,570	-320
7. Miscellaneous	Ø	60	-60	Ø	80	-80
NET INCOME FROM OPERATIONS						
INTEREST INCOME	1,250	1,125	-125	3,750	3,700	-50
INTEREST EXPENSE	1,500	1,425	+75	4,500	4,500	Ø
NET PROFIT (LOSS) BEFORE TAXES	35,850	38,825	+2,975	78,500	84,095	+5,595
TAXES	8,500	9,500	-1,000	25,500	28,500	-3,000
NET PROFIT (LOSS) AFTER TAXES	27,350	29,325	+1,975	53,000	55,595	+2,595
NON-INCOME STATEMENT ITEMS						
1. L-Term Asset Repay'ts	2,400	2,400	Ø	7,200	7,200	Ø
2. Loan Repayments	3,300	3,300	Ø	8,800	8,800	Ø
3. Owner Draws	6,000	6,000	Ø	18,000	18,000	Ø

Budget Deviations: 1. Current Quarter = $ _1,975_   2. Year-To-Date = $ _2,595_

THREE-YEAR INCOME PROJECTION

WHAT IS A THREE-YEAR INCOME PROJECTION?

The Pro Forma Income Statement (Profit & Loss Statement) differs from a cash flow statement in that the three-year projection includes only projected income and deductible expenses. The following examples will illustrate the difference.

Example 1: Your company plans to make loan repayments of $9,000 during the year, $3,000 of which will be interest. The full amount ($9,000) would be recorded on a cash flow statement. Only the interest ($3,000) is recorded on a projected income statement. The principal is not a deductible expense.

Example 2: Your company plans to buy a vehicle for $15,000 cash. The full amount is recorded on your cash flow statement. The vehicle is a depreciable asset and only the projected depreciation for the year will be recorded on the projected income statement.

Example 3: You plan to take owner draws of $2,000 per month. The draws will be recorded on your cash flow statement. They are not a deductible expense and will not be recorded on the projected income statement.

ACCOUNT FOR INCREASE AND DECREASES

Increases in income and expenses are only realistic and should be reflected in your projections. Industry trends can also cause decreases in both income and expenses. An example of this might be in the computer industry where heavy competition and standardization of components has caused a decrease in both cost and sale price of certain items. The state of the economy will also be a contributing factor in the outlook for your business.

SOURCES OF INFORMATION

Information for a Three-Year Projection can be developed from your Pro Forma Cash Flow Statement and your Business and Marketing Analysis. The first year's figures can be transferred from the totals of income and expense items. The second and third years' figures are derived by combining these totals with projected trends in your particular industry. Again, if you are an established business, you will also be able to use past financial statements to help you determine what you project for the future of your business. Be sure to take into account fluctuations anticipated in costs, efficiency of operation, changes in your market, etc.

SAMPLE THREE-YEAR INCOME PROJECTION FORM: On the next page is a sample form for your use. You may wish to compile all three years on a month-by-month basis. If you are diligent enough to do so, it will provide you with a more detailed annual projection that can be compared with actual monthly performance.

ABC COMPANY
THREE-YEAR INCOME PROJECTION

FOR THE YEARS 19_94_, 19_95_ AND 19_96_.	YEAR 1	YEAR 2	YEAR 3
INCOME			
1. NET SALES (Gross less ret. & allow.)	500,000	540,000	595,000
2. COST OF GOODS SOLD (c. minus d.)	312,000	330,000	365,000
a. Beginning Inventory	147,000	155,000	175,000
b. Purchases	320,000	350,000	375,000
c. C.O.G. Available for Sale (a+b)	467,000	505,000	550,000
d. Less End. Inv. (Dec. 31st)	155,000	175,000	185,000
3. GROSS PROFIT ON SALES (1 minus 2)	188,000	210,000	230,000
EXPENSES			
1. VARIABLE (Selling/Direct) (a. thru h.)			
a. Advertising/Marketing	9,000	12,000	12,000
b. Freight	22,000	25,500	26,500
c. Fulfillment	2,000	4,000	4,000
d. Packaging Costs	3,000	2,800	2,900
e. Salaries/Wages/Commissions	25,000	35,000	40,000
f. Travel	5,000	5,000	4,500
g. Miscellaneous Selling Exp.			
h. Depreciation (Product/Services Assets)			
2. FIXED (Administrative/Indirect) (a. thru h.)			
a. Insurance	9,000	9,000	9,000
b. Licenses & Permits	4,000	4,000	4,000
c. Office Salaries	16,000	16,000	16,800
d. Rent Expense	14,000	14,000	14,000
e. Financial Admin.	7,000	7,000	7,500
f. Utilities	3,000	3,500	4,000
g. Other Overhead			
h. Depreciation (Office Equipment)			
TOTAL OPERATING EXPENSES (Variable+Fixed)	119,000	137,800	145,200
NET INCOME FROM OPERATIONS (Gross Profit less Expenses)	69,000	72,200	84,800
OTHER INCOME (INTEREST)	+ 5,000	+ 5,000	+ 5,000
OTHER EXPENSE (INTEREST)	− 7,000	− 5,000	− 4,000
NET PROFIT (LOSS) BEFORE INCOME TAXES	67,000	72,200	85,800
TAXES (Federal, Self-Employment, State)	26,000	29,000	34,200
NET PROFIT (LOSS) AFTER TAXES	41,000	43,200	51,600

BREAK-EVEN ANALYSIS

WHAT IS A BREAK-EVEN POINT?

Break-even is the point at which a company's costs exactly match their sales volume. In other words, it is the point at which the business begins to make a profit. The break-even point can be calculated either in mathematical or graph form. It is expressed in either of two ways:

1. **TOTAL DOLLARS OF REVENUE** (exactly offset by total costs).

2. **TOTAL UNITS OF PRODUCTION** (cost of which exactly equals the income derived by their sale).

To apply a break-even analysis to an operation, you will need three projections. They are as follows:

1. **Fixed Costs for the Period** - (Admin. Overhead, Depreciation, Interest, etc.) These costs remain constant even if you have a slow period.
2. **Variable Costs** - (Cost of Goods + Direct Expenses). Usually varies. The greater the sales volume, the higher the cost.
3. **Total Sales Volume** - (Projected sales for same period).

SOURCE OF INFORMATION: All of your figures can be derived from your Three-Year Projection. Simply retrieve the figures and plug them into the formula or graph.

MATHEMATICALLY: Sales at break-even point can be computed using the following formula:

B-E Point (Sales) = Fixed Costs + [(Variable Costs/Est.Revenues) x Sales]

Terms Used: a. Sales = The volume of sales at Break-Even Point
                 b. Fixed Costs = Indirect Expense, Depreciation, Interest
                 c. Variable Costs = Cost of Goods Sold and Direct Expenses
                 d. Estimated Revenues = Income (from sales of goods/services)

Figures are: a. **S** (Sales at B-E Point) = The unknown
                 b. **FC** (Fixed Costs) = $25,000
                 c. **VC** (Variable Costs) = $45,000
                 d. **R** (Estimated Revenues) = $90,000

Using the formula, the computation would appear as follows:

S (at B-E Point) = $25,000 + [($45,000/$90,000) x S]
S = $25,000 + (1/2 x S)
S - 1/2 S = $25,000
1/2 **S** = $25,000
S = **$50,000** (**Break-Even Point in terms of dollars of revenue exactly offset by total costs**)

GRAPHICALLY: Break-Even Point can also be plotted as on the next page:

BREAK-EVEN ANALYSIS GRAPH

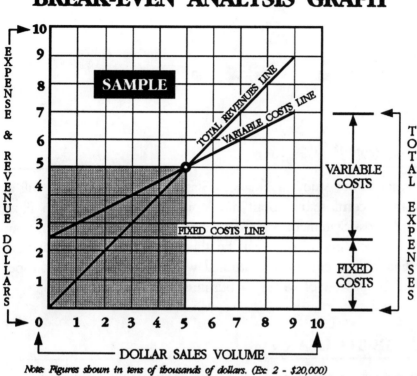

To Complete the Graph: Determine the following projections

1. Fixed Costs for Period - Those costs that usually remain constant and must be met regardless of your sales volume (administrative, rent, insurance, depreciation, interest, salaries, etc.). **Ex: $25,000**

2. Variable Costs - Cost associated with the production and selling of your products or services. If you have a product, you will include cost-of-goods (inventory purchases, labor, materials, freight, packaging, sales commissions, advertising, etc.). These costs may be expressed by multiplying the unit cost by the units to be sold for a product. **Ex: 1) $1.50 per unit x 30,000 units = $45,000; or 2) for a service, use total of projected direct expenses, no Cost of Goods.**

3. Total Sales Volume - This is the figure representing units of product to be sold by sale price per unit. **Ex: 30,000 units @ $3.00 = $90,000;** For a service, multiply your billable hours x your hourly rate. **900 hours x $100 = $90,000.**

To Draw Graph Lines

1. Draw Horizontal Line at point representing Fixed Costs (25).

2. Draw Variable Cost Line from left end of Fixed Cost Line sloping upward to point where Total Costs (Fixed + Variable) on vertical scale (7) meet Total Revenues on the horizontal scale (9).

3. Draw Total Revenues Line from zero through a point describing total Revenues on both scales (9).

Break-Even Point: The point on the graph where the Variable Cost Line intersects the Total Revenue Line. This business estimates that it will break even at the time sales volume reaches $50,000. The triangular area below and to the left of that point represents company losses. The triangular area above and to the right of the point represents potential profit.

■   ■   ■   ■   ■

CONGRATULATIONS!

You have now finished your study of Financial Statements and hopefully will at least feel a little more comfortable about developing a Pro Forma Cash Flow Statement, Profit & Loss Statement and Balance Sheet of your own from your General Records. These three records will be the backbone of your business. The rest of the financial statements you studied will also prove valuable, especially if you are in the process of writing a business plan.

IT TAKES TIME TO LEARN

Don't expect to remember and absorb all of this information right now. I'm sure that you are overwhelmed. As you set up and work with your records, everything will fall into place. Recordkeeping is not difficult. It is simply a matter of repetitive work that will soon become a matter of habit.

BUSINESS PLANNING

Before we close this chapter, we would like to say another word about business planning. Every now and then, throughout the text, we have mentioned the benefits of writing a business plan. Most entrepreneurs shudder at the thought of having to go through the formal planning process. It is a difficult task, but one that may ultimately make the difference between success and failure. A business plan is required if you are seeking a lender or investor. More importantly, however, it is the guide you will follow during the life of your business. Having learned about recordkeeping and financial statements, you will have made a significant step in the planning process.

Taxes and Recordkeeping

Warning!

Disclaimer

The information in this chapter is presented with the understanding that we are in no way rendering legal, accounting or other professional services. Our purpose is to introduce you to some of the common tax forms and publications and to provide you with a general guide for use in recordkeeping. Detailed information, along with legal advice, will have to be obtained from your accountant, attorney, or the IRS.

BASIC UNDERSTANDING OF THE U.S. TAX SYSTEM

If you are going to be in command of your business recordkeeping, it will be necessary for you to have a good basic understanding of the relationship between your finances and income tax accounting. When the Federal income tax came into being, it was structured according to accounting principles. This has served a double purpose. The records you keep enable you to retrieve the necessary information for filing taxes at the close of your tax year. By the same token, the tax forms that you will be required to submit will provide you with important clues as to how your records can be set up, not only in a usable format, but in a manner that will make it practical for you to analyze your records and determine what changes will have to be implemented for future growth and profit.

THE RELATIONSHIP BETWEEN TAX FORMS AND BUSINESS ANALYSIS

In order for you to better comprehend the relationship between the Tax System and analyzing your business, we will give you two examples of tax forms and how you can benefit from understanding those forms.

1. SCHEDULE C (Form 1040)

Entitled Profit or (Loss) from Business or Profession (required tax reporting form for Sole Proprietors).

IRS Information Required: Gross receipts or sales, beginning and ending inventories, labor, materials, goods purchased, returns and allowances, deductions, interest expense, income and net profit or loss.

Benefits of Understanding: In case you did not catch on, the required information listed above is exactly the same as the list of income and expenses on a Profit & Loss Statement. When the IRS has you fill out a business return, you are merely transferring information from the profit and loss. By understanding this, you can look through a Schedule C and see what categories of information are needed under expenses. This can help you to decide what categories you will use in your Revenue & Expense Journal. It will also help you after your accountant has sent your return back to you for submission to the IRS. Now you can put your knowledge of a Profit & Loss Statement to work and read and check it over for accuracy—a chore too frequently ignored by taxpayers. Since you have the final responsibility for the correctness of your return, knowing how to examine it can prevent mistakes that might prove costly.

Note: Form 1065 - *U.S. Partnership Return of Income* and Form 1120 or Form 1120-A, *U.S. Corporation Income Tax Returns,* are used for those legal structures.

2. SCHEDULE SE (Form 1040)

Entitled Computation of Social Security Self-Employment Tax.

IRS Information Required: Computation of contribution to social security.

Benefits of Understanding: Failure to familiarize yourself with the requirements on how to compute this tax and know what percentage of your net income will be owed will result in a false picture as to the net profit of your business. Don't forget—the IRS is interested in your Net Profit before taxes. You are concerned with Net Profit after taxes.

As you can see from the two examples, examination of required tax forms can lead to the discovery of many types of records that you will need and profit from in your business.

FEDERAL TAXES FOR WHICH YOU MAY BE LIABLE

The next section of this chapter will be devoted to providing you with tax calendars and to introducing you to the most common federal taxes for which a sole proprietor, partnership, or corporation may be liable.

We are not giving you complete information for filling out tax returns. What we are trying to do is make you aware of required reporting, familiarize you with some of the forms, and give you a frame of reference for any questions you have. To do this, we will discuss each requirement briefly and include the following:

a. Tax to be reported.

b. Forms used for reporting.

c. IRS Publications to be used for information.

d. Sample of each reporting form.

CALENDARS OF FEDERAL TAXES

For your convenience, we have provided tax calendars on the next four pages. They will serve as a guide to tell you when tax and information returns must be filed. There is a calendar for each of the four legal structures (sole proprietor, partnership, S corporation, and corporation). Copy the calendar that is appropriate to your business and post it near your recordkeeping area to remind you to file on the appropriate dates.

It should be noted that these calendars are compiled according to specific dates. If your tax year is not January 1st through December 31st, there are footnoted dates listed below the calendar that you can transpose to figure out filing dates. These calendars will be especially useful combined with your Recordkeeping Schedule that will be presented in the next chapter.

USING THE INDEX: If you are looking for information on a specific tax or form, you will find that text and forms are indexed in three ways: by form number, by subject matter and by legal structure.

SOLE PROPRIETOR

Calendar of Federal Taxes for Which You May Be Liable

January	15	Estimated tax	Form 1040ES
	31	Social security (FICA) tax and the withholding of income tax Note: See IRS rulings for deposit - Pub. 334	941, 941E, 942 & 943
	31	Providing information on social security (FICA) tax and the withholding of income tax	W-2 (to employee)
	31	Federal unemployment (FUTA) tax	940-EZ or 940
	31	Federal unemployment (FUTA) tax (only if liability for unpaid taxes exceeds $100)	8109 (to make deposits)
	31	Information returns to nonemployees and transactions with other persons	Form 1099 (to recipients)
February	28	Information returns to nonemployees and transactions with other persons	Form 1099 (to IRS)
	28	Providing information on social security (FICA) tax and the withholding income tax	W-2 & W-3 (to Soc. Sec. Admin.)
April	15	Income tax	Schedule C (Form 1040)
	15	Self-employment tax	Schedule SE (Form 1040)
	15	Estimated tax	Form 1040ES
	30	Social security (FICA) tax and the withholding of income tax Note: See IRS rulings for deposit - Pub. 334	941, 941E 942 & 943
	30	Federal unemployment (FUTA) tax (only if liability for unpaid taxes exceeds $100)	8109 (to make deposits)
June	15	Estimated tax	Form 1040ES
July	31	Social security (FICA) tax and the withholding of income tax Note: See IRS rulings for deposit - Pub. 334	941, 941E, 942 & 943
	31	Federal unemployment (FUTA) tax (only if liability for unpaid taxes exceeds $100)	8109 (to make deposits)
September	15	Estimated tax	Form 1040ES
October	31	Social security (FICA) tax and the withholding of income tax Note: See IRS rulings for deposit - Pub. 334	941, 941E, 941 & 943
	31	Federal unemployment (FUTA) tax (only if liability for unpaid taxes exceeds $100)	8109 (to make deposits)

If your tax year is not January 1st through December 31st:

- Schedule C (Form 1040) is due the 15th day of the 4th month after end of the tax year. Schedule SE is due same day as Form 1040.

- Estimated tax (1040ES) is due the 15th day of 4th, 6th, and 9th months of tax year, and the 15th day of 1st month after the end of tax year.

PARTNERSHIP

Calendar of Federal Taxes for Which You May Be Liable

January	15	Estimated tax (individual who is a partner)	Form 1040ES
	31	Social security (FICA) tax and the withholding of income tax Note: See IRS rulings for deposit - Pub. 334	941, 941E, 942 & 943
	31	Providing information on soc. security (FICA) tax and the withholding of income tax	W-2 (to employee)
	31	Federal unemployment (FUTA) tax	940-EZ or 940
	31	Federal unemployment (FUTA) tax (only if liability for unpaid taxes exceeds $100)	8109 (to make deposits)
	31	Information returns to nonemployees and transactions with other persons	Form 1099 (to recipients)
February	28	Information returns to nonemployees and transactions with other persons	Form 1099 (to IRS)
	28	Providing information on social security (FICA) tax and on withholding income tax	W-2 & W-3 (to Soc. Sec. Admin.)
April	15	Income tax (individual who is a partner)	Schedule C (Form 1040)
	15	Annual return of income	Form 1065
	15	Self-employment tax (individual who is partner)	Schedule SE (Form 1040)
	15	Estimated tax (individual who is partner)	Form 1040ES
	30	Social security (FICA) tax and the withholding of income tax Note: See IRS rulings for deposit - Pub. 334	941, 941E 942 & 943
	30	Federal unemployment (FUTA) tax (only if liability for unpaid taxes exceeds $100)	8109 (to make deposits)
June	15	Estimated tax (individual who is a partner)	Form 1040ES
July	31	Social security (FICA) tax and the withholding of income tax Note: See IRS rulings for deposit - Pub. 334	941, 941E, 942 & 943
	31	Federal unemployment (FUTA) tax (only if liability for unpaid taxes exceeds $100)	8109 (to make deposits)
September	15	Estimated tax (individual who is a partner)	Form 1040ES
October	31	Social security (FICA) tax and the withholding of income tax Note: See IRS rulings for deposit - Pub. 334	941, 941E, 941 & 943
	31	Federal unemployment (FUTA) tax (only if liability for unpaid taxes exceeds $100)	8109 (to make deposits)

If your Tax Year is not January 1st through December 31st:
- Income tax is due the 15th day of the 4th month after end of tax year.
- Self-employment tax is due the same day as income tax (Form 1040).
- Estimated tax (1040ES) is due the 15th day of the 4th, 6th, and 9th month of the tax year and the 15th day of 1st month after end of the tax year.

S CORPORATION

Calendar of Federal Taxes for Which You May Be Liable

January	15	Estimated tax (individual S corp. shareholder)	Form 1040ES
	31	Social security (FICA) tax and the withholding of income tax Note: See IRS rulings for deposit - Pub. 334	941, 941E, 942 & 943
	31	Providing information on social security (FICA) tax and the withholding of income tax	W-2 (to employee)
	31	Federal unemployment (FUTA) tax	940-EZ or 940
	31	Federal unemployment (FUTA) tax (only if liability for unpaid taxes exceeds $100)	8109 (to make deposits)
	31	Information returns to nonemployees and transactions with other persons	Form 1099 (to recipients)
February	28	Information returns to nonemployees and transactions with other persons	Form 1099 (to IRS)
	28	Providing information on social security (FICA) tax and the withholding of income tax	W-2 & W-3 (to Soc. Sec. Admin.)
March	15	Income tax	1120S
April	15	Income tax (individual S corp. shareholder)	Form 1040
	15	Estimated tax (individual S corp. shareholder)	Form 1040ES
	30	Social security (FICA) tax and the withholding of income tax Note: See IRS rulings for deposit - Pub. 334	941, 941E 942 & 943
	30	Federal unemployment (FUTA) tax (only if liability for unpaid taxes exceeds $100)	8109 (to make deposits)
June	15	Estimated tax (individual S corp. shareholder)	Form 1040ES
July	31	Social security (FICA) tax and the withholding of income tax Note: See IRS rulings for deposit - Pub. 334	941, 941E, 942 & 943
	31	Federal unemployment (FUTA) tax (only if liability for unpaid taxes exceeds $100)	8109 (to make deposits)
September	15	Estimated tax (individual S corp. shareholder)	Form 1040ES
October	31	Social security (FICA) tax and the withholding of income tax Note: See IRS rulings for deposit - Pub. 334	941, 941E, 941 & 943
	31	Federal unemployment (FUTA) tax (only if liability for unpaid taxes exceeds $100)	8109 (to make deposits)

If your tax year is not January 1st through December 31st:

- S corp. income tax (1120S) and individual S corp shareholder income tax (Form 1040) are due the 15th day of the 4th month after end of tax year.

- Estimated tax of indiv. shareholder (1040ES) is due 15th day of 4th, 6th, and 9th months of tax year and 15th day of 1st month after end of tax year.

CORPORATION

Calendar of Federal Taxes for Which You May Be Liable

January	31	Social security (FICA) tax and the withholding of income tax Note: See IRS rulings for deposit - Pub. 334	941, 941E, 942 & 943
	31	Providing information on social security (FICA) tax and the withholding of income tax	W-2 (to employee)
	31	Federal unemployment (FUTA) tax	940-EZ or 940
	31	Federal unemployment (FUTA) tax (only if liability for unpaid taxes exceeds $100)	8109 (to make deposits)
	31	Information returns to nonemployees and transactions with other persons	Form 1099 (to recipients)
February	28	Information returns to nonemployees and transactions with other persons	Form 1099 (to IRS)
	28	Providing information on social security (FICA) tax and the withholding of income tax	W-2 & W-3 (to Soc. Sec. Admin.)
March	15	Income tax	1120 or 1120-A
April	15	Estimated tax	1120-W
	30	Social security (FICA) tax and the withholding of income tax Note: See IRS rulings for deposit - Pub. 334	941, 941E 942 & 943
	30	Federal unemployment (FUTA) tax (only if liability for unpaid taxes exceeds $100)	8109 (to make deposits)
June	15	Estimated tax	1120-W
July	31	Social security (FICA) tax and the withholding of income tax Note: See IRS rulings for deposit - Pub. 334	941, 941E, 942 & 943
	31	Federal unemployment (FUTA) tax (only if liability for unpaid taxes exceeds $100)	8109 (to make deposits)
September	15	Estimated tax	1120-W
October	31	Social security (FICA) tax and the withholding of income tax Note: See IRS rulings for deposit - Pub. 334	941, 941E, 941 & 943
	31	Federal unemployment (FUTA) tax (only if liability for unpaid taxes exceeds $100)	8109 (to make deposits)
December	15	Estimated tax	1120-W

If your tax year is not January 1st through December 31st:

- Income tax (Form 1120 or 1120-A) is due on the 15th day of the 3rd month after the end of the tax year.
- Estimated tax (1120-W) is due the 5th day of the 4th, 6th, 9th, and 12th months of the tax year.

INCOME TAX (FOR SOLE PROPRIETORS)

File Schedule C (Form 1040), *Profit or (Loss) from Business or Profession.*

You are a sole proprietor if you are self-employed and are the sole owner of an unincorporated business.

If you are a sole proprietor, you report your income and expenses from your business or profession on Schedule C. File Schedule C with your Form 1040 and report the amount of net profit or (loss) from Schedule C on your 1040. If you operate more than one business as a sole proprietor, you prepare a separate Schedule C for each business.

Withdrawals: If you are a sole proprietor, there is no tax effect if you take money to or from your business, or transfer money to or from your business. You should set up a drawing account to keep track of amounts for personal use and not for business expenses.

Home-Office Deductions: If you claim a home office deduction, you must attach Form 8829. (Sample form is included after Schedule C.)

Estimated Tax: If you are a sole proprietor, you will have to make estimated tax payments if the total of your estimated income tax and self-employment tax for 1993 will exceed your total withholding and credits by $500 or more. Form 1040-ES is used to estimate your tax. See: "Estimated Tax for Sole Proprietors."

Self-Employment Tax: Generally required if you are a sole proprietor. See: "Self-Employment Tax," Schedule SE.

SCHEDULE C AND FORM 1040

Forms are due by April 15th. If you use a fiscal year, your return is due by the 15th day of the 4th month after the close of your tax year.

IRS PUBLICATION: See Publication 334, *Tax Guide for Small Business.* Chapter 28 discusses tax rules and Chapter 38 will illustrate how to fill in this form.

SAMPLE: Schedule C (Form 1040) can be seen on the next two pages.

FORM 1040 - SCHEDULE C
PROFIT OR LOSS FROM BUSINESS SOLE PROPRIETORSHIP

SCHEDULE C
(Form 1040)

Department of the Treasury
Internal Revenue Service (X)

Profit or Loss From Business
(Sole Proprietorship)
▶ Partnerships, joint ventures, etc., must file Form 1065.
▶ **Attach to Form 1040 or Form 1041.** ▶ **See Instructions for Schedule C (Form 1040).**

OMB No. 1545-0074
1992
Attachment
Sequence No. **09**

Name of proprietor

Social security number (SSN)

A Principal business or profession, including product or service (see page C-1)

B Enter principal business code
(from page 2) ▶

C Business name

D Employer ID number (Not SSN)

E Business address (including suite or room no.) ▶ ....
City, town or post office, state, and ZIP code

F Accounting method: (1) ☐ Cash (2) ☐ Accrual (3) ☐ Other (specify) ▶ ....

G Method(s) used to value closing inventory: (1) ☐ Cost (2) ☐ Lower of cost or market (3) ☐ Other (attach explanation) (4) ☐ Does not apply (if checked, skip line H) | Yes | No

H Was there any change in determining quantities, costs, or valuations between opening and closing inventory? If "Yes," attach explanation

I Did you "materially participate" in the operation of this business during 1992? If "No," see page C-2 for limitations on losses . .

J Was this business in operation at the end of 1992? . . . .

K How many months was this business in operation during 1992? . . . . ▶

L If this is the first Schedule C filed for this business, check here . . . . ▶ ☐

Part I Income

1	Gross receipts or sales. **Caution:** If this income was reported to you on Form W-2 and the "Statutory employee" box on that form was checked, see page C-2 and check here ▶ ☐	1	
2	Returns and allowances	2	
3	Subtract line 2 from line 1	3	
4	Cost of goods sold (from line 40 on page 2)	4	
5	**Gross profit.** Subtract line 4 from line 3	5	
6	Other income, including Federal and state gasoline or fuel tax credit or refund (see page C-2) . .	6	
7	**Gross Income.** Add lines 5 and 6 . . . . ▶	7	

Part II Expenses (Caution: *Do not enter expenses for business use of your home on lines 8–27. Instead, see line 30.*)

8	Advertising	8		21	Repairs and maintenance . .	21	
9	Bad debts from sales or services (see page C-3) . .	9		22	Supplies (not included in Part III) .	22	
				23	Taxes and licenses	23	
10	Car and truck expenses (see page C-3—also attach **Form 4562**) .	10		24	Travel, meals, and entertainment:		
				a	Travel	24a	
11	Commissions and fees. . .	11		b	Meals and entertainment .		
12	Depletion.	12		c	Enter 20% of line 24b subject to limitations (see page C-4) . .		
13	Depreciation and section 179 expense deduction (not included in Part III) (see page C-3) . .	13					
				d	Subtract line 24c from line 24b .	24d	
14	Employee benefit programs (other than on line 19) . . .	14		25	Utilities	25	
15	Insurance (other than health) .	15		26	Wages (less jobs credit) . .	26	
16	Interest:			27a	Other expenses (**list type and amount**):		
a	Mortgage (paid to banks, etc.) .	16a			....		
b	Other	16b			....		
17	Legal and professional services .	17			....		
18	Office expense	18			....		
19	Pension and profit-sharing plans .	19			....		
20	Rent or lease (see page C-4):				....		
a	Vehicles, machinery, and equipment	20a					
b	Other business property .	20b		27b	Total other expenses . . .	27b	

28	**Total expenses** before expenses for business use of home. Add lines 8 through 27b in columns ▶	28	
29	Tentative profit (loss). Subtract line 28 from line 7	29	
30	Expenses for business use of your home. Attach **Form 8829**	30	
31	**Net profit or (loss).** Subtract line 30 from line 29. If a profit, enter here and on Form 1040, line 12. Also, enter the net profit on Schedule SE, line 2 (statutory employees, see page C-5). If a loss, you MUST go on to line 32 (fiduciaries, see page C-5)	31	

32 If you have a loss, you MUST check the box that describes your investment in this activity (see page C-5)

If you checked 32a, enter the loss on Form 1040, line 12, and Schedule SE, line 2 (statutory employees, see page C-5). If you checked 32b, you MUST attach **Form 6198.**

} 32a ☐ All investment is at risk.
32b ☐ Some investment is not at risk

For Paperwork Reduction Act Notice, see Form 1040 instructions.   Cat. No. 11334P   **Schedule C (Form 1040) 1992**

FORM 1040 - SCHEDULE C - page 2
PROFIT OR LOSS FROM BUSINESS SOLE PROPRIETORSHIP

Schedule C (Form 1040) 1992   Page **2**

Part III   Cost of Goods Sold (see page C-5)

33	Inventory at beginning of year. If different from last year's closing inventory, attach explanation	33	
34	Purchases less cost of items withdrawn for personal use	34	
35	Cost of labor. Do not include salary paid to yourself	35	
36	Materials and supplies	36	
37	Other costs	37	
38	Add lines 33 through 37.	38	
39	Inventory at end of year.	39	
40	**Cost of goods sold.** Subtract line 39 from line 38. Enter the result here and on page 1, line 4	40	

Part IV   Principal Business or Professional Activity Codes

Locate the major category that best describes your activity. Within the major category, select the activity code that most closely identifies the business or profession that is the principal source of your sales or receipts. **Enter this 4-digit code on page 1, line B.** For example, real estate agent is under the major category of **"Real Estate,"** and the code is "5520." Note: *If your principal source of income is from farming activities, you should file Schedule F (Form 1040), Profit or Loss From Farming.*

Agricultural Services, Forestry, Fishing
Code
1990 Animal services, other than breeding
1933 Crop services
2113 Farm labor & management services
2246 Fishing, commercial
2238 Forestry, except logging
2212 Horticulture & landscaping
2469 Hunting & trapping
1974 Livestock breeding
0836 Logging
1958 Veterinary services, including pets

Construction
0018 Operative builders (for own account)
Building Trade Contractors, Including Repairs
0414 Carpentering & flooring
0455 Concrete work
0273 Electrical work
0299 Masonry, dry wall, stone, & tile
0257 Painting & paper hanging
0232 Plumbing, heating, & air conditioning
0430 Roofing, siding & sheet metal
0885 Other building trade contractors (excavation, glazing, etc.)
General Contractors
0075 Highway & street construction
0059 Nonresidential building
0034 Residential building
3889 Other heavy construction (pipe laying, bridge construction, etc.)

Finance, Insurance, & Related Services
6064 Brokers & dealers of securities
6080 Commodity contracts brokers & dealers; security & commodity exchanges
6148 Credit institutions & mortgage bankers
5702 Insurance agents or brokers
5744 Insurance services (appraisal, consulting, inspection, etc.)
6130 Investment advisors & services
5777 Other financial services

Manufacturing, Including Printing & Publishing
0679 Apparel & other textile products
1115 Electric & electronic equipment
1073 Fabricated metal products
0638 Food products & beverages
0810 Furniture & fixtures
0695 Leather footwear, handbags, etc.
0836 Lumber & other wood products
1099 Machinery & machine shops
0877 Paper & allied products
1057 Primary metal industries
0851 Printing & publishing
1032 Stone, clay, & glass products
0653 Textile mill products
1883 Other manufacturing industries

Mining & Mineral Extraction
1537 Coal mining
1511 Metal mining

1552 Oil & gas
1719 Quarrying & nonmetallic mining

Real Estate
5538 Operators & lessors of buildings, including residential
5553 Operators & lessors of other real property
5520 Real estate agents & brokers
5579 Real estate property managers
5710 Subdividers & developers, except cemeteries
6155 Title abstract offices

Services: Personal, Professional, & Business Services
Amusement & Recreational Services
9670 Bowling centers
9688 Motion picture & tape distribution & allied services
9597 Motion picture & video production
9639 Motion picture theaters
8557 Physical fitness facilities
9696 Professional sports & racing, including promoters & managers
9811 Theatrical performers, musicians, agents, producers & related services
9613 Video tape rental
9837 Other amusement & recreational services
Automotive Services
8813 Automotive rental or leasing, without driver
8953 Automotive repairs, general & specialized
8839 Parking, except valet
8896 Other automotive services (wash, towing, etc.)
Business & Personal Services
7658 Accounting & bookkeeping
7716 Advertising, except direct mail
7682 Architectural services
8318 Barber shop (or barber)
8110 Beauty shop (or beautician)
8714 Child day care
7872 Computer programming, processing, data preparation & related services
7922 Computer repair, maintenance, & leasing
7286 Consulting services
7799 Consumer credit reporting & collection services
8755 Counseling (except health practitioners)
7732 Employment agencies & personnel supply
7518 Engineering services
7773 Equipment rental & leasing (except computer or automotive)
8532 Funeral services & crematories
7633 Income tax preparation
7914 Investigative & protective services
7617 Legal services (or lawyer)
7856 Mailing, reproduction, commercial art, photography, & stenographic services
7245 Management services
8771 Ministers & chaplains
8334 Photographic studios
7260 Public relations
8733 Research services

7708 Surveying services
8730 Teaching or tutoring
7880 Other business services
6882 Other personal services

Hotels & Other Lodging Places
7237 Camps & camping parks
7096 Hotels, motels, & tourist homes
7211 Rooming & boarding houses

Laundry & Cleaning Services
7450 Carpet & upholstery cleaning
7419 Coin-operated laundries & dry cleaning
7435 Full-service laundry, dry cleaning, & garment service
7476 Janitorial & related services (building, house, & window cleaning)

Medical & Health Services
9274 Chiropractors
9233 Dentist's office or clinic
9217 Doctor's (M.D.) office or clinic
9456 Medical & dental laboratories
9472 Nursing & personal care facilities
9290 Optometrists
9258 Osteopathic physicians & surgeons
9241 Podiatrists
9415 Registered & practical nurses
9431 Offices & clinics of other health practitioners (dieticians, midwives, speech pathologists, etc.)
9886 Other health services

Miscellaneous Repair, Except Computers
9019 Audio equipment & TV repair
9035 Electrical & electronic equipment repair, except audio & TV
9050 Furniture repair & reupholstery
2881 Other equipment repair

Trade, Retail—Selling Goods to Individuals & Households
3038 Catalog or mail order
3012 Selling door to door, by telephone or party plan, or from mobile unit
3053 Vending machine selling
Selling From Showroom, Store, or Other Fixed Location
Apparel & Accessories
3921 Accessory & specialty stores & furriers for women
3939 Clothing, family
3772 Clothing, men's & boys'
3913 Clothing, women's
3756 Shoe stores
3954 Other apparel & accessory stores
Automotive & Service Stations
3558 Gasoline service stations
3319 New car dealers (franchised)
3533 Tires, accessories, & parts
3335 Used car dealers
3517 Other automotive dealers (motorcycles, recreational vehicles, etc.)
Building, Hardware, & Garden Supply
4416 Building materials dealers
4457 Hardware stores
4473 Nurseries & garden supply stores
4432 Paint, glass, & wallpaper stores

Food & Beverages
0612 Bakeries selling at retail
3086 Catering services
3095 Drinking places (bars, taverns, pubs, saloons, etc.)
3079 Eating places, meals & snacks
3210 Grocery stores (general line)
3251 Liquor stores
3236 Specialized food stores (meat, produce, candy, health food, etc.)
Furniture & General Merchandise
3988 Computer & software stores
3970 Furniture stores
4317 Home furnishings stores (china, floor coverings, drapes)
4119 Household appliance stores
4333 Music & record stores
3996 TV, audio & electronic stores
3715 Variety stores
3731 Other general merchandise stores
Miscellaneous Retail Stores
4812 Boat dealers
5017 Book stores, excluding newsstands
4853 Camera & photo supply stores
3277 Drug stores
5058 Fabric & needlework stores
4655 Florists
5090 Fuel dealers (except gasoline)
4630 Gift, novelty & souvenir stores
4838 Hobby, toy, & game shops
4671 Jewelry stores
4895 Luggage & leather goods stores
5074 Mobile home dealers
4879 Optical goods stores
4697 Sporting goods & bicycle shops
5033 Stationery stores
4614 Used merchandise & antique stores (except motor vehicle parts)
5884 Other retail stores

Trade, Wholesale—Selling Goods to Other Businesses, etc.
Durable Goods, Including Machinery Equipment, Wood, Metals, etc.
2634 Agent or broker for other firms—more than 50% of gross sales on commission
2618 Selling for your own account
Nondurable Goods, Including Food, Fiber, Chemicals, etc.
2675 Agent or broker for other firms—more than 50% of gross sales on commission
2659 Selling for your own account

Transportation, Communications, Public Utilities, & Related Services
6619 Air transportation
6312 Bus & limousine transportation
6676 Communication services
6395 Courier or package delivery
6361 Highway passenger transportation (except chartered service)
6536 Public warehousing
6114 Taxicabs
6510 Trash collection without own dump
6635 Travel agents & tour operators
6338 Trucking (except trash collection)
6692 Utilities (dumps, snow plowing, road cleaning, etc.)
6551 Water transportation
6650 Other transportation services
8888 **Unable to classify**

HOME OFFICE DEDUCTION

File Form 8829, *Expenses for Business Use of Your Home* (with Schedule C).

If you use your home for business, you may be able to deduct some of your expenses for its business use. But you cannot deduct more than you receive in gross income from its business use.

USE TESTS

To take a deduction for the use of part of your home in business, you must meet certain tests. That part of your home that you deduct must be used **exclusively** and **regularly** as the principal place of business for the trade in which you engage, as a place to meet and deal with customers in the normal course of your trade, or in connection with your trade if you are using a separate structure that is not attached to your house or residence.

FIGURE BUSINESS PERCENTAGE

To figure deductions for the business use of your home, you will have to divide the expenses of operating your home between personal and business use. Some expenses are divided on an area basis. Some are further divided on a time usage basis. To find the business percentage, divide the area used for the business by the total area of your home.

DEDUCTIBLE EXPENSES

Certain expenses are totally deductible, such as painting or repairs made to the specific area used for business. You can deduct indirect expenses based on percentage of usage, including real estate taxes, mortgage interest, casualty losses, utilities, telephone, insurance and security systems and depreciation. Unrelated expenses cannot be deducted.

FORM 8829

This form, entitled *Expenses for Business Use of Your Home,* is filed with Schedule C (Form 1040) on April 15th.

IRS PUBLICATIONS: Publication 587, *Business Use of Your Home,* will give you more detailed information on what is and is not deductible.

SAMPLE: A copy of Form 8829 is provided on the next page.

FORM 8829
EXPENSES FOR BUSINESS USE OF YOUR HOME

Form **8829**	**Expenses for Business Use of Your Home**	OMB No. 1545-1266
Department of the Treasury Internal Revenue Service	▶ File with Schedule C (Form 1040). Use a separate Form 8829 for each home you used for business during the year. ▶ See instructions on back.	**1992** Attachment Sequence No. **66**

Name(s) of proprietor(s)   Your social security number

Part I   Part of Your Home Used for Business

1	Area used exclusively for business (see instructions). Include area that does not meet exclusive use test and either used for inventory storage or regularly used as part of a day-care facility	1	
2	Total area of home	2	
3	Divide line 1 by line 2. Enter the result as a percentage	3	%

• For day-care facilities not used exclusively for business, also complete lines 4–6.
• All others, skip lines 4–6 and enter the amount from line 3 on line 7.

4	Multiply days used for day care during year by hours used per day .	4		hr.
5	Total hours available for use during the year (366 days × 24 hours). See instructions	5	8,784	hr.
6	Divide line 4 by line 5. Enter the result as a decimal amount . . .	6	.	
7	Business percentage. For day-care facilities not used exclusively for business, multiply line 6 by line 3 (enter the result as a percentage). All others, enter the amount from line 3 . . . . ▶	7		%

Part II   Figure Your Allowable Deduction

		(a) Direct expenses	(b) Indirect expenses	
8	Enter the amount from Schedule C, line 29, **plus** any net gain or (loss) derived from the business use of your home and shown on Schedule D or Form 4797. If more than one place of business, see instructions		8	
	See instructions for columns (a) and (b) before completing lines 9–20.			
9	Casualty losses. See instructions	9		
10	Deductible mortgage interest. See instructions .	10		
11	Real estate taxes. See instructions	11		
12	Add lines 9, 10, and 11.	12		
13	Multiply line 12, column (b) by line 7		13	
14	Add line 12, column (a) and line 13.			14
15	Subtract line 14 from line 8. If zero or less, enter -0- .			15
16	Excess mortgage interest. See instructions . .	16		
17	Insurance	17		
18	Repairs and maintenance	18		
19	Utilities	19		
20	Other expenses. See instructions	20		
21	Add lines 16 through 20	21		
22	Multiply line 21, column (b) by line 7	22		
23	Carryover of operating expenses from 1991 Form 8829, line 41 . .	23		
24	Add line 21 in column (a), line 22, and line 23			24
25	Allowable operating expenses. Enter the **smaller** of line 15 or line 24			25
26	Limit on excess casualty losses and depreciation. Subtract line 25 from line 15			26
27	Excess casualty losses. See instructions	27		
28	Depreciation of your home from Part III below	28		
29	Carryover of excess casualty losses and depreciation from 1991 Form 8829, line 42	29		
30	Add lines 27 through 29			30
31	Allowable excess casualty losses and depreciation. Enter the **smaller** of line 26 or line 30 . .			31
32	Add lines 14, 25, and 31			32
33	Casualty loss portion, if any, from lines 14 and 31. Carry amount to **Form 4684**, Section B .			33
34	Allowable expenses for business use of your home. Subtract line 33 from line 32. Enter here and on Schedule C, line 30. If your home was used for more than one business, see instructions ▶			34

Part III   Depreciation of Your Home

35	Enter the **smaller** of your home's adjusted basis or its fair market value. See instructions . .	35	
36	Value of land included on line 35	36	
37	Basis of building. Subtract line 36 from line 35	37	
38	Business basis of building. Multiply line 37 by line 7	38	
39	Depreciation percentage. See instructions	39	%
40	Depreciation allowable. Multiply line 38 by line 39. Enter here and on line 28 above. See instructions	40	

Part IV   Carryover of Unallowed Expenses to 1993

41	Operating expenses. Subtract line 25 from line 24. If less than zero, enter -0-	41	
42	Excess casualty losses and depreciation. Subtract line 31 from line 30. If less than zero, enter -0- .	42	

For Paperwork Reduction Act Notice, see back of form.   Cat. No. 13232M   Form **8829** (1992)

INCOME TAX (FOR PARTNERSHIPS)

File Form 1065, *U.S. Partnership Return of Income.*

A partnership is the relationship between two or more persons who join together to carry on a trade or business with each person contributing money, property, labor or skill, and each expecting to share in the profits and losses of the business.

Every partnership doing business in or having income from sources within the United States is required to file Form 1065 for its tax year. This is mainly an information return. Partnership profits are not taxed to the partnership. Each partner must take into account his distributive share of partnership items and report it on his own income tax return.

Estimated Tax: As a result of partnership distributions, partners may have to make estimated tax payments. See: "Self-Employment Tax," Schedule SE.

Self-Employment Tax: A partner's distributive share of income is usually included in figuring net earnings from self-employment. See: "Self-Employment Tax," Schedule SE.

SCHEDULES K AND K-1 (FORM 1065)

These forms are used to show partners distributive shares of reportable partnership items. Form 1065 and its Schedules K or K-1 are filed separately and not attached to your income tax return.

SCHEDULE E (FORM 1040)

Supplemental Income Schedule, Part II is used to report partnership items on your individual tax return. Failure to treat your individual and partnership returns consistently will allow the IRS to assess and take action to collect deficiencies and penalties.

IRS PUBLICATIONS: See Chapters 4 and 29, Publication 334, *Tax Guide for Small Business.* Chapter 39 contains examples of filled-in forms. Also, see Publication 541, *Tax Information on Partnerships.*

SAMPLE: Form 1065 and Schedule K follow on the next two pages.

FORM 1065
U.S. PARTNERSHIP RETURN OF INCOME

Form **1065**	**U.S. Partnership Return of Income**	OMB No. 1545-0099
Department of the Treasury Internal Revenue Service	For calendar year 1992, or tax year beginning .... , 1992, and ending .... , 19 .... ▶ See separate instructions.	**1992**

A Principal business activity	Use the IRS label. Otherwise, please print or type.	Name of partnership	**D** Employer identification number
B Principal product or service		Number, street, and room or suite no. (If a P.O. box, see page 9 of the instructions.)	**E** Date business started
C Business code number		City or town, state, and ZIP code	**F** Total assets (see Specific Instructions) $

G Check applicable boxes: **(1)** ☐ Initial return **(2)** ☐ Final return **(3)** ☐ Change in address **(4)** ☐ Amended return
H Check accounting method: **(1)** ☐ Cash **(2)** ☐ Accrual **(3)** ☐ Other (specify) ▶ ....
I Number of partners in this partnership . . . . ▶ ....

Caution: *Include only trade or business income and expenses on lines 1a through 22 below. See the instructions for more information.*

Income

1a Gross receipts or sales	**1a**		
b Less returns and allowances.	**1b**	**1c**	
2 Cost of goods sold (Schedule A, line 8)		**2**	
3 Gross profit. Subtract line 2 from line 1c.		**3**	
4 Ordinary income (loss) from other partnerships and fiduciaries *(attach schedule)*		**4**	
5 Net farm profit (loss) *(attach Schedule F (Form 1040))*		**5**	
6 Net gain (loss) from Form 4797, Part II, line 20.		**6**	
7 Other income (loss) (see instructions) *(attach schedule)*		**7**	
8 **Total income (loss).** Combine lines 3 through 7		**8**	

Deductions (see instructions for limitations)

9a Salaries and wages (other than to partners).	**9a**		
b Less jobs credit	**9b**	**9c**	
10 Guaranteed payments to partners		**10**	
11 Repairs		**11**	
12 Bad debts		**12**	
13 Rent		**13**	
14 Taxes		**14**	
15 Interest		**15**	
16a Depreciation (see instructions)	**16a**		
b Less depreciation reported on Schedule A and elsewhere on return	**16b**	**16c**	
17 Depletion **(Do not deduct oil and gas depletion.)**		**17**	
18 Retirement plans, etc.		**18**	
19 Employee benefit programs		**19**	
20 Other deductions *(attach schedule)*		**20**	
21 **Total deductions.** Add the amounts shown in the far right column for lines 9c through 20 .		**21**	
22 **Ordinary income (loss)** from trade or business activities. Subtract line 21 from line 8 . .		**22**	

Please Sign Here

Under penalties of perjury, I declare that I have examined this return, including accompanying schedules and statements, and to the best of my knowledge and belief, it is true, correct, and complete. Declaration of preparer (other than general partner) is based on all information of which preparer has any knowledge.

▶ _____ Signature of general partner ▶ _____ Date

Paid Preparer's Use Only

Preparer's signature ▶	Date	Check if self-employed ▶ ☐	Preparer's social security no.
Firm's name (or yours if self-employed) and address ▶		E.I. No. ▶	
		ZIP code ▶	

For Paperwork Reduction Act Notice, see page 1 of separate instructions.   Cat. No. 11390Z   Form **1065** (1992)

SCHEDULE K - FORM 1065
PARTNERS' SHARES OF INCOME, CREDITS, DEDUCTIONS, ETC.

Form 1065 (1992) Page **3**

Schedule K	Partners' Shares of Income, Credits, Deductions, Etc.		
	(a) Distributive share items		**(b) Total amount**

Income (Loss)

1	Ordinary income (loss) from trade or business activities (page 1, line 22)	1	
2	Net income (loss) from rental real estate activities (attach Form 8825)	2	
3a	Gross income from other rental activities	3a	
b	Expenses from other rental activities (attach schedule)	3b	
c	Net income (loss) from other rental activities. Subtract line 3b from line 3a	3c	
4	Portfolio income (loss) (see instructions): a Interest income	4a	
b	Dividend income	4b	
c	Royalty income	4c	
d	Net short-term capital gain (loss) (attach Schedule D (Form 1065))	4d	
e	Net long-term capital gain (loss) (attach Schedule D (Form 1065))	4e	
f	Other portfolio income (loss) (attach schedule)	4f	
5	Guaranteed payments to partners	5	
6	Net gain (loss) under section 1231 (other than due to casualty or theft) (attach Form 4797)	6	
7	Other income (loss) (attach schedule)	7	

Deductions

8	Charitable contributions (see instructions) (attach schedule)	8	
9	Section 179 expense deduction (attach Form 4562)	9	
10	Deductions related to portfolio income (see instructions) (itemize)	10	
11	Other deductions (attach schedule)	11	

Investment Interest

12a	Interest expense on investment debts	12a	
b (1)	Investment income included on lines 4a through 4f above	12b(1)	
(2)	Investment expenses included on line 10 above	12b(2)	

Credits

13a	Credit for income tax withheld	13a	
b	Low-income housing credit (see instructions):		
(1)	From partnerships to which section 42(j)(5) applies for property placed in service before 1990	13b(1)	
(2)	Other than on line 13b(1) for property placed in service before 1990	13b(2)	
(3)	From partnerships to which section 42(j)(5) applies for property placed in service after 1989	13b(3)	
(4)	Other than on line 13b(3) for property placed in service after 1989	13b(4)	
c	Qualified rehabilitation expenditures related to rental real estate activities (attach Form 3468)	13c	
d	Credits (other than credits shown on lines 13b and 13c) related to rental real estate activities (see instructions)	13d	
e	Credits related to other rental activities (see instructions)	13e	
14	Other credits (see instructions)	14	

Self-Employment

15a	Net earnings (loss) from self-employment	15a	
b	Gross farming or fishing income	15b	
c	Gross nonfarm income	15c	

Adjustments and Tax Preference Items

16a	Depreciation adjustment on property placed in service after 1986	16a	
b	Adjusted gain or loss	16b	
c	Depletion (other than oil and gas)	16c	
d (1)	Gross income from oil, gas, and geothermal properties	16d(1)	
(2)	Deductions allocable to oil, gas, and geothermal properties	16d(2)	
e	Other adjustments and tax preference items (attach schedule)	16e	

Foreign Taxes

17a	Type of income ▶ .... b Foreign country or U.S. possession ▶		
c	Total gross income from sources outside the United States (attach schedule)	17c	
d	Total applicable deductions and losses (attach schedule)	17d	
e	Total foreign taxes (check one): ▶ ☐ Paid ☐ Accrued	17e	
f	Reduction in taxes available for credit (attach schedule)	17f	
g	Other foreign tax information (attach schedule)	17g	

Other

18a	Total expenditures to which a section 59(e) election may apply	18a	
b	Type of expenditures ▶		
19	Tax-exempt interest income	19	
20	Other tax-exempt income	20	
21	Nondeductible expenses	21	
22	Other items and amounts required to be reported separately to partners (see instructions) (attach schedule)		

Analysis

23a	Income (loss). Combine lines 1 through 7 in column (b). From the result, subtract the sum of lines 8 through 12a, 17e, and 18a	23a	

b Analysis by type of partner:	(a) Corporate	(b) Individual		(c) Partnership	(d) Exempt organization	(e) Nominee/Other
		i. Active	ii. Passive			
(1) General partners						
(2) Limited partners						

INCOME TAX (S CORPORATIONS)

File Form 1120S, *U.S. Income Tax Return for an S Corporation.*

Some corporations may elect not to be subject to income tax. If a corporation qualifies and chooses to become an S corporation, its income usually will be taxed to the shareholders.

The formation of an S corporation is only allowable under certain circumstances.

1. It must be a domestic corporation either organized in the United States or organized under federal or state law.

2. It must have only one class of stock.

3. It must have no more than 35 shareholders.

4. It must have as shareholders only individuals, estates and certain trusts. Partnerships and corporations cannot be shareholders in an S corporation.

5. It must have shareholders who are citizens or residents of the United States. Nonresident aliens cannot be shareholders.

The formation of an S corporation can be an advantage form of legal structure, but if entered into without careful planning, it can result in more taxes instead of less, as anticipated.

FORM 1120S

This form is used to file an income tax return for an S corporation. Schedule K and K-1 are extremely important parts of Form 1120S. Schedule K summarizes the corporation's income, deductions, credits, etc., reportable by the shareholders. Schedule K-1 shows each shareholders separate share. The individual shareholder reports their income tax on Form 1040. Form 1120S is due on the 15th day of the third month after the end of the tax year.

IRS PUBLICATIONS: The following publications available for use are, Publication 589, *Tax Information on S Corporations* and Publication 334, *Tax Guide for Small Business*, Chapters 31 and 42.

SAMPLE: A copy of Form 1120S follows.

FORM 1120S
U.S. INCOME TAX RETURN FOR AN S CORPORATION

Form **1120S**	U.S. Income Tax Return for an S Corporation	OMB No. 1545-0130
Department of the Treasury Internal Revenue Service	For calendar year 1992, or tax year beginning .... , 1992, and ending .... , 19 ..... ▶ See separate instructions.	**1992**

A Date of election as an S corporation	Use IRS label. Otherwise, please print or type.	Name	**C** Employer Identification number
		Number, street, and room or suite no. (If a P.O. box, see page 8 of the instructions.)	**D** Date incorporated
B Business code no. (see Specific Instructions)		City or town, state, and ZIP code	**E** Total assets (see Specific Instructions) $

F Check applicable boxes: (1) ☐ Initial return (2) ☐ Final return (3) ☐ Change in address (4) ☐ Amended return

G Check this box if this S corporation is subject to the consolidated audit procedures of sections 6241 through 6245 (see instructions before checking this box) . ▶ ☐

H Enter number of shareholders in the corporation at end of the tax year . . . . ▶

Caution: *Include only trade or business income and expenses on lines 1a through 21. See the instructions for more information.*

Income

1a Gross receipts or sales [____] **b** Less returns and allowances [____] **c** Bal ▶	**1c**	
2 Cost of goods sold (Schedule A, line 8)	**2**	
3 Gross profit. Subtract line 2 from line 1c	**3**	
4 Net gain (loss) from Form 4797, Part II, line 20 *(attach Form 4797)*	**4**	
5 Other income (loss) (see instructions) *(attach schedule)* . .	**5**	
6 Total income (loss). Combine lines 3 through 5 . . . . . ▶	**6**	

Deductions (See instructions for limitations.)

7 Compensation of officers	**7**	
8a Salaries and wages [____] **b** Less jobs credit [____] **c** Bal ▶	**8c**	
9 Repairs	**9**	
10 Bad debts	**10**	
11 Rents	**11**	
12 Taxes	**12**	
13 Interest	**13**	
14a Depreciation (see instructions) . . . . **14a** [____]		
b Depreciation claimed on Schedule A and elsewhere on return . **14b** [____]		
c Subtract line 14b from line 14a	**14c**	
15 Depletion (**Do not deduct oil and gas depletion.**) . .	**15**	
16 Advertising	**16**	
17 Pension, profit-sharing, etc., plans	**17**	
18 Employee benefit programs	**18**	
19 Other deductions (see instructions) *(attach schedule)* . .	**19**	
20 Total deductions. Add lines 7 through 19 . . . . . . ▶	**20**	
21 Ordinary income (loss) from trade or business activities. Subtract line 20 from line 6 .	**21**	

Tax and Payments

22 Tax:		
a Excess net passive income tax *(attach schedule)* . . . . . **22a** [____]		
b Tax from Schedule D (Form 1120S) . . . . **22b** [____]		
c Add lines 22a and 22b (see instructions for additional taxes) .	**22c**	
23 Payments:		
a 1992 estimated tax payments . . . . **23a** [____]		
b Tax deposited with Form 7004 . . . . **23b** [____]		
c Credit for Federal tax paid on fuels *(attach Form 4136)* . . . **23c** [____]		
d Add lines 23a through 23c . . . . ▶	**23d**	
24 Estimated tax penalty (see instructions). Check if Form 2220 is attached. . . . . ▶ ☐	**24**	
25 Tax due. If the total of lines 22c and 24 is larger than line 23d, enter amount owed. See instructions for depositary method of payment . . . . ▶	**25**	
26 Overpayment. If line 23d is larger than the total of lines 22c and 24, enter amount overpaid ▶	**26**	
27 Enter amount of line 26 you want: **Credited to 1993 estimated tax** ▶ [____] **Refunded** ▶	**27**	

Please Sign Here

Under penalties of perjury, I declare that I have examined this return, including accompanying schedules and statements, and to the best of my knowledge and belief, it is true, correct, and complete. Declaration of preparer (other than taxpayer) is based on all information of which preparer has any knowledge.

▶ _____	_____	▶ _____
Signature of officer	Date	Title

Paid Preparer's Use Only

Preparer's signature ▶		Date	Check if self-employed ▶ ☐	Preparer's social security number
Firm's name (or yours if self-employed) and address ▶			E.I. No. ▶	
			ZIP code ▶	

For Paperwork Reduction Act Notice, see page 1 of separate Instructions.   Cat. No. 11510H   Form **1120S** (1992)

INCOME TAX (CORPORATIONS)

File Form 1120 or 1120-A, *Corporation Income Tax Return*, or *Corporations Short-Form Income Tax Return*.

Every corporation, unless it is specifically exempt or has dissolved, must file a tax return even if it has no taxable income for the year and regardless of the amount of its gross income. Corporate profits normally are taxed to the corporation. When the profits are distributed as dividends, the dividends are then taxed to the shareholders.

Estimated Tax: Every corporation whose tax is expected to be $500 or more must make estimated tax payments. If a corporation's estimated tax is $500 or more, its estimated tax payments are deposited with an authorized financial institution or Federal Reserve. Each deposit must be accompanied by Form 8109.

Contributions to the Capital of a Corporation: Contributions are "paid in capital" and are not taxable income to the corporation.

FORM 1120 OR 1120-A

The income tax return for ordinary corporations is Form 1120. Form 1120-A is for companies having gross receipts, total income and total assets that are all under $500,000.

Corporation returns are due on March 15th. A corporation using a fiscal year not beginning January 1st and ending December 31st, will have to file it on or before the 15th of the third month following the close of its fiscal year.

IRS PUBLICATIONS: See Publication 334, *Tax Guide for Small Business*, Chapter 30 for explanation of the application of various tax provisions to corporations (filing requirements, tax computations, estimated tax payments, corporate distribution and retained earnings). For a more complete discussion of corporation taxation, as well as liquidations and stock redemptions, see Publication 542, *Tax Information on Corporations*. For filled-in examples see Chapters 39 and 40 of Publication 334.

SAMPLE: See Forms 1120 and 1120A on the following pages.

FORM 1120

U.S. CORPORATION INCOME TAX RETURN

Form **1120**	**U.S. Corporation Income Tax Return**	OMB No. 1545-0123
Department of the Treasury Internal Revenue Service	For calendar year 1992 or tax year beginning ...., 1992, ending ...., 19 ... ▶ Instructions are separate. See page 1 for Paperwork Reduction Act Notice.	**1992**

A Check if a:	Use IRS label. Other-wise, please print or type.	Name		B Employer identification number
(1) Consolidated return (attach Form 851) ☐				
(2) Personal holding co. (attach Sch. PH) ☐		Number, street, and room or suite no. (If a P.O. box, see page 6 of instructions.)		C Date incorporated
(3) Personal service corp. (as defined in Temporary Regs. sec. 1.441-4T—see instructions) ☐		City or town, state, and ZIP code		D Total assets (see Specific Instructions)

E Check applicable boxes: (1) ☐ Initial return (2) ☐ Final return (3) ☐ Change in address $

	1a Gross receipts or sales	**b** Less returns and allowances	**c** Bal ▶	**1c**	
	2 Cost of goods sold (Schedule A, line 8)	**2**	
	3 Gross profit. Subtract line 2 from line 1c	**3**	
	4 Dividends (Schedule C, line 19)	**4**	
Income	**5** Interest	**5**	
	6 Gross rents	**6**	
	7 Gross royalties	**7**	
	8 Capital gain net income (attach Schedule D (Form 1120))	**8**	
	9 Net gain or (loss) from Form 4797, Part II, line 20 (attach Form 4797) . . .	**9**	
	10 Other income (see instructions—attach schedule)	**10**	
	11 **Total income.** Add lines 3 through 10 . . . . ▶	**11**	

Deductions (See instructions for limitations on deductions.)		
12 Compensation of officers (Schedule E, line 4).	**12**	
13a Salaries and wages **b** Less jobs credit **c** Balance ▶	**13c**	
14 Repairs	**14**	
15 Bad debts	**15**	
16 Rents	**16**	
17 Taxes	**17**	
18 Interest	**18**	
19 Charitable contributions (see instructions for 10% limitation)	**19**	
20 Depreciation (attach Form 4562) **20**		
21 Less depreciation claimed on Schedule A and elsewhere on return . . **21a**	**21b**	
22 Depletion	**22**	
23 Advertising	**23**	
24 Pension, profit-sharing, etc., plans	**24**	
25 Employee benefit programs	**25**	
26 Other deductions (attach schedule)	**26**	
27 **Total deductions.** Add lines 12 through 26 . . . . ▶	**27**	
28 Taxable income before net operating loss deduction and special deductions. Subtract line 27 from line 11	**28**	
29 **Less: a** Net operating loss deduction (see instructions) **29a**		
b Special deductions (Schedule C, line 20) **29b**	**29c**	

Tax and Payments		
30 **Taxable income.** Subtract line 29c from line 28	**30**	
31 **Total tax** (Schedule J, line 10)	**31**	
32 **Payments: a** 1991 overpayment credited to 1992 **32a**		
b 1992 estimated tax payments . . **32b**		
c Less 1992 refund applied for on Form 4466 **32c** ( ) **d** Bal ▶ **32d**		
e Tax deposited with Form 7004 . . . . **32e**		
f Credit from regulated investment companies (attach Form 2439) . . . **32f**		
g Credit for Federal tax on fuels (attach Form 4136). See instructions . . **32g**	**32h**	
33 Estimated tax penalty (see instructions). Check if Form 2220 is attached . . . . ▶ ☐	**33**	
34 **Tax due.** If line 32h is smaller than the total of lines 31 and 33, enter amount owed	**34**	
35 **Overpayment.** If line 32h is larger than the total of lines 31 and 33, enter amount overpaid . . .	**35**	
36 Enter amount of line 35 you want: **Credited to 1993 estimated tax** ▶ Refunded ▶	**36**	

Please Sign Here

Under penalties of perjury, I declare that I have examined this return, including accompanying schedules and statements, and to the best of my knowledge and belief, it is true, correct, and complete. Declaration of preparer (other than taxpayer) is based on all information of which preparer has any knowledge.

▶ Signature of officer	Date	▶ Title

Paid Preparer's Use Only	Preparer's signature ▶	Date	Check if self-employed ☐	Preparer's social security number
	Firm's name (or yours if self-employed) and address ▶		E.I. No. ▶	
			ZIP code ▶	

Cat. No. 11450Q

FORM 1120-A
U.S. CORPORATION SHORT-FORM INCOME TAX RETURN

Form **1120-A** Department of the Treasury Internal Revenue Service	**U.S. Corporation Short-Form Income Tax Return** See separate instructions to make sure the corporation qualifies to file Form 1120-A. For calendar year 1992 or tax year beginning .... , 1992, ending .... , 19.....	OMB No. 1545-0890 19**92**

A Check this box if corp. is a personal service corp. (as defined in Temporary Regs. section 1.441-4T—see instructions) ▶ ☐

Use IRS label. Otherwise, please print or type.	Name	**B** Employer identification number
	Number, street, and room or suite no. (If a P.O. box, see page 6 of instructions.)	**C** Date incorporated
	City or town, state, and ZIP code	**D** Total assets (see Specific Instructions) $

E Check applicable boxes: **(1)** ☐ Initial return **(2)** ☐ Change in address

F Check method of accounting: **(1)** ☐ Cash **(2)** ☐ Accrual **(3)** ☐ Other (specify) . . ▶

Income

1a	Gross receipts or sales [ ] **b** Less returns and allowances [ ] **c** Balance ▶	1c	
2	Cost of goods sold (see instructions)	2	
3	Gross profit. Subtract line 2 from line 1c	3	
4	Domestic corporation dividends subject to the 70% deduction	4	
5	Interest	5	
6	Gross rents	6	
7	Gross royalties	7	
8	Capital gain net income (attach Schedule D (Form 1120))	8	
9	Net gain or (loss) from Form 4797, Part II, line 20 (attach Form 4797) . .	9	
10	Other income (see instructions)	10	
11	**Total income.** Add lines 3 through 10 . . . . ▶	11	

Deductions (See Instructions for limitations on deductions.)

12	Compensation of officers (see instructions)	12	
13a	Salaries and wages [ ] **b** Less jobs credit [ ] **c** Balance ▶	13c	
14	Repairs	14	
15	Bad debts	15	
16	Rents	16	
17	Taxes	17	
18	Interest	18	
19	Charitable contributions **(see instructions for 10% limitation)** . . .	19	
20	Depreciation (attach Form 4562) 20		
21	Less depreciation claimed elsewhere on return 21a	21b	
22	Other deductions (attach schedule)	22	
23	**Total deductions.** Add lines 12 through 22 . . . . ▶	23	
24	Taxable income before net operating loss deduction and special deductions. Subtract line 23 from line 11	24	
25	**Less: a** Net operating loss deduction (see instructions) 25a		
	b Special deductions (see instructions) 25b	25c	

Tax and Payments

26	**Taxable income.** Subtract line 25c from line 24	26	
27	**Total tax** (from page 2, Part I, line 7)	27	
28	**Payments:**		
a	1991 overpayment credited to 1992 28a		
b	1992 estimated tax payments . 28b		
c	Less 1992 refund applied for on Form 4466 28c ( ) Bal ▶	28d	
e	Tax deposited with Form 7004	28e	
f	Credit from regulated investment companies (attach Form 2439) .	28f	
g	Credit for Federal tax on fuels (attach Form 4136). See instructions	28g	
h	**Total payments.** Add lines 28d through 28g	28h	
29	Estimated tax penalty (see instructions). Check if Form 2220 is attached . . . . ▶ ☐	29	
30	**Tax due.** If line 28h is smaller than the total of lines 27 and 29, enter amount owed	30	
31	**Overpayment.** If line 28h is larger than the total of lines 27 and 29, enter amount overpaid . . .	31	
32	Enter amount of line 31 you want: **Credited to 1993 estimated tax** ▶ [ ] **Refunded** ▶	32	

Please Sign Here

Under penalties of perjury, I declare that I have examined this return, including accompanying schedules and statements, and to the best of my knowledge and belief, it is true, correct, and complete. Declaration of preparer (other than taxpayer) is based on all information of which preparer has any knowledge.

▶ _____   _____   _____
Signature of officer   Date   Title

Paid Preparer's Use Only	Preparer's signature ▶	Date	Check if self-employed ▶ ☐	Preparer's social security number
	Firm's name (or yours if self-employed) and address ▶		E.I. No. ▶	
			ZIP code ▶	

For Paperwork Reduction Act Notice, see page 1 of the instructions.   Cat. No. 11456E   Form **1120-A** (1992)

ESTIMATED TAX (FOR SOLE PROPRIETOR, INDIVIDUAL WHO IS A PARTNER OR S CORPORATION SHAREHOLDER)

File Form 1040-ES, *Estimated Tax for Individuals.*

If you are a sole proprietor, an individual who is a partner, or a shareholder in an S corporation, you probably will have to make estimated tax payments if the total of your estimated income tax and self-employment tax is in excess of a certain amount (in 1992, if it exceeds your total withholding and credits by $500 or more).

Underpayment of Tax: If you do not pay enough income tax and self-employment tax for the current year by withholding or by making estimated tax payments, you may have to pay a penalty on the amount not paid. IRS will figure the penalty and send you a bill.

FORM 1040-ES

IRS Form 1040-ES is used to estimate your tax. There are four vouchers and they are filed on April 15th, June 15th, September 15th and January 15th. (Notice that there are only two months between the second and third payments and four months between the third and fourth payments.)

Your estimated tax payments include both federal income tax and self-employment tax liabilities.

ESTIMATED TAX WORKSHEET

You can use the *Estimated Tax Worksheet* to figure your estimated tax liability. Keep it for your own records and revise if your actual income is very far over or under your estimate. After the first filing, Form 1040-ES will be sent to you each year.

IRS PUBLICATIONS: See Publication 505, *Tax Withholding and Estimated Tax,* for information. Also see instructions accompanying Form 1040-ES.

SAMPLE: Samples of an Estimated Tax Worksheet and a 1040-ES can be seen on the following pages.

1993
ESTIMATED TAX WORKSHEET

1993 Estimated Tax Worksheet (keep for your records)

1	Enter amount of adjusted gross income you expect in 1993	**1**
2	• If you plan to itemize deductions, enter the estimated total of your itemized deductions. **Caution:** If line 1 above is over $108,450 ($54,225 if married filing separately), your deduction may be reduced. See Pub. 505 for details. • If you do not plan to itemize deductions, see **Standard Deduction for 1993** on page 2, and enter your standard deduction here.	**2**
3	Subtract line 2 from line 1	**3**
4	Exemptions. Multiply $2,350 by the number of personal exemptions. If you can be claimed as a dependent on another person's 1993 return, your personal exemption is not allowed. **Caution:** If line 1 above is over $162,700 ($135,600 if head of household; $108,450 if single; $81,350 if married filing separately), get Pub. 505 to figure the amount to enter . . .	**4**
5	Subtract line 4 from line 3	**5**
6	**Tax.** Figure your tax on the amount on line 5 by using the 1993 Tax Rate Schedules below. DO NOT use the Tax Table or the Tax Rate Schedules in the 1992 Form 1040 or Form 1040A instructions. **Caution:** If you have a net capital gain and line 5 is over $89,150 ($76,400 if head of household; $53,500 if single; $44,575 if married filing separately), get Pub. 505 to figure the tax	**6**
7	Additional taxes (see line 7 instructions)	**7**
8	Add lines 6 and 7	**8**
9	Credits (see line 9 instructions). Do not include any income tax withholding on this line	**9**
10	Subtract line 9 from line 8. Enter the result, but not less than zero	**10**
11	Self-employment tax. Estimate of 1993 net earnings from self-employment $ .... ; If **$57,600 or less,** multiply the amount by .153; if **more than $57,600,** see line 11 instructions for the amount to enter. **Caution:** If you also have wages subject to social security or Medicare tax, get Pub. 505 to figure the amount to enter . .	**11**
12	Other taxes (see line 12 instructions)	**12**
13a	Add lines 10 through 12	**13a**
b	Earned income credit and credit from **Form 4136**	**13b**
c	Subtract line 13b from line 13a. Enter the result, but not less than zero. **THIS IS YOUR TOTAL 1993 ESTIMATED TAX** ▶	**13c**
14a	Multiply line 13c by 90% (66⅔% for farmers and fishermen)	**14a**
b	Enter 100% of the tax shown on your 1992 tax return	**14b**
	Caution: If 14b is **smaller** than 14a **and** line 1 above is over $75,000 ($37,500 if married filing separately), stop here and see **Limit on Use of Prior Year's Tax** on page 1 before continuing.	
c	Enter the **smaller** of line 14a or 14b. **THIS IS YOUR REQUIRED ANNUAL PAYMENT TO AVOID A PENALTY** ▶ **Caution:** Generally, if you do not prepay at least the amount on line 14c, you may owe a penalty for not paying enough estimated tax. To avoid a penalty, make sure your estimate on line 13c is as accurate as possible. Even if you pay the required annual payment, you may still owe tax when you file your return. If you prefer, you may pay the amount shown on line 13c. For more details, get Pub. 505.	**14c**
15	Income tax withheld and estimated to be withheld during 1993 (including income tax withholding on pensions, annuities, certain deferred income, etc.)	**15**
16	Subtract line 15 from line 14c. (**Note:** If zero or less, or line 13c minus line 15 is less than $500, stop here. You are not required to make estimated tax payments.)	**16**
17	If the first payment you are required to make is due April 15, 1993, enter ¼ of line 16 (minus any 1992 overpayment that you are applying to this installment) here and on your payment voucher(s)	**17**

1993 Tax Rate Schedules

Caution: Do not use these Tax Rate Schedules to figure your 1992 taxes. Use only to figure your 1993 estimated taxes.

Single—Schedule X

If line 5 is: Over—	But not over—	The tax is:	of the amount over—
$0	$22,100	..........15%	$0
22,100	53,500	$3,315.00 + 28%	22,100
53,500	....	12,107.00 + 31%	53,500

Head of household—Schedule Z

If line 5 is: Over—	But not over—	The tax is:	of the amount over—
$0	$29,600	..........15%	$0
29,600	76,400	$4,440.00 + 28%	29,600
76,400	....	17,544.00 + 31%	76,400

Married filing jointly or Qualifying widow(er)—Schedule Y-1

If line 5 is: Over—	But not over—	The tax is:	of the amount over—
$0	$36,900	..........15%	$0
36,900	89,150	$5,535.00 + 28%	36,900
89,150	....	20,165.00 + 31%	89,150

Married filing separately—Schedule Y-2

If line 5 is: Over—	But not over—	The tax is:	of the amount over—
$0	$18,450	..........15%	$0
18,450	44,575	$2,767.50 + 28%	18,450
44,575	....	10,082.50 + 31%	44,575

Page 3

FORM 1040ES
ESTIMATED TAX PAYMENT RECORD & SAMPLE VOUCHER

ESTIMATED TAX PAYMENT DUE DATES
1st Payment . . . . April 15, 1993
2nd Payment . . . .June 15, 1993
3rd Payment Sept.15, 1993
4th Payment . . . . Jan 15, 1994

Record of Estimated Tax Payments

Payment number	(a) Date	(b) Amount paid	(c) 1992 overpayment credit applied	(d) Total amount paid and credited (add (b) and (c))
1				
2				
3				
4				
Total . . . . ▶				

Where To File Your Payment Voucher

Mail your payment voucher to the Internal Revenue Service at the address shown below for the place where you live. **Do not** mail your tax return to this address. Also, do not mail your estimated tax payments to the address shown in the Form 1040 or 1040A instructions.

Note: *For proper delivery of your estimated tax payment, you must include the P.O. box number, if any, in the address.*

If you live in: ▼	Use this address: ▼
New Jersey, New York (New York City and counties of Nassau, Rockland, Suffolk, and Westchester)	P.O. Box 162 Newark, NJ 07101-0162
New York (all other counties), Connecticut, Maine, Massachusetts, New Hampshire, Rhode Island, Vermont	P.O. Box 371999 Pittsburgh, PA 15250-7999
Delaware, District of Columbia, Maryland, Pennsylvania, Virginia	P.O. Box 839 Newark, NJ 07101-0839
Florida, Georgia, South Carolina	P.O. Box 970004 St. Louis, MO 63197-0004
Indiana, Kentucky, Michigan, Ohio, West Virginia	P.O. Box 7422 Chicago, IL 60680-7422

Alabama, Arkansas, Louisiana, Mississippi, North Carolina, Tennessee	P.O. Box 371300M Pittsburgh, PA 15250-7300
Illinois, Iowa, Minnesota, Missouri, Wisconsin	P.O. Box 6413 Chicago, IL 60680-6413
Kansas, New Mexico, Oklahoma, Texas	P.O. Box 970001 St. Louis, MO 63197-0001
Alaska, Arizona, California (counties of Alpine, Amador, Butte, Calaveras, Colusa, Contra Costa, Del Norte, El Dorado, Glenn, Humboldt, Lake, Lassen, Marin, Mendocino, Modoc, Napa, Nevada, Placer, Plumas, Sacramento, San Joaquin, Shasta, Sierra, Siskiyou, Solano, Sonoma, Sutter, Tehama, Trinity, Yolo, and Yuba), Colorado, Idaho, Montana, Nebraska, Nevada, North Dakota, Oregon, South Dakota, Utah, Washington, Wyoming	P.O. Box 510000 San Francisco, CA 94151-5100
California (all other counties), Hawaii	P.O. Box 54030 Los Angeles, CA 90054-0030
American Samoa	P.O. Box 839 Newark, NJ 07101-0839

Guam	Commissioner of Revenue and Taxation 855 West Marine Drive Agana, GU 96910
The Commonwealth of the Northern Mariana Islands	P.O. Box 839 Newark, NJ 07101-0839
Puerto Rico (or if excluding income under section 933)	P.O. Box 839 Newark, NJ 07101-0839
Virgin Islands: Nonpermanent residents	P.O. Box 839 Newark, NJ 07101-0839
Permanent residents*	V.I. Bureau of Internal Revenue Lockharts Garden No. 1A Charlotte Amalie St. Thomas, VI 00802

* You must prepare separate vouchers for estimated income tax and self-employment tax payments. Send the income tax vouchers to the V.I. address and the self-employment tax vouchers to the address for V.I. nonpermanent residents shown above.

All A.P.O. and F.P.O. addresses	P.O. Box 839 Newark, NJ 07101-0839
Foreign country: U.S. citizens and those filing Form 2555, Form 2555-EZ, or Form 4563	P.O. Box 839 Newark, NJ 07101-0839

Tear off here

Form **1040-ES**
Department of the Treasury
Internal Revenue Service

1993 Payment Voucher 4

OMB No. 1545-0087

Calendar year—Due Jan. 18, 1994

Return this voucher with check or money order payable to the **"Internal Revenue Service."** Please write your social security number and "1993 Form 1040-ES" on your check or money order. Please do not send cash. Enclose, but do not staple or attach, your payment with this voucher. File only if you are making a payment of estimated tax.

Amount of payment	Please type or print			
		Your first name and initial	Your last name	Your social security number
		If joint payment, complete for spouse		
		Spouse's first name and initial	Spouse's last name	Spouse's social security number
		Address (number, street, and apt. no.)		
$		City, state, and ZIP code		

ESTIMATED TAX (FOR CORPORATIONS)

File Form 1120-W, *Corporation Estimated Tax* (Worksheet).

Every corporation whose tax is expected to be $500 or more must make estimated tax payments. A corporation's estimated tax is the amount of its expected tax liability (including alternative minimum tax and environmental tax) less its allowable tax credits.

DEPOSITS

If a corporation's estimated tax is $500 or more, its estimated tax payments must be deposited with an authorized financial institution or a Federal Reserve Bank. Each deposit must be accompanied by a federal tax deposit coupon and deposited according to the instructions in the coupon book.

The due dates of deposits are the 15th day of the 4th, 6th, 9th and 12th months of the tax year. Depending on when the $500 requirement is first met, a corporation will make either four, three, two or one installment deposits. Amounts of estimated tax should be refigured each quarter and amended to reflect changes.

Penalty: A corporation that fails to pay in full a correct installment of estimated tax by the due date is generally subject to a penalty. The penalty is figured at a rate of interest published quarterly by the IRS.

FORM 1120-W (WORKSHEET)

This form is filled out as an aid in determining the estimated tax and required deposits. The form should be retained and not filed with IRS. As an aid in determining its estimated alternative minimum tax and environmental tax, a corporation should get a copy of Form 4626-W. Retain this form and do not file with IRS.

IRS PUBLICATIONS: See Publication 334, *Tax Guide for Small Business,* Chapter 30. For a more complete discussion of corporation taxation, as well as liquidations and stock redemptions, see Publication 542, *Tax Information on Corporations.*

SAMPLE: See Sample of Form 1120-W (Worksheet) on the next page.

FORM 1120-W
CORPORATION ESTIMATED TAX WORKSHEET

Form **1120-W** (WORKSHEET) Department of the Treasury Internal Revenue Service	**Corporation Estimated Tax** For calendar year 1993, or tax year beginning .... , 1993, and ending .... , 19 ..... (Keep for the Corporation's Records—Do *Not* Send to the Internal Revenue Service)	OMB No. 1545-0975 **1993**

1	Taxable income expected in the tax year . . . . **Qualified personal service corporations (as defined in the instructions): Skip lines 2 through 9 and go to line 10.**	**1**
2	Enter the smaller of line 1 or $50,000 (members of a controlled group, see instructions) . . .	**2**
3	Subtract line 2 from line 1	**3**
4	Enter the smaller of line 3 or $25,000 (members of a controlled group, see instructions) . . .	**4**
5	Subtract line 4 from line 3	**5**
6	Multiply line 2 by 15%	**6**
7	Multiply line 4 by 25%	**7**
8	Multiply line 5 by 34%	**8**
9	If line 1 is greater than $100,000, enter the smaller of 5% of the excess over $100,000 or $11,750 (members of a controlled group, see instructions)	**9**
10	**Total.** Add lines 6 through 9 (Qualified personal service corporations: Multiply line 1 by 34%.) .	**10**
11	Estimated tax credits (see instructions)	**11**
12	Subtract line 11 from line 10	**12**
13	Recapture of: **a** Investment credit, and **b** Low-income housing credit	**13**
14a	Alternative minimum tax (see instructions)	**14a**
b	Environmental tax (see instructions)	**14b**
15	**Total.** Add lines 12 through 14b	**15**
16	Credit for Federal tax paid on fuels (see instructions)	**16**
17	Subtract line 16 from line 15. **Note:** *If the result is less than $500, the corporation is not required to make estimated tax payments.*	**17**

		18a		18c
18a	Multiply line 17 by 97% .	**18a**		
b	Enter the tax shown on the corporation's 1992 tax return. **CAUTION:** *See instructions before completing this line*	**18b**		
c	Enter the smaller of line 18a or line 18b. If the corporation is required to skip line 18b, enter the amount from line 18a on line 18c		**18c**	

		(a)	(b)	(c)	(d)
19	**Installment due dates** (see instructions) . . . . ▶ **19**				
20	**Required installments.** Enter 25% of line 18c in columns (a) through (d) (less any 1992 overpayment credited to 1993 estimated tax) unless **a** or **b** below applies to the corporation. (See instructions.)				
a	If the annualized income installment method and/or the adjusted seasonal installment method is used, complete Schedule A and enter the amounts from line 45 in each column of line 20.				
b	If the corporation is a "large corporation," see the instructions for the amount to enter in each column of line 20 . . . . . **20**				

For Paperwork Reduction Act Notice, see the instructions on page 4.   Cat. No. 11525G   Form **1120-W** (1993)

SELF-EMPLOYMENT TAX (FOR SOLE PROPRIETOR, INDIVIDUAL WHO IS A PARTNER OR S CORPORATION SHAREHOLDER)

File Schedule SE (Form 1040), *Computation of Social Security Self-Employment Tax.*

The self-employment tax is a social security tax for individuals who work for themselves. Social Security benefits are available to the self-employed individual just as they are to wage earners. Your payments of self-employment tax contribute to your coverage under the social security system. That coverage provides you with retirement benefits and with medical insurance benefits.

Note: You may be liable for paying self-employment tax even if you are now fully insured under social security and are now receiving benefits.

WHO MUST PAY THE TAX?

If you carry on a trade or business, except as an employee, you will have to pay self-employment tax on your self-employment income. A trade or business is generally an activity that is carried on for a livelihood, or in good faith to make a profit. The business does not need to actually make a profit, but the profit motive must exist and you must be making ongoing efforts to further your business. Regularity of activities and transactions and the production of income are key elements.

You are probably self-employed if you are a 1) sole proprietor, 2) independent contractor, 3) member of a partnership, or 4) are otherwise in business for yourself.

INCOME LIMITS

You must pay self-employment tax if you have net earnings from self-employment of $400 or more. The self-employment tax rate for 1992 is 15.3% (a total of 12.4% for social security on net earnings up to a maximum of $55,500 and 2.9% for Medicare on net earnings up to a maximum of $130,200). If you are also a wage earner and those earnings were subject to social security tax, you will not be taxed on that amount under self-employment income.

Note: There are two deductions on your income tax return relating to self-employment tax. Both deductions result in a reduction of your total income tax burden.

1. On Schedule E: A deduction of 7.65% of your net earnings from self-employment is taken directly on Schedule SE, reducing the self-employment tax itself by that percentage.

2. On Form 1040: There is a nice deduction that reduces your Adjusted Gross Income on Form 1040 by allowing one-half the amount of your Self-Employment Tax liability to be deducted as a business expense.

JOINT RETURNS

You **may not** file a joint Schedule SE (Form 1040) even if you file a joint income tax return. Your spouse is not considered self-employed just because you are. If you both have self-employment income, each of you must file a separate Schedule SE (Form 1040).

SOCIAL SECURITY NUMBER

You must have a social security number if you have to pay self-employment tax. You may apply for one at the nearest Social Security Office. Form SS-5, *Application for a Social Security Card*, may be obtained from any Social Security office.

SCHEDULE SE (FORM 1040)

Schedule SE, *Computation of Social Security Self-Employment Tax*, is used to compute self-employment tax. If you are required to pay estimated income tax (see Estimated Tax, section) you must also figure any self-employment tax you owe and include that amount when you send in your 1040-ES vouchers. If you are not required to pay estimated taxes, the full payment is remitted with your annual tax return.

IRS PUBLICATION: See Publication 334 (Rev. Nov., 1992), *Tax Guide for Small Business*, Chapter 33. For more detailed information, read Publication 533, *Self-Employment Tax*. Included in the publication is an illustrated Schedule SE.

SAMPLE: A sample of Schedule SE (Form 1040) can be seen on the next page. For information on 1040-ES, refer back a few pages to the information on Estimated Taxes for your legal structure.

SCHEDULE SE - FORM 1040
COMPUTATION OF SELF-EMPLOYMENT TAX

SCHEDULE SE (Form 1040) Department of the Treasury Internal Revenue Service (X)	Self-Employment Tax ▶ See Instructions for Schedule SE (Form 1040). ▶ Attach to Form 1040.	OMB No. 1545-0074 1992 Attachment Sequence No. 17

Name of person with **self-employment** income (as shown on Form 1040)	Social security number of person with **self-employment** income ▶	

Who Must File Schedule SE

You must file Schedule SE if:

● Your wages (and tips) subject to social security AND Medicare tax (or railroad retirement tax) were less than $130,200; **AND**

● Your *net earnings from self-employment from other than church employee income* (line 4 of Short Schedule SE or line 4c of Long Schedule SE) were $400 or more;
  OR

● You had church employee income (as defined on page SE-1) of $108.28 or more.

Exception. If your only self-employment income was from earnings as a minister, member of a religious order, or Christian Science practitioner, AND you filed **Form 4361** and received IRS approval not to be taxed on those earnings, DO NOT file Schedule SE. Instead, write "Exempt–Form 4361" on Form 1040, line 47.

May I Use Short Schedule SE or MUST I Use Long Schedule SE?

Did you receive wages or tips in 1992?

No → Are you a minister, member of a religious order, or Christian Science practitioner who received IRS approval **not** to be taxed on earnings from these sources, **but** you owe self-employment tax on other earnings? **Yes** →

No ↓ Are you using one of the optional methods to figure your net earnings (see page SE-3)? **Yes** →

No ↓ Did you receive church employee income reported on Form W-2 of $108.28 or more? **Yes** →

No ↓ **YOU MAY USE SHORT SCHEDULE SE BELOW**

Yes → Was the total of your wages and tips subject to social security or railroad retirement tax **plus** your net earnings from self-employment more than $55,500? **Yes** →

No ↓ Was the total of your wages and tips subject to Medicare tax **plus** your net earnings from self-employment more than $130,200? **Yes** →

No ↓ Did you receive tips subject to social security or Medicare tax that you **did not** report to your employer? **No** ← / **Yes** →

YOU MUST USE LONG SCHEDULE SE ON THE BACK

Section A—Short Schedule SE. Caution: *Read above to see if you must use Long Schedule SE on the back (Section B).*

1	Net farm profit or (loss) from Schedule F, line 36, and farm partnerships, Schedule K-1 (Form 1065), line 15a	**1**
2	Net profit or (loss) from Schedule C, line 31; Schedule C-EZ, line 3; and Schedule K-1 (Form 1065), line 15a (other than farming). See page SE-2 for other income to report	**2**
3	Combine lines 1 and 2	**3**
4	**Net earnings from self-employment.** Multiply line 3 by 92.35% (.9235). If less than $400, **do not** file this schedule; you do not owe self-employment tax . . . . ▶	**4**
5	**Self-employment tax.** If the amount on line 4 is: ● $55,500 or less, multiply line 4 by 15.3% (.153) and enter the result. ● More than $55,500 but less than $130,200, multiply the amount in excess of $55,500 by 2.9% (.029). Then, add $8,491.50 to the result and enter the total. ● $130,200 or more, enter $10,657.80. Also, enter this amount on Form 1040, line 47 . . . . **Note:** *Also, enter **one-half** of the amount from line 5 on **Form 1040, line 25.***	**5**

For Paperwork Reduction Act Notice, see Form 1040 instructions.   Cat. No. 11358Z   **Schedule SE (Form 1040) 1992**

Social Security (FICA) Tax and Withholding of Income Tax

File Form 941 (941E, 942 or 943), *Employers Quarterly Federal Tax Return.* Also: W-2, W-3, and W-4.

If you have one or more employees, you will be required to withhold federal income tax from their wages. You also must collect and pay the employee's part and your matching share of Social Security (FICA) and Medicare taxes.

You are liable for the payment of these taxes.
See: "Liability for Taxes Withheld" on p. 117.

Who Are Employees?

Under common law rules, every individual who performs services that are subject to the will and control of an employer, as to both what must be done and how it must be done, is an employee. Two of the usual characteristics of an employer-employee relationship are that the employer has the right to discharge the employee and the employer supplies tools and a place to work. It does not matter if the employee is called an employee, or a partner, co-adventurer, agent, or independent contractor. It does not matter how the payments are measured, how they are made, or what they are called. Nor does it matter whether the individual is employed full time or part time.

Note: For an in-depth discussion and examples of employer-employee relationships, see Publication 937, *Business Reporting*. If you want the IRS to determine whether a worker is an employee, file Form SS-8 with the District Director for the area in which your business is located.

Social Security Taxes

The Federal Insurance Contributions Act (FICA) provides for a federal system of old age, survivors, disability and hospital insurance. This system is financed through social security taxes, also known as FICA taxes. Social security taxes are levied on both you and your employees. You as an employer must collect and pay the employee's part of the tax. You must withhold it from wages. You are also liable for your own (employer's) share of social security taxes.

TAX RATE

The tax rate for social security is 6.2% each for employers and employees (12.4% total) and the wage base for 1992 is $55,500. The tax rate for Medicare is 1.45% each for employers and employees (2.9% total) and the 1992 wage base is $130,200. Social Security taxes and withheld income taxes are reported and paid together. For more detailed information, read Publication 334, *Tax Guide for Small Business*, Chapter 34 and Publication 937, *Business Reporting*.

WITHHOLDING OF INCOME TAX

Generally, you must withhold income from wages you pay employees if their wages for any payroll period are more than the amount of their withholding allowance for that period. The amount to be withheld is figured separately for each payroll period. You should figure withholding on gross wages before any deductions for social security tax, pension, union dues, insurance, etc. are made. Circular E, *Employer's Tax Guide*, contains the applicable tables and detailed instructions for using withholding methods. Publication 937, *Business Reporting*, will also give you more information.

TAX FORMS

The following are the forms used to report social security taxes and withheld income tax.

Form 941, Employees Quarterly Federal Tax Return

Generally, social security (FICA) taxes and withheld income tax are reported together on Form 941. Forms 941E, 942, and 943 are used for other than the usual type of employee. (See Publication 334, Chapter 34). Form 943 (for Agricultural Employees) is an annual return due one month after the end of the calendar year. The other forms are quarterly returns and are due one month after the end of each calendar quarter. Due dates are April 30, July 31, October 31, and January 31. An extra 10 days are given if taxes are deposited on time and in full.

Form 8109, Federal Tax Deposit Coupon

You generally will have to make deposits of social security taxes and withheld income taxes before the return is due. Deposits are not required for taxes reported on Form 942. You must deposit both your part and your employee's part of social security taxes in an authorized financial institution or a Federal Reserve bank. See Publication 334, *Tax Guide for Small Business*, Chapter 34, and

Publication 937, *Business Reporting*, for more detailed information on deposits. Forms 8109, *Federal Tax Deposit Coupons*, are used to make deposits.

Form W-2

You must furnish copies of Form W-2 to each employee from whom income tax or social security tax has been withheld. Detailed information for preparation of this form is contained in the instructions for Forms W-2 and W-2P. Furnish copies of Form W-2 to employees as soon as possible after December 31, so they may file their income tax returns early. It must be sent to the employee no later than January 31st. W-2s must also be transmitted annually to the Social Security Administration (see number d).

Form W-3

Employers must file Form W-3 annually to transmit forms W-2 and W-2P to the Social Security Administration. These forms will be processed by the Social Security Administration, which will then furnish the Internal Revenue Service with the income tax data that it needs from the forms. Form W-3 and its attachments must be filed separately from Form 941 by the last day of February, following the calendar year for which the Forms W-2 and W-2P are prepared.

Form W-4

Each new employee should give you a form W-4, Employee's Withholding Allowance Certificate, on or before his first day of work. The certificates must include the employees social security number. Copies of W-4 that are required to be submitted because of a large number of allowances or claims of exemption from income tax withholding are sent in with quarterly employment tax returns (Form 941 and 941E), Withholding is then figured on gross wages before deductions for social security, tax pension, insurance, etc.

LIABILITY FOR TAX WITHHELD

You are required by law to deduct and withhold income tax from the salaries and wages of your employees. You are liable for payment of that tax to the Federal government whether or not you collect it from your employees.

IRS PUBLICATIONS: For publication references in this section, see above text under each separate heading.

SAMPLE: You will find samples of Form 941, W-2 and W-3 and W-4 on the following pages.

FORM 941
EMPLOYER'S QUARTERLY FEDERAL TAX RETURN

Form **941**
(Rev. January 1992)
Department of the Treasury
Internal Revenue Service

4141

Employer's Quarterly Federal Tax Return
▶ See Circular E for more information concerning employment tax returns.
Please type or print.

Your name, address, employer identification number, and calendar quarter of return. (If not correct, please change.)

Name (as distinguished from trade name)
Date quarter ended

Trade name, if any
Employer identification number

Address (number and street)
City, state, and ZIP code

OMB No. 1545-0029
Expires 5-31-93

T
FF
FD
FP
I
T

If address is different from prior return, check here ▶

IRS Use

1 1 1 1 1 1 1 1 1 1 2 3 3 3 3 3 3 4 4 4
5 5 5 6 7 8 8 8 8 8 9 9 9 10 10 10 10 10 10 10 10 10 10

If you do not have to file returns in the future, check here . ▶ ☐   Date final wages paid . . . ▶ _____

If you are a seasonal employer, see **Seasonal employers** on page 2 and check here . . ▶ ☐

1	Number of employees (except household) employed in the pay period that includes March 12th ▶	1	
2	Total wages and tips subject to withholding, plus other compensation . . . . ▶	2	
3	Total income tax withheld from wages, tips, pensions, annuities, sick pay, gambling, etc. . ▶	3	
4	Adjustment of withheld income tax for preceding quarters of calendar year (see instructions) . ▶	4	
5	Adjusted total of income tax withheld (line 3 as adjusted by line 4—see instructions) . .	5	
6a	Taxable social security wages **(Complete line 7)** $ _____ × 12.4% (.124) =	6a	
b	Taxable social security tips $ _____ × 12.4% (.124) =	6b	
7	Taxable Medicare wages and tips . . . . $ _____ × 2.9% (.029) =	7	
8	Total social security and Medicare taxes (add lines 6a, 6b, and 7).	8	
9	Adjustment of social security and Medicare taxes (see instructions for required explanation) .	9	
10	Adjusted total of social security and Medicare taxes (line 8 as adjusted by line 9—see instructions) . ▶	10	
11	Backup withholding (see instructions)	11	
12	Adjustment of backup withholding tax for preceding quarters of calendar year	12	
13	Adjusted total of backup withholding (line 11 as adjusted by line 12)	13	
14	**Total taxes** (add lines 5, 10, and 13)	14	
15	Advance earned income credit (EIC) payments made to employees, if any . . . . . . ▶	15	
16	Net taxes (subtract line 15 from line 14). **This should equal line IV below** (plus line IV of Schedule A (Form 941) if you have treated backup withholding as a separate liability) . .	16	
17	**Total deposits for quarter,** including overpayment applied from a prior quarter, from your records . ▶	17	
18	**Balance due** (subtract line 17 from line 16). This should be less than $500. Pay to Internal Revenue Service . . ▶	18	
19	**Overpayment,** if line 17 is more than line 16, enter excess here ▶ $ _____ and check if to be:		

☐ Applied to next return   **OR**   ☐ Refunded.

Record of Federal Tax Liability (You must complete if line 16 is $500 or more and Schedule B is not attached.) See instructions before checking these boxes.
If you made deposits using the 95% rule, check here ▶ ☐   If you are a first time 3-banking-day depositor, check here . . ▶ ☐

Show tax liability here, **not deposits.** The IRS gets deposit data from FTD coupons.

Date wages paid	First month of quarter		Second month of quarter		Third month of quarter	
1st through 3rd	A		I		Q	
4th through 7th	B		J		R	
8th through 11th	C		K		S	
12th through 15th	D		L		T	
16th through 19th	E		M		U	
20th through 22nd	F		N		V	
23rd through 25th	G		O		W	
26th through the last	H		P		X	
Total liability for month	I		II		III	

DO NOT Show Federal Tax Deposits Here

IV Total for quarter (add lines **I, II,** and **III**). This should equal line 16 above . . . . . . ▶

Sign Here
Under penalties of perjury, I declare that I have examined this return, including accompanying schedules and statements, and to the best of my knowledge and belief, it is true, correct, and complete.

Signature ▶

Print Your Name and Title ▶

Date ▶

FORM W-2
WAGE AND TAX STATEMENT 1992

1 Control number		**Copy 1 For State, City or Local Tax Dept.**
	OMB No. 1545-0008	Employee's and employer's copy compared ☐

2 Employer's name, address, and ZIP code	**6** Statutory Deceased Pension Legal 942 Subtotal Deferred Void employee plan rep. emp. compensation
	7 Allocated tips **8** Advance EIC payment
	9 Federal income tax withheld **10** Wages, tips, other compensation

3 Employer's identification number	**4** Employer's state I.D. number	**11** Social security tax withheld	**12** Social security wages
5 Employee's social security number		**13** Social security tips	**14** Medicare wages and tips
19 Employee's name, address, and ZIP code		**15** Medicare tax withheld	**16** Nonqualified plans
		17	**18** Other

20	**21**	**22** Dependent care benefits	**23** Benefits included in Box 10
24 State income tax	**25** State wages, tips, etc.	**26** Name of state	**27** Local income tax	**28** Local wages, tips, etc.	**29** Name of locality

Department of the Treasury—Internal Revenue Service

Form **W-2 Wage and Tax Statement 1992** (Rev. 4-92)

---

1 Control number		**Copy 1 For State, City or Local Tax Dept.**
	OMB No. 1545-0008	Employee's and employer's copy compared ☐

2 Employer's name, address, and ZIP code	**6** Statutory Deceased Pension Legal 942 Subtotal Deferred Void employee plan rep. emp. compensation
	7 Allocated tips **8** Advance EIC payment
	9 Federal income tax withheld **10** Wages, tips, other compensation

3 Employer's identification number	**4** Employer's state I.D. number	**11** Social security tax withheld	**12** Social security wages
5 Employee's social security number		**13** Social security tips	**14** Medicare wages and tips
19 Employee's name, address, and ZIP code		**15** Medicare tax withheld	**16** Nonqualified plans
		17	**18** Other

20	**21**	**22** Dependent care benefits	**23** Benefits included in Box 10
24 State income tax	**25** State wages, tips, etc.	**26** Name of state	**27** Local income tax	**28** Local wages, tips, etc.	**29** Name of locality

Department of the Treasury—Internal Revenue Service

Form **W-2 Wage and Tax Statement 1992** (Rev. 4-92)

FORM W-3
TRANSMITTAL OF INCOME AND TAX STATEMENTS 1992

1 Control number		OMB No. 1545-0008	

Kind of Payer ▶	2 941/941E ☐ Military ☐ 943 ☐ CT-1 ☐ 942 ☐ Medicare govt. emp. ☐	3 Employer's state I.D. number 4	5 Total number of statements

6 Establishment number	7 Allocated tips	8 Advance EIC payments
9 Federal income tax withheld	10 Wages, tips, and other compensation	11 Social security tax withheld
12 Social security wages	13 Social security tips	14 Medicare wages and tips
15 Medicare tax withheld	16 Nonqualified plans	17 Deferred compensation
18 Employer's identification number		19 Other EIN used this year
20 Employer's name		21 Dependent care benefits
		23 Adjusted total social security wages and tips
YOUR COPY		24 Adjusted total Medicare wages and tips
		25 Income tax withheld by third-party payer
22 Employer's address and ZIP code		

Form **W-3** Transmittal of Income and Tax Statements **1992** Department of the Treasury Internal Revenue Service

General Instructions

This form is a transmittal form to be filed with Copy A of Forms W-2.

Note: *Amounts reported on related employment tax Forms (W-2, 941, 942, or 943) should agree with the amounts reported on Form W-3. If there are differences, you may be contacted by the IRS. The reason for the differences may be valid. You should retain your reconciliation for future reference.*

Employers filing privately printed Forms W-2 must file Forms W-3 that are the same width as Form W-2. The forms must meet the requirements in Revenue Procedure 91-45 printed in Publication 1141.

Who Must File.—Employers and other payers must file Form W-3 to send Copy A of Forms W-2.

A transmitter or sender (including a service bureau, paying agent, or disbursing agent) may sign Form W-3 for the employer or payer only if the sender:

(a) Is authorized to sign by an agency agreement (either oral, written, or implied) that is valid under state law; and

(b) Writes "For (name of payer)" next to the signature.

If an authorized sender signs for the payer, the payer is still responsible for filing, when due, a correct and complete Form W-3 and attachments, and is subject to any penalties that result from not complying with these requirements. Be sure the payer's name and employer identification number on Forms W-2 and W-3 are the same as those used on the Form 941, 942, or 943 filed by or for the payer.

A household employer is not required to file a Form W-3 if filing a single Form W-2.

If you buy or sell a business during the year, see Rev. Proc. 84-77, 1984-2 C.B. 753, for details on who should file the employment tax returns.

Reporting on Magnetic Media.—You must file Forms W-2 with the SSA on magnetic media instead of using the paper Copy A of Forms W-2 and Form W-3 if you file **250 or more forms.** You may be charged a penalty if you fail to file on magnetic media when required.

If you are filing Forms W-2 using magnetic media, you may also need **Form 6559,** Transmitter Report and Summary of Magnetic Media Filing, and **Form 6559-A,** Continuation Sheet for Form 6559 etc.

You can get magnetic media reporting specifications at most SSA offices. You may also get this information by writing to the Social Security Administration, P.O. Box 2317, Baltimore, MD 21235, Attn: Magnetic Media Coordinator.

When To File.—File Form W-3, with Copy A of Forms W-2, by March 1, 1993. You may be penalized if you do not include the correct information on the return or if you file the return late.

You may request an extension of time to file by sending **Form 8809,** Request for Extension of Time To File Information Returns, to the address shown on that form. You must request the extension before the due date of the returns for your request to be considered. See Form 8809 for more details.

Shipping and Mailing.—If you send more than one type of form, please group forms of the same type and send them in separate groups. See the specific instructions for Box 2.

Please do not staple Form W-3 to the related Forms W-2. These forms are machine read, and staple holes or tears cause the machine to jam.

If you have a large number of Forms W-2 to send with one Form W-3, you may send them in separate packages. Show your name and employer identification number on each package. Number them in order (1 of 4, 2 of 4, etc.) and place Form W-3 in package one. Show the number of packages at the bottom of Form W-3 below the title. If you mail them, you must send them first class.

Specific Instructions

This form is read by optical scanning machines, so please type entries if possible. Send the whole first page of Form W-3 with Copy A of Forms W-2. Make all dollar entries without the dollar sign and comma but with the decimal point (0000.00).

The following instructions are for boxes on the form. If any entry does not apply to you, leave it blank. (Household employers, see the instructions on Form 942. Third-party payers of sick pay, see **Sick Pay,** later.)

Box 1—Control number.—This is an optional box which you may use for numbering the whole transmittal.

Box 2—Kind of Payer.—Put an "X" in the checkbox that applies to you. **Check only one box.** If you have more than one type, send each with a separate Form W-3.

941/941E.—Check this box if you file **Form 941,** Employer's Quarterly Federal Tax Return, or **941E,** Quarterly Return of Withheld Federal Income and Medicare Tax, and none of the other five categories applies.

Military.—Check this box if you are a military employer sending Forms W-2 for members of the uniformed services.

943.—Check this box if you file **Form 943,** Employer's Annual Tax Return for Agricultural Employees, and you are

FORM W-4
EMPLOYEE'S WITHHOLDING ALLOWANCE CERTIFICATE

19**93** Form W-4

Department of the Treasury
Internal Revenue Service

Purpose. Complete Form W-4 so that your employer can withhold the correct amount of Federal income tax from your pay.

Exemption From Withholding. Read line 7 of the certificate below to see if you can claim exempt status. *If exempt, complete line 7; but do not complete lines 5 and 6.* No Federal income tax will be withheld from your pay. Your exemption is good for one year only. It expires February 15, 1994.

Basic Instructions. Employees who are not exempt should complete the Personal Allowances Worksheet. Additional worksheets are provided on page 2 for employees to adjust their withholding allowances based on itemized deductions, adjustments to income, or two-earner/two-job situations. Complete all worksheets that apply to your situation. The worksheets will help you figure

the number of withholding allowances you are entitled to claim. However, you may claim fewer allowances than this.

Head of Household. Generally, you may claim head of household filing status on your tax return only if you are unmarried and pay more than 50% of the costs of keeping up a home for yourself and your dependent(s) or other qualifying individuals.

Nonwage Income. If you have a large amount of nonwage income, such as interest or dividends, you should consider making estimated tax payments using Form 1040-ES. Otherwise, you may find that you owe additional tax at the end of the year.

Two-Earner/Two-Jobs. If you have a working spouse or more than one job, figure the total number of allowances you are entitled to claim on

all jobs using worksheets from only one Form W-4. This total should be divided among all jobs. Your withholding will usually be most accurate when all allowances are claimed on the W-4 filed for the highest paying job and zero allowances are claimed for the others.

Advance Earned Income Credit. If you are eligible for this credit, you can receive it added to your paycheck throughout the year. For details, get Form W-5 from your employer.

Check Your Withholding. After your W-4 takes effect, you can use Pub. 919, Is My Withholding Correct for 1993?, to see how the dollar amount you are having withheld compares to your estimated total annual tax. Call 1-800-829-3676 to order this publication. Check your local telephone directory for the IRS assistance number if you need further help.

Personal Allowances Worksheet

For 1993, the value of your personal exemption(s) is reduced if your income is over $108,450 ($162,700 if married filing jointly, $135,600 if head of household, or $81,350 if married filing separately). Get Pub. 919 for details.

A Enter "1" for **yourself** if no one else can claim you as a dependent . . . . **A** _____

B Enter "1" if:
- You are single and have only one job; or
- You are married, have only one job, and your spouse does not work; or
- Your wages from a second job or your spouse's wages (or the total of both) are $1,000 or less.

B _____

C Enter "1" for your **spouse.** But, you may choose to enter -0- if you are married and have either a working spouse or more than one job (this may help you avoid having too little tax withheld) . . . . **C** _____

D Enter number of **dependents** (other than your spouse or yourself) whom you will claim on your tax return . . . . . **D** _____

E Enter "1" if you will file as **head of household** on your tax return (see conditions under **Head of Household,** above) . **E** _____

F Enter "1" if you have at least $1,500 of **child or dependent care expenses** for which you plan to claim a credit . . **F** _____

G Add lines A through F and enter total here. Note: *This amount may be different from the number of exemptions you claim on your return* ▶ **G** _____

For accuracy, do all worksheets that apply.
- If you plan to **itemize or claim adjustments to income** and want to reduce your withholding, see the Deductions and Adjustments Worksheet on page 2.
- If you are **single** and have **more than one job** and your combined earnings from all jobs exceed $30,000 OR if you are **married** and have a **working spouse or more than one job,** and the combined earnings from all jobs exceed $50,000, see the Two-Earner/Two-Job Worksheet on page 2 if you want to avoid having too little tax withheld.
- If **neither** of the above situations applies, **stop here** and enter the number from line G on line 5 of Form W-4 below.

. . . . **Cut here and give the certificate to your employer. Keep the top portion for your records.** . . . .

Form **W-4**
Department of the Treasury
Internal Revenue Service

Employee's Withholding Allowance Certificate

▶ **For Privacy Act and Paperwork Reduction Act Notice, see reverse.**

OMB No. 1545-0010

19**93**

1 Type or print your first name and middle initial	Last name	2 Your social security number

Home address (number and street or rural route)

3 ☐ Single ☐ Married ☐ Married, but withhold at higher Single rate.
Note: *If married, but legally separated, or spouse is a nonresident alien, check the Single box.*

City or town, state, and ZIP code

4 If your last name differs from that on your social security card, check here and call 1-800-772-1213 for more information . . . ▶ ☐

5 Total number of allowances you are claiming (from line G above or from the worksheets on page 2 if they apply) . **5** _____

6 Additional amount, if any, you want withheld from each paycheck . . . . **6** $ _____

7 I claim exemption from withholding for 1993 and I certify that I meet **ALL** of the following conditions for exemption:
- Last year I had a right to a refund of **ALL** Federal income tax withheld because I had **NO** tax liability; **AND**
- This year I expect a refund of **ALL** Federal income tax withheld because I expect to have **NO** tax liability; **AND**
- This year if my income exceeds $600 and includes nonwage income, another person cannot claim me as a dependent.

If you meet all of the above conditions, enter "EXEMPT" here . . . . ▶ **7** _____

Under penalties of perjury, I certify that I am entitled to the number of withholding allowances claimed on this certificate or entitled to claim exempt status.

Employee's signature ▶

Date ▶ _____ , 19 ___

8 Employer's name and address (Employer: Complete 8 and 10 only if sending to the IRS)

9 Office code (optional)

10 Employer identification number

Cat. No. 10220Q

FEDERAL UNEMPLOYMENT (FUTA) TAX

File Form 940, *Employers Annual Federal Unemployment (FUTA) Tax Return.* Also, use Form 8109 to make deposits.

The federal unemployment tax system, together with the state systems, provides for payments of unemployment compensation to workers who have lost their jobs. Most employers pay both a state and the federal unemployment tax.

In general you are subject to FUTA tax on the wages you pay employees who are not farm workers or household workers if: 1) in any calendar quarter, the wages you paid to employees in this category totalled $1,500 or more; or 2) in each of 20 different calendar weeks, there was at least a part of a day in which you had an employee in this category. See Circular E, Employer's Tax Guide, for lists of payments excluded from FUTA and types of employment not subject to the tax.

FIGURING THE TAX

The federal unemployment tax is figured on the first $7,000 in wages paid to each employee during 1992. The tax is imposed on you as the employer. You must not collect it or deduct it from the wages of your employees.

TAX RATE

The gross federal unemployment tax rate for 1992 is 6.2%. However, you are given a credit of up to 5.4% for the state unemployment tax you pay. The next tax rate, therefore, can be as low as 0.8% (6.2% minus 5.4%) if your state is not subject to a credit reduction. Study rules applying to liability for this tax (i.e., credit reduction, success of employer, concurrent employment by related corporations. See Publication 334, Chapter 35, *Tax Guide for Small Business.* More information on federal unemployment tax can be found in the instructions to Form 940.

FORM 940

Employers Annual Federal Unemployment (FUTA) Tax Return, is used for reporting. This form covers one calendar year and is generally due one month after the year ends. However, you may have to make deposits of this tax before filing the return if at the end of any calendar quarter, you owe, but have not yet deposited, more than $100 in federal unemployment (FUTA) tax for the year.

DEPOSITS

If at the end of any calendar quarter, you owe but have not yet deposited, more than $100 in Federal unemployment (FUTA) tax for the year, you must make a deposit by the end of the next month.

Due dates are as follows:

If your undeposited FUTA tax is more than $100 on:	Deposit full amount by
March 31	April 30
June 30	July 31
September 30	October 31
December 31	January 31

If the tax is $100 or less at the end of the quarter, you need not deposit it, but you must add it to the tax for the next quarter and deposit according to the $100 rule. (See Publication 334, *Tax Guide for Small Business*, Chapter 356). Use a Federal Tax Deposit Coupon Book containing Form 8109, Federal Tax Deposit Coupons to deposit taxes to an authorized financial institution or Federal Reserve Bank.

FORM 8109

Federal Tax Deposit Coupons are used to make deposits to an authorized financial institution or Federal Reserve Bank. You can get the names of authorized institutions from a Federal Reserve Bank. Each deposit must be accompanied by a Federal tax deposit (FTD) coupon. Clearly mark the correct type of tax and tax period on each deposit coupon. The FUTA tax must be deposited separately from the social security and withheld income tax deposits. A federal Tax Deposit Coupon Book containing Form 8109 coupons and instructions will automatically be sent to you after you apply for an employer identification member (EIN): see p. 128).

IRS PUBLICATIONS: Form 940, *FUTA Tax Return* (Instructions); Publication 334, *Tax Guide for Small Business*, Chapter 35; Publication 15, *Employer's Tax Guide (Circular E)*; Form 8109, *Federal Tax Deposit Coupon* (Instructions); and Publication 937, *Business Reporting* (under social security taxes).

SAMPLE: The next page shows a sample Form 940, *Employers Annual Federal Unemployment (FUTA) Tax Return*.

FORM 940 - EMPLOYER'S ANNUAL FEDERAL UNEMPLOYMENT (FUTA) TAX RETURN

Form **940**	**Employer's Annual Federal Unemployment (FUTA) Tax Return**	OMB No. 1545-0028
Department of the Treasury Internal Revenue Service	► For Paperwork Reduction Act Notice, see separate instructions.	**1992**

If incorrect, make any necessary change. ►

Name (as distinguished from trade name)   Calendar year

Trade name, if any

Address and ZIP code   Employer identification number

	T	
	FF	
	FD	
	FP	
	I	
	T	

A Are you required to pay unemployment contributions to only one state? . . . . ☐ Yes ☐ No

B Did you pay all state unemployment contributions by February 1, 1993? (If a 0% experience rate is granted check "Yes.") . . . . ☐ Yes ☐ No

C Were all wages that were taxable for FUTA tax also taxable for your state's unemployment tax? . . . . . ☐ Yes ☐ No

D Did you pay all wages in a state other than Michigan? . . . . ☐ Yes ☐ No

If you answered "No" to any of these questions, you must file Form 940. If you answered "Yes" to all the questions, you may file Form 940-EZ which is a simplified version of Form 940. You can get Form 940-EZ by calling 1-800-TAX-FORM (1-800-829-3676).

If you will not have to file returns in the future, check here, complete, and sign the return . . . . ► ☐

If this is an Amended Return, check here . . . . ► ☐

Part I   Computation of Taxable Wages

1 Total payments (including exempt payments) during the calendar year for services of employees.   **1**

2 Exempt payments. (Explain each exemption shown, attach additional sheets if necessary.) ► .... **2**   Amount paid

3 Payments of more than $7,000 for services. Enter only amounts over the first $7,000 paid to each employee. Do not include payments from line 2. The $7,000 amount is the Federal wage base. Your state wage base may be different. Do not use the state wage limitation **3**

4 Total exempt payments (add lines 2 and 3) . , . , ... **4**

5 Total taxable wages (subtract line 4 from line 1) . . . . ► **5**

6 Additional tax resulting from credit reduction for unpaid advances to the State of Michigan. Enter the wages included on line 5 for Michigan and multiply by .011. (See the separate Instructions for Form 940.) Enter the credit reduction amount here and in Part II, line 5: Michigan wages   × .011 = ... ► **6**

Part II   Tax Due or Refund

1 Gross FUTA tax. Multiply the wages in Part I, line 5, by .062 . . . . **1**

2 Maximum credit. Multiply the wages in Part I, line 5, by .054. . . . | **2** |

3 Computation of tentative credit

(a) Name of state	(b) State reporting number(s) as shown on employer's state contribution returns	(c) Taxable payroll (as defined in state act)	(d) State experience rate		(e) State experience rate	(f) Contributions if rate had been 5.4% (col. (c) x .054)	(g) Contributions payable at experience rate (col. (c) x col. (e))	(h) Additional credit (col. (f) minus col.(g). If 0 or less, enter 0.	(i) Contributions actually paid to state
			From	To					

3a Totals . . . ►

3b Total tentative credit (add line 3a, columns (h) and (i) only—see instructions for limitations on late payments) ►

4 Credit: Enter the smaller of the amount in Part II, line 2, or line 3b. | **4** |

5 Enter the amount from Part I, line 6 . . . . **5**

6 Credit allowable (subtract line 5 from line 4). (If zero or less, enter 0.) **6**

7 Total FUTA tax (subtract line 6 from line 1) **7**

8 Total FUTA tax deposited for the year, including any overpayment applied from a prior year . **8**

9 Balance due (subtract line 8 from line 7). This should be $100 or less. Pay to the Internal Revenue Service . . . . ► **9**

10 Overpayment (subtract line 7 from line 8). Check if it is to be: ☐ Applied to next return, or ☐ Refunded . . . . ► **10**

Part III   Record of Quarterly Federal Tax Liability for Unemployment Tax (Do not include state liability)

Quarter	First	Second	Third	Fourth	Total for year
Liability for quarter					

Under penalties of perjury, I declare that I have examined this return, including accompanying schedules and statements, and to the best of my knowledge and belief, it is true, correct, and complete, and that no part of any payment made to a state unemployment fund claimed as a credit was or is to be deducted from the payments to employees.

Signature ►   Title (Owner, etc.) ►   Date ►

PAYMENTS TO NON-EMPLOYEES FOR SERVICES RENDERED

File Form 1099-MISC, *Statement for Recipients of Miscellaneous Income* together with Form 1096, *Annual Summary and Transmittal of U.S. Information Returns.*

Payments made by you in your trade or business activities that are not for wages must be reported to the IRS. Payments include fees, commissions, prizes, awards or other forms of compensation for services rendered for your company by an individual who is not your employee.

This also includes fair market value of exchanges (bartering) of property or services between individuals in the course of a trade or business. Exempt payments include inventory, utilities, telephone, employee travel expense reimbursements and payments to corporations.

Note: If the following four conditions are met, a payment is generally reported as nonemployee compensation:

1. You made the payment to a nonemployee.
2. You made the payment for services rendered in your business.
3. You made the payment to a payee who is not a corporation.
4. You made payments to the payee totaling $600 or more during the year.

FORM 1099 MISC

Statement for Recipient of Miscellaneous Income is an information form used to report payments in the course of your trade or business to nonemployees (or for which you were a nominee/middleman, or from which you withheld federal income tax or foreign tax).

WHEN AND HOW TO FILE

File 1099-MISC on or before the last day of February. Transmit these forms to your IRS Service Center with Form 1096, *Annual Summary and Transmittal of U.S. Information Return.* A 1099-MISC copy must be sent to the recipient by January 31st. For payments in the form of barter, file Form 1099-B, *Proceeds From Broker and Barter Exchange.*

IRS PUBLICATIONS: Publication 334, *Tax Guide for Small Business,* Chapter 37. For more information on 1099s, See Publication 916, *Information Returns,* and the current year's Instructions for Forms 1099 and 1096.

SAMPLES: The following pages show samples of Form 1099-MISC and 1096.

FORM 1096
ANNUAL SUMMARY AND TRANSMITTAL OF
U.S. INFORMATION RETURNS

DO NOT STAPLE   6969

Form **1096** Department of the Treasury Internal Revenue Service	Annual Summary and Transmittal of U.S. Information Returns	OMB No. 1545-0108 19**92**

ATTACH IRS LABEL HERE

⌈ FILER'S name   ⌉

    Street address (including room or suite number)

    City, state, and ZIP code

⌊   ⌋

If you are not using a preprinted label, enter in Box 1 or 2 below the identification number you used as the filer on the information returns being transmitted. Do not fill in both Boxes 1 and 2.

Name of person to contact if the IRS needs more information

Telephone number
( )

For Official Use Only

1 Employer identification number	2 Social security number	3 Total number of forms	4 Federal income tax withheld $	5 Total amount reported with this Form 1096 $

Check only one box below to indicate the type of form being transmitted.   If this is your FINAL return, check here . . . . ▶ ☐

☐	☐	☐	☐	☐	☐	☐	☐	☐	☐	☐	☐	☐
W-2G 32	1098 81	1099-A 80	1099-B 79	1099-DIV 91	1099-G 86	1099-INT 92	1099-MISC 95	1099-OID 96	1099-PATR 97	1099-R 98	1099-S 75	5498 28

Please return this entire page to the Internal Revenue Service. Photocopies are NOT acceptable.

Under penalties of perjury, I declare that I have examined this return and accompanying documents, and, to the best of my knowledge and belief, they are true, correct, and complete.

Signature ▶ ....   Title ▶ ....   Date ▶ ....

Instructions

Purpose of Form.—Use this form to transmit paper Forms 1099, 1098, 5498, and W-2G to the Internal Revenue Service. DO NOT USE FORM 1096 TO TRANSMIT MAGNETIC MEDIA. See **Form 4804,** Transmittal of Information Returns Reported Magnetically/Electronically.

Use of Preprinted Label.—If you received a preprinted label from the IRS with Package 1099, place the label in the name and address area of this form inside the brackets. Make any necessary changes to your name and address on the label. However, do not use the label if the taxpayer identification number (TIN) shown is incorrect. **Do not prepare your own label. Use only the IRS-prepared label that came with your Package 1099.**

If you are not using a preprinted label, enter the filer's name, address (including room, suite, or other unit number), and TIN in the spaces provided on the form.

Filer.—The name, address, and TIN of the filer on this form must be the same as those you enter in the upper left area of Form 1099, 1098, 5498, or W-2G. A filer includes a payer, a recipient of mortgage interest payments (including points), a broker, a barter exchange, a person reporting real estate transactions, a trustee or issuer of an individual retirement arrangement (including an IRA or SEP), and a lender who acquires an interest in secured property or who has reason to know that the property has been abandoned.

Transmitting to the IRS.—Group the forms by form number and transmit each group with a **separate** Form 1096. For example, if you must file both Forms 1098 and 1099-A, complete one Form 1096 to transmit your Forms 1098 and another Form 1096 to transmit your Forms 1099-A. You need not submit original and corrected returns separately.

Box 1 or 2.—Complete only if you are not using a preprinted IRS label. Individuals not in a trade or business must enter their social security number in Box 2; sole proprietors and all others must enter their employer identification number in Box 1. However, sole proprietors who do not have an employer identification number must enter their social security number in Box 2.

Box 3.—Enter the number of forms you are transmitting with this Form 1096. Do not include blank or voided forms or the Form 1096 in your total. Enter the number of correctly completed forms, not the number of pages, being transmitted. For example, if you send one page of three-to-a-page Forms 5498 with a Form 1096 and you have correctly completed two Forms 5498 on that page, enter 2 in Box 3 of Form 1096.

Box 4.—Enter the total Federal income tax withheld shown on the forms being transmitted with this Form 1096.

Box 5.—No entry is required if you are filing Form 1099-A or 1099-G. For all other forms, enter the total of the amounts from the specific boxes of the forms listed below:

Form W-2G	Box 1
Form 1098	Boxes 1 and 2
Form 1099-B	Boxes 2 and 3
Form 1099-DIV	Boxes 1a, 5, and 6
Form 1099-INT	Boxes 1 and 3
Form 1099-MISC	Boxes 1, 2, 3, 5, 6, 7, 8, and 10
Form 1099-OID	Boxes 1 and 2
Form 1099-PATR	Boxes 1, 2, 3, and 5
Form 1099-R	Box 1
Form 1099-S	Box 2
Form 5498	Boxes 1 and 2

For Paperwork Reduction Act Notice, see the Instructions for Forms 1099, 1098, 5498, and W-2G.   Cat. No. 14400O   Form **1096** (1992)

FORM 1099-MISC
STATEMENT TO RECIPIENTS OF MISCELLANEOUS INCOME

9595　☐ VOID　☐ CORRECTED

PAYER'S name, street address, city, state, and ZIP code	1 Rents $	OMB No. 1545-0115	Miscellaneous Income
	2 Royalties $	1992	
	3 Prizes, awards, etc. $		
PAYER'S Federal identification number	RECIPIENT'S identification number	4 Federal income tax withheld $	5 Fishing boat proceeds $	Copy A For Internal Revenue Service Center File with Form 1096.
RECIPIENT'S name	6 Medical and health care payments $	7 Nonemployee compensation $	For Paperwork Reduction Act Notice and instructions for completing this form, see Instructions for Forms 1099, 1098, 5498, and W-2G.
Street address (including apt. no.)	8 Substitute payments in lieu of dividends or interest $	9 Payer made direct sales of $5,000 or more of consumer products to a buyer (recipient) for resale ▶ ☐	
City, state, and ZIP code	10 Crop insurance proceeds $	11 State income tax withheld $	
Account number (optional)	2nd TIN Not. ☐	12 State/Payer's state number	

Form 1099-MISC　**Do NOT Cut or Separate Forms on This Page**　Department of the Treasury—Internal Revenue Service 13-2678063

9595　☐ VOID　☐ CORRECTED

PAYER'S name, street address, city, state, and ZIP code	1 Rents $	OMB No. 1545-0115	Miscellaneous Income
	2 Royalties $	1992	
	3 Prizes, awards, etc. $		
PAYER'S Federal identification number	RECIPIENT'S identification number	4 Federal income tax withheld $	5 Fishing boat proceeds $	Copy A For Internal Revenue Service Center File with Form 1096.
RECIPIENT'S name	6 Medical and health care payments $	7 Nonemployee compensation $	For Paperwork Reduction Act Notice and instructions for completing this form, see Instructions for Forms 1099, 1098, 5498, and W-2G.
Street address (including apt. no.)	8 Substitute payments in lieu of dividends or interest $	9 Payer made direct sales of $5,000 or more of consumer products to a buyer (recipient) for resale ▶ ☐	
City, state, and ZIP code	10 Crop insurance proceeds $	11 State income tax withheld $	
Account number (optional)	2nd TIN Not. ☐	12 State/Payer's state number	

Form 1099-MISC　**Do NOT Cut or Separate Forms on This Page**　Department of the Treasury—Internal Revenue Service 13-2678063

9595　☐ VOID　☐ CORRECTED

PAYER'S name, street address, city, state, and ZIP code	1 Rents $	OMB No. 1545-0115	Miscellaneous Income
	2 Royalties $	1992	
	3 Prizes, awards, etc. $		
PAYER'S Federal identification number	RECIPIENT'S identification number	4 Federal income tax withheld $	5 Fishing boat proceeds $	Copy A For Internal Revenue Service Center File with Form 1096.
RECIPIENT'S name	6 Medical and health care payments $	7 Nonemployee compensation $	For Paperwork Reduction Act Notice and instructions for completing this form, see Instructions for Forms 1099, 1098, 5498, and W-2G.
Street address (including apt. no.)	8 Substitute payments in lieu of dividends or interest $	9 Payer made direct sales of $5,000 or more of consumer products to a buyer (recipient) for resale ▶ ☐	
City, state, and ZIP code	10 Crop insurance proceeds $	11 State income tax withheld $	
Account number (optional)	2nd TIN Not. ☐	12 State/Payer's state number	

Form 1099-MISC　**Do NOT Cut or Separate Forms on This Page**　Department of the Treasury—Internal Revenue Service 13-2678063

TAXPAYER IDENTIFICATION NUMBER (EIN)

Form SS-4, *Application for Employer Identification Number.*

SOCIAL SECURITY NUMBER

If you are a sole proprietor, you will generally use your social security number as your taxpayer identification number. You must put this number on each of your individual income tax forms, such as Form 1040 and its schedules.

EMPLOYEE INDENTIFICATION NUMBER (EIN)

Every partnership, S corporation, corporation and certain sole proprietors must have an "employer identification number" (EIN) to use as a taxpayer identification number.

Sole proprietors must have EINs, if they pay wages to one or more employees or must file pension or excise tax returns. Otherwise they can use their social security number.

NEW EIN

You may need to get a new EIN if either the form or the ownership of your business changes.

1. Change in organization: A new EIN is required if a sole proprietor incorporates, a sole proprietorship takes in partners and operates as a partnership, a partnership incorporates, a partnership is taken over by one of the partners and is operated as a sole proprietorship, or a corporation changes to a partnership or to a sole proprietorship.

2. Change in ownership: A new EIN is required if you buy or inherit an existing business that you will operate as a sole proprietorship, you represent an estate that operates a business after the owner's death, or you terminate an old partnership and begin a new one.

APPLICATION FOR AN EIN

Use Form SS-4, *Application for Employer Identification Number.* SS-5 is used to apply for a Social Security Number Card. These forms are available from Social Security Administration Offices.

If you are under 18 years of age, you must furnish evidence, along with this form, of age, identity and U.S. citizenship. If you are 18 or older, you must appear in person with this evidence at a Social Security office. If you are an alien, you must appear in person and bring your birth certificate and either your alien registration card or your U.S. immigration form.

FREE TAX PUBLICATIONS
AVAILABLE FROM THE IRS

The following is a list of the publications referred to in the preceding material, along with others that may prove helpful to you in the course of your business. Make it a point to keep a file of tax information. Send for these free publications and update your file with new publications at least once a year. The United States Government has spent a great deal of time and money to make this information available to you for preparation of income tax returns.

Information on ordering these publications can be found following this listing. If you prefer, you may call IRS toll free at 1-800-TAX-FORM (1-800-829-3676).

FOR A COMPLETE LISTING: Ask for Publication 910, *Guide to Free Tax Services*

Begin by reading these two publications. They will give you the most comprehensive information. Publication 334 - *Tax Guide for Small Business* and Publication 910 - *Guide to Free Tax Services.*

The following publications are good to have on hand as reference material and will answer most questions that you have relating to specific topics. Call the IRS and order them by publication number.

15 - *Circular E., Employers Tax Guide*

17 - *Your Federal Income Tax*

463 - *Travel, Entertainment and Gift Expenses*

505 - *Tax Withholding and Estimated Tax*

508 - *Educational Expenses*

509 - *Tax Calendars for 1993*

510 - *Excise Taxes for 1993*

533 - *Self-Employment Tax*

534 - *Depreciation*

535 - *Business Expenses*

536 - *Net Operating Losses*

538 - *Accounting Periods and Methods*

541 - *Taxes on Partnerships*

542 - *Tax Information on Corporations*

545 - *Deduction for Bad Debts*

553 - *Highlights of 1992 Tax Changes*

557 - *Tax-Exempt Status for Your Organization*

560 - *Retirement Plans for the Self-Employed*

583 - *Information for Business Taxpayers*

587 - *Business Use of Your Home*

589 - *Tax Information on S Corporations*

594 - *The Collection Process (Employment Tax Accounts)*

596 - *Earned Income Credit*

908 - *Bankruptcy and other Debt Cancellation*

911 - *Tax Information for Direct Sellers*

917 - *Business Use of a Car*

925 - *Passive Activity and At Risk Rules*

937 - *Business Reporting (Employment Taxes, Information Returns)*

946 - *How to Begin Depreciating Your Property*

947 - *Power of Attorney and Practice Before the IRS*

1544 - *Reporting Cash Payments of Over $10,000* (Received in a Trade or Business)

Order Information
for
IRS Forms and Publications

Resource:

IRS Pub. 910
(Rev. 11-91)

If you live in:	Send to:	For other locations, see below:
Alaska, Arizona, California, Colorado, Hawaii, Idaho, Montana, Nevada, New Mexico, Oregon, Utah, Washington, Wyoming	Western Area Distribution Center Rancho Cordova, CA 95743-0001	**Foreign Addresses—** Taxpayers with mailing addresses in foreign countries should send this order blank to either: Eastern Area Distribution Center, P.O. Box 85074, Richmond, VA 23261-5074; or Western Area Distribution Center, Rancho Cordova, CA 95743-0001, whichever is closer. Send letter requests for other forms and publications to: Eastern Area Distribution Center, P.O. Box 85074, Richmond, VA 23261-5074.
Alabama, Arkansas, Illinois, Indiana, Iowa, Kansas, Kentucky, Louisiana, Michigan, Minnesota, Mississippi, Missouri, Nebraska, North Dakota, Ohio, Oklahoma, South Dakota, Tennessee, Texas, Wisconsin	Central Area Distribution Center P.O. Box 9903 Bloomington, IL 61799	
Connecticut, Delaware, District of Columbia, Florida, Georgia, Maine, Maryland, Massachusetts, New Hampshire, New Jersey, New York, North Carolina, Pennsylvania, Rhode Island, South Carolina, Vermont, Virginia, West Virginia	Eastern Area Distribution Center P.O. Box 85074 Richmond, VA 23261-5074	**Puerto Rico—Eastern** Area Distribution Center, P.O. Box 85074, Richmond, VA 23261-5074. **Virgin Islands—V.I. Bureau** of Internal Revenue, Lockharts Garden No. 1A, Charlotte Amalie, St. Thomas, VI 00802

Distribution Centers

Where to Send Your Order for Free Forms and Publications

Save Time

Participating libraries have IRS tax forms available for copying and reference sets of Tax Information Publications. Also, participating banks, post offices, and libraries stock Forms 1040, 1040A, 1040EZ, their instructions, Schedules A&B, and EIC, and Schedules 1 and 2.

Detach at this Line

- -

Circle Desired Forms, Instructions, and Publications

We will send you two copies of each form and one copy of each publication or set of instructions you circle. Please cut the order blank on the dotted line and be sure to print or type your name and address accurately on the other side.

To help reduce waste, please order only the items you think you will need to prepare your return. Use the blank spaces to order items not listed. If you need more space, attach a separate sheet of paper listing the additional items you need.

Order Blank

1040	Schedule F (1040)	Schedule 3 (1040A) & instructions	2210 & instructions	8582 & instructions	Pub. 508	Pub. 590
Instructions for 1040 & Schedules	Schedule R (1040) & instructions	1040EZ	2441 & instructions	8822	Pub. 521	Pub. 596
Schedules A&B (1040)	Schedule SE (1040)	Instructions for 1040EZ	3903 & instructions	Pub. 1	Pub. 523	Pub. 910
Schedule C (1040)	1040A	1040-ES (1992)	4562 & instructions	Pub. 17	Pub. 525	Pub. 917
Schedule D (1040)	Instructions for 1040A & Schedules	1040X & instructions	4868	Pub. 334	Pub. 527	Pub. 929
Schedule E (1040)	Schedule 1 (1040A)	2106 & instructions	8283 & instructions	Pub. 463	Pub. 529	
Schedule EIC (1040A or 1040)	Schedule 2 (1040A)	2119 & instructions	8332	Pub. 505	Pub. 553	

Detach at this Line

- -

Print or type your name and address on this label. It will be used to speed your order for forms to you.

_____

Name

_____

Number, Street, and Apartment Number

_____

City, Town or Post Office, State and ZIP Code

SUMMARY

The purpose of this chapter has been to introduce you to the tax requirements pertaining to your business. It is important to keep abreast of revisions in the tax laws that will effect your business.

IRS WORKSHOPS

The IRS holds tax seminars on a regular basis for small business owners who would like to learn more about current regulations and requirements. You can call the local IRS office and ask them to mail you a schedule of coming workshops.

KNOW WHAT IS HAPPENING

Planning for your business is an ongoing process requiring the implementation of many changes. You may rest assured that many of those changes will be a direct result of new tax laws. Today, many small businesses are having to examine their hiring policies because of the regulatory legislation that is being passed or considered regarding employee benefits, workman's compensation, contract services, etc. Business owners need to understand what is happening and take active positions to impact legislation that is pertinent to their operations and can ultimately lead to their success or failure.

You have taken the first step. You would not be reading this book unless you had already committed yourself to organizing and understanding your recordkeeping. You are one of the lucky ones—the entrepreneurs who know that every decision leads to the bottom line.

WHAT'S NEXT?

Now that you are familiar with basic records, statements and tax returns, it is time to combine your information and utilize it to formulate recordkeeping and tax reporting schedules for your business. Setting up your records and keeping them current are two different pieces of the same pie.

To help you get started, the next chapter will be devoted to providing you with written guides to follow while you are getting into the habit of doing all the unfamiliar chores required to keep your records current.

Recordkeeping and Tax Reporting Schedules

You should now have a basic understanding of the interrelationship of each of the phases of recordkeeping. Up to this point, you have been introduced to the following:

BASICS OF RECORDKEEPING
    a. Functions and types of recordkeeping
    b. When does the recordkeeping begin and who should do it

ESSENTIAL RECORDS FOR SMALL BUSINESS
    a. What records are required
    b. What their purposes are
    c. Format for recording information

DEVELOPMENT OF FINANCIAL STATEMENTS
    a. What they are
    b. How they are developed
    c. Information sources

TAXES AND RECORDKEEPING
    a. Federal taxes for which you may be liable
    b. Forms to be used for reporting
    c. Publications available as tax aids

ORGANIZING YOUR RECORDKEEPING

Just as timing is important to all other phases of your business, it also is important when you deal with recordkeeping. You cannot haphazardly throw all of your paperwork into a basket and deal with it in a sporadic nature. You will have to organize your recordkeeping into a system that will allow you to proceed through the tax year in an orderly fashion. That system will have to provide for retrieval and verification of tax information and, at the same time, form a picture of your business that will help you to analyze trends and implement changes to make your venture grow and become more profitable.

BUILDING YOUR SYSTEM

The information in this book was presented in a particular order for a specific reason. Just as a homebuilder must first lay the foundation, do the framing, put up the walls, and then do the finish work, you, too, must build your foundation first and learn the Basics of Recordkeeping. The frame can be likened to your General Records. They are the underlying material without which there could be no walls. In the same way, General Records are the basis (source of information) for forming Financial Statements. At last, the builder finishes the home and makes some rooms into a limited space for each family member, and other rooms into common areas where the whole family will meet. This is Tax Accounting, with different legal structures functioning within their limited areas, but meeting in areas common to all businesses. The house is complete—and so is your recordkeeping. Now a schedule needs to be made to maintain your home or it will soon be a shambles. To keep your business in a maintained state, it too must have scheduled upkeep. To keep maintenance at an optimum, you will need to set up a Recordkeeping and Tax Reporting Schedule.

Proceeding on the assumption that you have never done recordkeeping and that you have no idea in what order it must be done, we will give you a basic format to follow while you learn this task.

DOING TASKS IN SEQUENCE

There is a specific order to recordkeeping, and you must follow that order if your records are going to be effective. Since the two goals of recordkeeping are retrieval for tax purposes and the analyzing of information for internal planning, your schedule will have to provide for the reaching of those goals.

We have provided a General Recordkeeping and Tax Reporting Schedule on the following pages that will do just that if you will follow it. There are two things that you must keep in mind to insure success:

1. Do not fail to do any of the tasks.

2. Be sure to do them on time.

POST your schedule on the wall in your office and refer to it every day for what needs to be done. Before long those chores will become automatic. All of the information presented in this book will have assimilated in your mind and you will begin to see the overall picture. At the end of the year, if you have followed the schedule, you will have every piece of financial information at your fingertips. It can be done—and you can do it!

SCHEDULE FORMAT

The General Recordkeeping Schedule is divided into tasks according to frequency. There are two basic divisions:

1. GENERAL RECORDKEEPING

Daily: Tasks you should be aware of and do every day.

Weekly: The tasks you do when you do your regular bookkeeping. Timing may vary according to the needs of your business.

Monthly: Closing out your books at the end of the month.

Quarterly: Analysis of past quarter and revision of budget.

End of Year: Closing out your books for the year and setting up records for the new year.

2. TAX REPORTING

Monthly: Payroll reporting and deposits, Sales Tax Reporting (sales tax may be monthly, quarterly or annually).

Quarterly: Sending in required tax reports.

Annually: Filing information and tax returns.

Every business has individual needs. You may have to shift the frequency of some tasks. To begin with, however, follow the progression in the schedule we have provided and it should adequately cover most of your needs.

NOTE FOR DIFFERENT LEGAL STRUCTURES: Since some recordkeeping tasks are different for different legal structures (i.e., - sole proprietorship, partnership, S corporation, and corporation), it will be noted as to which apply. If there is no notation accompanying the task, it applies to all legal structures.

IF YOU NEED HELP, REFER BACK: Keep in mind when you are using the General Recordkeeping Schedule that all the items on the schedule have been covered in one of the previous sections. You need only refer back to the appropriate record, statement, or tax return information to refresh your memory and complete your task. Be sure to keep reference materials mentioned in those sections close at hand in case you need more detailed information.

SAMPLE SCHEDULE: The next five pages contain a General Recordkeeping and Tax Reporting Schedule. Copy it! Post it!

Use These Schedules!

The following schedules are meant to serve as guides for you until you are familiar with the recordkeeping process. There may be other jobs for you to do, but this should get you off to a good start.

RECORDKEEPING SCHEDULE

DAILY

1. Go through mail and file for appropriate action.

2. Unpack and put away incoming inventory.

3. Record inventory information in Inventory Record.

4. Pay any invoices necessary to meet discount deadlines.

5. Record daily invoices sent out in Accounts Receivable. **Note**: It would be a good idea to keep invoice copies in an envelope or folder behind its corresponding Accounts Receivable record.*

*Double Entry: Enter invoices sent out in General Journal and post to individual General Ledger accounts. Invoices may be kept together and posted weekly (depends on volume).

WEEKLY

1. Prepare bank deposit for income received and take it to the bank.

2. Enter deposit in Checkbook and Revenue & Expense Journal.*

3. Enter sales information in Inventory Record.*

4. Enter week's checking transactions in Revenue & Expense Journal.*

5. Record Petty Cash purchases in Petty Cash Record and file receipts.*

7. Record purchase of any depreciable purchases in your Fixed Asset Log.*

6. Pay invoices due. Be aware of discount dates.

*Double Entry: Week's checking transactions (income and deposits) are entered in the General Journal and posted to individual General Ledger accounts.

MONTHLY

1. Balance checkbook (reconcile with bank statement).

2. Enter any interest earned and any bank charges in Checkbook and in your Revenue & Expense Journal.

3. Total and Balance all Revenue & Expense Journal columns.*

4. Enter monthly income and expense totals on 12-month Profit and Loss Statement. Prepare a separate one-month Profit & Loss if you wish.

5. If you wish to look at assets and liabilities, prepare a Balance Sheet. It is only required at year end for those who are not Sole Proprietors or filers of Schedule C. (see: End of the Year)

6. Check Accounts Payable and send Statements to open accounts.

   *Double Entry: Total and Balance accounts in ledger.

QUARTERLY

1. Do a Quarterly Budget Analysis. Compare actual income and expenses with projections.

2. Revise your cash flow statement (budget) accordingly.

END OF TAX YEAR

1. Pay all invoices, sales taxes and other expenses that you wish to use as deductions for the current tax year.

2. Prepare annual Profit & Loss Statement. (Add income and expense totals from the twelve monthly reports.)*

3. Prepare a Balance Sheet for your business. A balance sheet is **required** for all but Sole Proprietors or filers of Schedule C.

4. Prepare a Pro Forma Cash Flow Statement (Budget) for next year. Use your Profit & Loss information from the current year to help you make decisions.

5. Set up your new records for the coming year. It is a good idea to buy new journals and files early before the supply runs out. Begin recordkeeping in the first week. **Do not get behind.**

   *Double Entry: Transfer balances from individual income and expense ledger accounts (numbered 400 and 500) to your Profit & Loss (Income) Statement.

TAX REPORTING SCHEDULE

Warning!

The following Tax Reporting Schedule is not meant for use as a final authority. Requirements may change. Also you may be responsible for reports and returns that are not listed below. This is meant only to be used as a general guide to help keep you on track until you become familiar with the specific requirements for your business.

NOTE: This schedule refers to tax reports and reporting dates. In the tax chapter, there are tax reporting calendars for all legal structures. Post your calendar with this schedule and refer to it for required forms and dates. Also refer to information on individual forms which are listed in the index by subject and by form number.

MONTHLY

1. Check your payroll tax liability. If it exceeds $500, a deposit is due on the 15th of the month. (If you work with an accountant or payroll service, information on payments and withholding amounts needs to be provided to them as early in the month as possible so you can receive information back as to what your deposits should be.) See information on "Payroll Records" in Chapter 3.

2. Sales Tax Reports: You may be required to file monthly, quarterly or annually, according to your sales volume. In some cases, you may be required to be bonded or prepay sales tax. Fill out and send in your sales tax report to the State Board of Equalization (or in some states sales tax may be administered through the Department of Revenue) with a check for monies collected (or in due) for the sale of taxable goods or services for the previous period. This is for those businesses holding a Seller's Permit. The subject of sales tax is not covered in this book. (See Chapter 9 in our business start-up book, *Out of Your Mind...and Into the Marketplace™*, Tustin, CA: Out of Your Mind . . ., 1988.) Report forms are furnished by the collecting agency and will generally be due somewhere around 30 days after the end of the reporting period.

QUARTERLY

1. Estimated Taxes (Form 1040ES): File estimated taxes with the Internal Revenue Service (You must also file with your state, if applicable).

a. Sole proprietor, individual who is a partner or S corporation shareholder file on 15th day of 4th, 6th, and 9th months of tax year, and 15th day of 1st month after the end of tax year. For most businesses the due dates would be April 15, June 15, September 15 and January 15. If the due date falls on a weekend day, the due date will be the following Monday.

b. Corporations file the 15th day of 4th, 6th, 9th and 12th months of the tax year. For most businesses this will be April 15, June 15, September 15 and December 15; the same weekend rules apply.

Note: Take special note that only two months lapse between 1st and 2nd quarter filing.

2. FICA and Withholding Returns (Form 941): File Employer's Quarterly Federal Tax Returns reporting social security (FICA) tax and the withholding of income tax. Check early to see if you are required to make deposits.

3. FUTA Deposits (Form 8109): Make Federal Unemployment (FUTA) tax deposits. Make deposits on April 30th, July 31st, October 31st and January 31st, but only if the liability for unpaid tax is more than $100.

4. Sales Tax Reports: If you are on a quarterly reporting basis, reports will be due by April 30th, July 31st, October 31st and January 31st for the previous quarter. If you are only required to file annually, it will generally be due on January 31st for the previous calendar year.

ANNUALLY

1. FICA and Withholding Information Returns: Provide information on social security (FICA) tax and the withholding of income tax. (Also, make it your business to be aware of any additional state requirements.)

a. W-2 to employees on January 31st.

b. W-2 and W-3 to Social Security Administration on the last day of February.

2. 1099 Information Returns: Send information for payments to nonemployees and transactions with other persons.

    a. Forms 1099 due to recipient by 1-31.

    b. Forms 1099 and transmittals 1096 due to IRS on the last day of February.

3. FUTA Tax Returns: File Federal unemployment (FUTA) tax returns with the IRS, Due date is January 31st.

4. Income Tax Returns (Form 1040): File Income Tax Returns with the IRS (and your state, if applicable).

    a. Sole Proprietor, Individual who is a partner, S Corporation shareholder file on 15th day of 4th month after end of tax year (generally April 15th, Schedule C, Form 1040).

    b. Partnership returns due on the 15th day of the 4th month after the end of tax year (generally April 15th, Form 1065).

    c. S corporations (Form 1120S) and corporations (Form 1120) file on the 15th day of the 3rd month after end of the tax year (generally March 15th).

5. Self-Employment Tax Forms (Form SE): Self-Employment Tax Forms are filed with Form 1040 (see above).

    a. For sole proprietors or individuals who are partners.

    b. Self-Employment Forms are only applicable if your business shows a taxable profit in excess of $400.

Preparing
for Uncle Sam

This book would not be complete without giving you information on getting ready to do your income tax. As was stated earlier, one of the two main purposes of recordkeeping is for income tax retrieval and verification.

When all your end-of-the-year work has been done, it is time to begin work on income taxes. By no means are we suggesting that you do it all yourself. As a matter of fact, we strongly suggest that you hire a C.P.A., Enrolled Agent or other tax professional to do the final preparation and aid you in maximizing your tax benefits. Not very many of us are well enough informed to have a good command of all the tax regulations and changes. However, you can do a great deal of the preliminary work. This will be of benefit to you in two different ways: 1) You will save on accounting fees; and 2) You will learn a lot about your business by working on your taxes.

There will be a great deal of variation in what you can do yourself, due not only to the complexity of your particular business, but also to the abilities of the individual doing your recordkeeping. For this reason, we will not attempt to give directions for preliminary tax preparations. However, there is some sound advice that we can give you at this point.

You have spent the year keeping General Records and developing Financial Statements. These are the records that provide all the information you need for income tax accounting. In fact, if the IRS regulations weren't so fast changing and complicated, you could probably fill out your own tax return.

However, since you will need a professional preparer to make sure that your return is correct and to maximize your benefits, your task is to gather and pass on the information that is needed to get the job done.

Many tax preparers complain that the assignment is made difficult because customers do not prepare their material. They bring in bags full of receipts and disorganized information. What do you need in order to be prepared for the accountant?

WHAT TO GIVE YOUR ACCOUNTANT

The information needed by your accountant will come from sources that you should already have if you have kept your General Records and generated Financial Statements as presented in Chapters 3 and 4.

ALL BUSINESSES

There are two things that your accountant will need from you regardless of your type of business:

1. Annual Profit & Loss Statement: This gives your accountant a list of all of the income and expenses your business has had for the tax year. If you are in a product industry, your accountant will be need to compute your cost of goods sold for your return. You are required to do a beginning and ending inventory every year. Before you complete your Profit & Loss Statement, you will need the following two items:

    a. **Beginning Inventory:** Inventory as of January 1 of the current year. It must match the figure you listed as "Ending Inventory" last year.

    b. **Ending Inventory:** Inventory as of December 31st of this year. This is done by physical inventory. It will become your beginning inventory for next year.

    c. **Amount of Inventory Purchased:** List the cost of all inventory purchased by your company during the tax year.

    Note: Your Profit & Loss Statement should already have the computation for "Cost of Goods Sold." However, giving your accountant a list of the above three items will help in checking your understanding and accuracy.

2. Copy of Your Fixed Asset Log: Lists all of the depreciable assets your company has purchased during the current year, with date purchased, purchase price, etc. Your accountant needs to know whether or not you have listed any of these costs in your Profit & Loss Statement. Both of you can then decide whether to depreciate these items or expense them under Section 179.

HOME-BASED BUSINESSES

List of Home-Office Expenses: You will have to gather information on taxes, insurance and interest paid (rent if you are not a home owner). You will also need amounts on maintenance and utilities. Before you decide to depreciate your home as a home-office deduction, ask your accountant to explain the recapture if you subsequently sell. You must also measure your office space and calculate the percentage of your home that is used exclusively for your business. Your accountant will need this information to fill out the required form that must accompany your income tax return if you are claiming home-office deduction.

PARTNERSHIPS, S CORPORATIONS AND FULL CORPORATIONS

Record of Owner Equity Deposits and Owner Draws: The three legal structures listed are required to have a balance as part of the return, listing the equity of each owner. In order to compute equity, your accountant will have to have the total contributed and withdrawn by each owner. Using last year's equity account balances as a base, deposits will be added and withdrawals subtracted to arrive at the owners' new balances.

It is best to provide the accountant with the above information as soon as possible after the new year. This allows extra time for any questions that might arise while your returns are being prepared. It also allows you to forget about income taxes and get on with the new business year.

THE LAST CHORE

The IRS requires us to keep all income tax information for a period of three years. During that time, (and longer, in come cases, such as fraud) our past returns are subject to audit. In addition, several records are retained for longer periods, mostly determined by administrative decision. It is a good idea to keep many of them for the life of your business. Remember that the other purpose of records is that of analyzing trends and implementing changes. They are only useful if they are still in your possession.

We have found it to be very effective to file all of the information for one year together. Put the following things in your file, mark it with the year date and put it away.

1. Income Tax Returns
2. All Receipts
3. Bank Statements
4. Revenue & Expense Journal
5. Petty Cash Record
6. Fixed Assets Record, Inventory Record, etc.
7. All information pertinent to verification of your return

RECORDS RETENTION SCHEDULE: The schedule on the next page will help you to decide what records you should retain and how long you should keep them.

RECORDS
RETENTION SCHEDULE

RETENTION PERIOD	AUTHORITY TO DISPOSE	
1-10 - No. Years to be Retained PR - Retain Permanently EOY - Retain Until End of Year CJ - Retain Until Completion of Job EXP - Retain Until Expiration ED - Retain Until Equipment Disposal	AD - Administrative Decision FLSA - Fair Labor Standards Act CFR - Code of Federal Regulators IR - Insurance Regulation	
TYPE OF RECORD	RETAIN FOR	BY WHOSE AUTHORITY
BANK DEPOSIT RECORDS	7	AD
BANK STATEMENTS	7	AD
BUSINESS LICENSES	EXP	AD
CATALOGS	EXP	AD
CHECK REGISTER	PR	AD
CHECKS (CANCELLED)	3	FLSA, STATE
CONTRACTS	EXP	AD
CORRESPONDENCE	5	AD
DEPRECIATION RECORDS	PR	CFR
ESTIMATED TAX RECORDS	PR	AD
EXPENSE RECORDS	7	AD
INSURANCE (CLAIMS RECORDS)	11	IR
INSURANCE POLICIES	EXP	AD
INVENTORY RECORDS	10	AD
INVENTORY REPORTS	PR	CFR
INVOICES (ACCT. PAYABLE)	3	FLSA, STATE
INVOICES (ACCT. RECEIVABLE)	7	AD
LEDGER (GENERAL)	PR	CFR
MAINTENANCE RECORDS	ED	AD
OFFICE EQUIPMENT RECORDS	5	AD
PATENTS	PR	AD
PETTY CASH RECORD	PR	AD
POSTAL RECORDS	1	AD, CFR
PURCHASE ORDERS	3	CFR
SALES TAX REPORTS TO STATE	PR	STATE
SHIPPING DOCUMENTS	2-10	AD, CFR
TAX BILLS & STATEMENTS	PR	AD
TAX RETURNS (FED. & STATE)	PR	AD
TRADEMARKS & COPYRIGHTS	PR	AD
TRAVEL RECORDS	7	AD
WORK PAPERS (PROJECTS)	CJ	AD
YEAR-END REPORTS	PR	AD

Financial Statement Analysis

Marilyn J. Dauber is a C.P.A. in Butte, Montana and the author of this chapter on Financial Statement Analysis. Her success at helping businesses that are in trouble has been greatly enhanced by her ability to analyze financial statements and implement the appropriate changes. We would like to thank her for sharing her expertise with us through the contribution of this chapter. Because of her generosity, the user of this book has the opportunity not only to set up and maintain the proper records, but to gain the maximum benefits from those records through financial statement analysis.

FINANCIAL STATEMENTS

Your financial statements contain the information you need to help make decisions regarding your business. Many small business owners think of their financial statements as requirements for creditors, bankers, or tax preparers only, but they are much more than that. When analyzed, your financial statements can give you key information needed on the financial condition and the operations of your business.

Financial statement analysis requires measures to be expressed as ratios or percentages. For example, consider the situation where total assets on your balance sheet are $10,000. Cash is $2,000; Accounts Receivable are $3,000; and Fixed Assets are $5,000. The relationships would be expressed as follows:

	Ratio	Ratio Relationship	Percentages
Cash	.2	.2:1	20%
Accounts Receivable	.3	.3:1	30%
Fixed Assets	.5	.5:1	50%

Financial statement analysis involves the studying of relationships and comparisons of 1) items in a single year's financial statement, 2) comparative financial statements for a period of time, and 3) your statements with those of other businesses.

Many analytic tools are available, but we will focus on the following measures that are of most importance to a small business owner:

> **Liquidity Analysis**
> **Profitability Analysis**
> **Measures of Debit**
> **Measures of Investment**
> **Vertical Financial Statement Analysis**
> **Horizontal Financial Statement Analysis**

Lets take a look, on the next few pages, at some ratios that may help you to evaluate your business. To illustrate, we will use the following statements from a small business. We will call it Mary's Flower Shop and we will use small figures that will be easy to examine.

Mary's Flower Shop
Comparative Balance
12/31/92 and 12/31/91

	1992	1991
ASSETS		
Current Assets		
Cash	$2,000	$5,000
Accounts Receivable	3,000	1,000
Inventory	5,000	3,000
Total Current Assets	$10.000	$9,000
Fixed Assets	8,000	5,000
Total Assets	$18,000	$14,000
LIABILITIES & OWNER'S EQUITY		
Current Liabilities		
Accounts Payable	$4,000	$2,000
Taxes Payable	220	300
Total Current Liabilities	$4,220	$2,300
Long Term Liabilities	10,000	8,000
Total Liabilities	$14,220	$10,300
OWNER'S EQUITY	$3,780	$3,700
TOTAL LIABILITIES & OWNER'S EQUITY	$18,000	$14,000

Mary's Flower Shop
Comparative Income Statement
For Years Ended 12/31/92 and 12/31/91

	1992	1991
SALES	$8,000	$6,000
Cost of Goods Sold	-6,000	-3,900
Gross Profit	$2,000	$2,100
EXPENSES		
Selling (Variable) Expenses		
Advertising	$100	$50
Freight	50	40
Salaries	150	150
Total Selling Expenses	$300	$240
Administrative (Fixed) Expenses		
Rent	$450	$250
Insurance	150	125
Utilities	150	100
Total Administrative Expenses	$750	$475

	1992	1991
INCOME FROM OPERATIONS	$950	$1,385
Interest Income	+ 0	+ 0
Interest Expense	- 720	- 450
NET INCOME BEFORE TAXES	$230	$935
TAXES	- 150	- 180
NET PROFIT (LOSS) AFTER TAXES	$80	$755

Now You Are Ready to

Analyze Mary's Financial Statements

LIQUIDITY ANALYSIS

The liquidity of a business is the ability it has to meet financial obligations. The analysis focuses on the balance sheet relationships for the current assets and current liabilities.

NET WORKING CAPITAL

The excess of current assets over current liabilities is net working capital. The more net working capital a business has, the less risky it is, as it has the ability to cover current liabilities as they come due. Lets take a look at the net working capital for Mary's Flower Shop:

	1992	1991
Current Assets	$10,000	$9,000
Current Liabilities	- 4,220	- 2,300
Net Working Capital	**$5,780**	**$6,700**

In both years, net working capital was present, which would indicate a good position. But lets analyze this a bit more to get a clear picture of the liquidity of Mary's Flower Shop.

CURRENT RATIO

The current ratio is a more dependable indication of liquidity than the net working capital. The current ratio is computed with the following formula:

$$\text{Current Ratio} = \frac{\text{Current Assets}}{\text{Current Liabilities}}$$

For Mary's Flower Shop, the current ratios are:

$$1991: \quad \frac{\$9,000}{\$2,300} = 3.91$$

$$1992: \quad \frac{\$10,000}{\$4,220} = 2.37$$

As you can see, the business was in a more liquid position in 1991. In 1992, the business did experience an increase in current assets, but it also had a increase in current liabilities.

There is no set criteria for the **normal** current ratio, as that is dependent on the business you are in. If you have predictable cash flows, you can operate with a lower current ratio.

The ratio of 2.0 is considered acceptable for most businesses. A ratio of 2.0 would allow a company to lose 50% of its current assets and still be able to cover current liabilities. For most businesses, this is an adequate margin of safety.

For Mary's Flower Shop, the **decrease** in the current ratio would cause the owner to investigate further.

QUICK RATIO

Since inventory is the most difficult current asset to dispose of quickly, it is subtracted from the current assets in the quick ratio to give a tougher list of liquidity. The quick ratio is computed as follows:

$$\text{Quick Ratio} = \frac{\text{Current Assets - Inventory}}{\text{Current Liabilities}}$$

The quick Ratios for our case are:

1992: $\dfrac{\$10,000 - 5,000}{\$4,220} = 1.18$

1991: $\dfrac{\$9,000 - 3,000}{\$2,300} = 2.61$

A quick ratio of 1.00 or greater is usually recommended, but that is dependent upon the business you are in.

From the analysis of the liquidity measures (net working capital, current ratio and quick ratio), we see that the 1992 results are within acceptable limits. The business did experience a decrease in liquidity, and is viewed as more risky than in 1991.

You can use these ratios to see if your business is in any risk of insolvency. You will also be able to assess your ability to increase or decrease current assets for your business strategy. How would these moves affect your liquidity?

Your creditors will use these ratios to determine whether or not to extend credit to you. They will compare the ratios for previous periods and with those of similar businesses.

PROFITABILITY ANALYSIS

A Profitability Analysis will measure the ability of a business to make a profit.

GROSS PROFIT MARGIN

The gross profit margin indicates the percentage of each sales dollar remaining after a business has paid for its goods.

$$\text{Gross Profit Margin} = \frac{\text{Gross Profit}}{\text{Sales}}$$

The higher the gross profit margin, the better. For Mary's Flower Shop, the gross profit margins were:

$$1992: \quad \frac{\$2,000}{\$8,000} = 25\%$$

$$1991: \quad \frac{\$2,100}{\$6,000} = 35\%$$

The normal rate is dependent on the business you are in. The Gross Profit Margin is the actual mark-up you have on the goods sold.

In 1992, our case has a 25% contribution margin, which means that 25 cents of every dollar in sales is left to cover the direct, indirect, and other expenses. Mary's Flower Shop can be viewed as "less profitable" in 1992 as compared to 1991.

OPERATING PROFIT MARGIN

This ratio represents the pure operations profits, ignoring interest and taxes. A high operating profit margin is preferred.

$$\text{Operating Profit Margin} = \frac{\text{Income from Operations}}{\text{Sales}}$$

Mary's Flower Shop has the following ratios:

1992: $\dfrac{\$950}{\$8,000}$ = 11.88%

1991 $\dfrac{\$1,385}{\$6,000}$ = 23.08%

Again our case is showing a less profitable position in 1992 than it did in 1991.

NET PROFIT MARGIN

The net profit margin is clearly the measure of a business success with respect to earnings on sales.

$$\text{Net Profit Margin} = \frac{\text{Net Profit}}{\text{Sales}}$$

A higher margin means the firm is more profitable. The net profit margin will differ according to your specific type of business. A one percent margin for a grocery store is not unusual due to the large quantity of items handled; while a ten percent margin for a jewelry store would be considered low.

Mary's Flower Shop has the following net profit margins:

1992: $\dfrac{\$80}{\$8,000}$ = 1%

1991: $\dfrac{\$755}{\$6,000}$ = 12.6%

Clearly, Mary's Flower Shop is in trouble. All the ratios indicate a significant decrease in profitability from 1991. The next step is to determine reasons for that decrease.

As a business owner, you can see just how profitable your business is. If the ratios are too low, you will want to analyze why.

Did you mark up your goods sold enough? Check your gross profit margin.

Are your operating expenses too high? Check your operating profit margin.

Are your interest expenses too high? Check your net profit margin.

For Mary's Flower shop, all of the above questions can be answered using the ratios we computed. Your creditors will look at these ratios to see just how profitable your business is. Without profits, a business can't attract outside financing.

DEBT MEASURES

The debt position of a business indicates the amount of other people's money that is being used to generate profits. Many new businesses assume too much debt too soon in an attempt to grow too quickly. The measures of debt will tell a business how indebted it is and how able it is to service the debts. The more indebtedness, the greater the risk of failure.

DEBT RATIO

This is a key financial ratio used by creditors.

$$\text{Debt Ratio} = \frac{\text{Total Liabilities}}{\text{Total Assets}}$$

The higher this ratio, the more risk of failure. For Mary's Flower Shop, the debt ratios are:

1992: $\dfrac{\$14,200}{\$18,000}$ = 79%

1991: $\dfrac{\$10,300}{\$14,000}$ = 74%

The acceptable ratio is dependent upon the policies of your creditors and bankers. The rates of 79% and 74% above are excessively high and show a very high risk of failure. Clearly three quarters of the company is being financed by others' money, and it does not put the business in a good position for acquiring new debt.

If your business plan includes the addition of long-term debt at a future point, you will want to monitor your debt ratio. Is it within the limits acceptable to your banker?

INVESTMENT MEASURES

As a small business owner, you have invested money to acquire assets, and you should be getting a return on these assets. Even if the owner is taking a salary from the business, he/she also should be earning an additional amount for the investment in the company.

RETURN-ON-INVESTMENT (ROI)

The Return-on-Investment measures the effectiveness of you as the business owner, to generate profits from the available assets.

$$ROI = \frac{\text{Net Profits}}{\text{Total Assets}}$$

The higher the ROI, the better. The business owner should get a target for the ROI. What do you want your investment to earn?

For Mary's Flower Shop, the ROI is as follows:

1992: $\dfrac{\$80}{\$18,000} = .4\%$

1991: $\dfrac{\$755}{\$14,000} = 5.4\%$

We do no know Mary's target for ROI, but .4% would seem unacceptable. She could put her money in a savings account and earn 5%, so it doesn't appear that a .4% return on her investment is good. Many small business owners have successfully created jobs for themselves, but still don't earn a fair return on their investment. Set your target for ROI, and work towards it.

VERTICAL FINANCIAL STATEMENT ANALYSIS

Percentage analysis is used to show the relationship of the components in a single financial statement.

For a balance sheet, each asset is stated as a percent of total assets, and each liability and equity item is stated as a percent of total liabilities and equity.

In vertical analysis of the income statement, each item is stated as a percent of net sales.

Let's do a vertical analysis of the income statements for Mary's Flower Shop as shown below.

Mary's Flower Shop
Comparative Income Statement
For Years Ended 12/31/92 and 12/31/91

	1992		1991	
	AMOUNT	**PERCENT**	**AMOUNT**	**PERCENT**
Sales	$8,000	100.0%	$6,000	100.0%
Cost of Goods Sold	6,000	75.0%	3,900	65.0%
Gross Profit	$2,000	25.0%	$2,100	35.0%
Selling Expenses				
Advertising	$ 100	1.3%	$ 50	4.2%
Freight	50	.6%	40	2.1%
Salaries	150	1.9%	150	1.7%
Total Selling Expenses	$ 300	3.8%	$ 240	7.9%
Administrative Expenses				
Rent	$ 450	5.6%	$ 250	5.6%
Insurance	150	1.9%	125	1.9%
Utilities	150	1.9%	100	1.9%
Total Direct Expenses	$ 750	9.4%	$ 475	9.4%
Income from Operations	$ 950	11.9%	$1,385	23.0%
Interest (Paid)	720	9.0%	450	7.5%
Taxes	150	1.9%	180	3.0%
Net Profit (Loss)	$ 80	1.0%	$ 755	12.6%

EVALUATION OF VERTICAL FINANCIAL STATEMENT

From the vertical analysis of Mary's income statements, we can see the following:

1. The components of cost of goods sold and gross profit showed significant difference.

There's a ten percent increase in cost of goods sold. Should alert the owner to investigate.

Did the cost of the items really increase ten percent?

Is there a possibility of theft which caused the variance?

The ten percent decrease in gross profit should trigger the owner to look at the mark-up.

Is it too low?

2. The composition of variable expenses changed.

The owner would want to evaluate the appropriateness of the increase in advertising and decrease in salaries.

3. The composition of fixed expenses would alert the owner to evaluate the increase in rent.

Why did this occur?

Is it necessary?

4. The increase in interest should be analyzed.

The most likely reason for the increase would probably be an increase in debt.

HORIZONTAL FINANCIAL STATEMENT ANALYSIS

Horizontal analysis is a percentage analysis of the increases and decreases in the items on comparative financial statements.

The increase or decrease of the item is listed, and the earlier statement is used as the base. The percentage of increase or decrease is listed.

A horizontal analysis of the income statements for Mary's Flower Shop can be seen below.

Mary's Flower Shop
Comparative Income Statement
For Years Ended 12/31/92 and 12/31/91

	1992	1991	INCREASE / (DECREASE) AMOUNT	PERCENT
Sales	$ 8,000	$ 6,000	$ 2,000	33.3%
Cost of Goods Sold	6,000	3,900	2,100	53.8%
Gross Profit	$ 2,000	$ 2,100	($ 100)	(4.8%)
Selling Expenses				
Advertising	$ 100	$ 50	$ 50	100.0%
Freight	50	40	10	25.0%
Salaries	150	150	same	same
Total Selling Expenses	$ 300	$ 240	$ 60	25.0%
Administrative Expenses				
Rent	$ 450	$ 250	200	80.0%
Insurance	150	125	25	20.0%
Utilities	150	100	50	50.0%
Total Direct Expenses	$ 750	$ 475	$ 275	57.9%
Income from Operations	$ 950	$ 1,385	(435)	(31.4%)
Interest (Paid)	720	450	270	60.0%
Taxes	150	180	(30)	(16.7%)
Net Profit (Loss)	$ 80	$ 755	($ 675)	(89.4%)

EVALUATION OF HORIZONTAL FINANCIAL STATEMENT ANALYSIS

From the horizontal analysis of Mary's income statements, we should evaluate the following:

1. **The 33.3% increase in sales resulted in a 4.8% gross profit.**

   a. This would alert the owner that something is wrong.

   b. Is the mark-up sufficient?

   c. Was there an according adjustment?

2. **The 100% increase in advertising expense was steep.**

   a. Did this expense increase sales?

   b. Was it justified?

3. **The 80% rent increase and 50% utilities increase should be looked at.**

   a. Are they justified?

4. **The 60% interest increase is most likely a result of increased debt.**

   a. The owner would want to analyze the components.

   b. Decide if the interest level is correct.

   c. Decide if some debt should be retired.

5. **The 89.4% decrease in net profit is not acceptable.**

   a. A serious decrease will require that the owner re-evaluate the business.

SUMMARY

Now, you can see how financial statement analysis can be a tool to help you manage your business.

If the analysis produces results that don't meet your expectation or if the business is in danger of failure, you must analyze your expenses and your use of assets. Your first stop should be to cut expenses and increase the productivity of your assets.

If your return on investment is too low, examine how you could make your assets (equipment, machinery, fixtures, inventory, etc.) work better for your benefits.

If your profit is low, be sure that your mark-up is adequate, analyze your operating expenses to see that they are not to high and review your interest expenses.

If your liquidity is low, you could have a risk of becoming insolvent. Examine the level and composition of current assets and current liabilities.

The vertical and horizontal financial statement analysis will reveal trends and compositions that signify trouble. Using your management skills, you can take corrective action.

Glossary of Accounting Terms

Account: A separate record showing the increases and decreases in each asset, liability, owner's equity, revenue and expense item.

Accounting: The process by which financial information about a business is recorded, classified, summarized, interpreted by a business.

Accounting period: The period of time covered by the income statement and other financial statements that report operating results.

Accounts payable: Amounts owed by a business to its creditors on open account for goods purchased or services rendered.

Accounts receivable: Amounts owed to the business on open account as a result of extending credit to a customer who purchases your products or services.

Accrual basis of accounting: The method of accounting in which all revenues and expenses are recognized on the income statement in the period when they are earned and incurred regardless of when the cash related to the transactions is received or paid.

Accrued expenses: Expenses that have been incurred but not paid (such as employee salaries, commissions, taxes, interest, etc.).

Accrued income: Income that has been earned but not received.

Aging accounts receivable: The classification of accounts receivable according to how long they have been outstanding. An appropriate rate of loss can then be applied to each age group in order to estimate probable loss from uncollectible accounts.

Assets: Everything owned by or owed to a business that has cash value.

Audit trail: A chain of references that makes it possible to trace information about transactions through an accounting system.

Balance sheet: The financial statement that shows the financial position of a business as of a fixed date. It is usually done at the close of an accounting period by summarizing its assets, liabilities, and owners' equity.

Bottom line: A business's net profit or loss after taxes for a specific accounting period.

Break-even point: That point at which a business no longer incurs at loss but has yet to make a profit. The break-even point can be expressed in total dollars of revenue exactly offset by total expenses or total units of production the cost of which exactly equals the income derived from their sale.

Budget: The development of a set of financial goals. A business is then evaluated by measuring its performance in terms of these goals. The budget contains projections for cash inflow and outflow and other balance sheet items. Also known as Cash Flow Statement.

Business financial history: A summary of financial information about a company from its start to the present.

Capital: See "Owner's equity."

Capital expenditures: An expenditure for a purchase of an item of property, plant or equipment that has a useful life of more than one year (Fixed assets).

Cash flow statement: See "Budget."

Chart of accounts: A list of the numbers and titles of a business's general ledger accounts.

Closing entries: Entries made at the end of an accounting period to reduce the balances of the revenue and expense accounts to zero. Most businesses close books at the end of each month and at the end of the year.

Comparative financial statements: Financial statements that include information for two or more periods or two or more companies.

Corporation: A business structure that is granted separate legal status under state law and whose owners are stockholders of the corporation.

Cost of goods sold: The cost of inventory sold during an accounting period. It is equal to the beginning inventory for the period plus the cost of purchases made during the period minus the ending inventory for the period.

Credit: An amount entered on the right side of an account in double-entry accounting. A decrease in asset and expense accounts. An increase in liability, capital and income accounts.

Creditor: A company or individual to whom a business owes money.

Current assets: Cash plus any assets that will be converted into cash within one year plus any assets that you plan to use up within one year.

Current liabilities: Debts that must be paid within one year.

Current ratio: A dependable indication of liquidity computed by dividing current assets by current liabilities. A ratio of 2.0 is acceptable for most businesses.

Debit: An amount entered on the left side of an account in double-entry accounting. A decrease in liabilities, capital and income accounts. An increase in asset and expense accounts.

Debt measures: The indication of the amount of other people's money that is being used to generate profits for a business. The more indebtedness, the greater the risk of failure.

Debt ratio: The key financial ratio used by creditors in determining how indebted a business is and how able it is to service the debts. The debt ratio is calculated by dividing total liabilities by total assets. Ths higher the ratio, the more risk of failure. The acceptable ratio is dependent upon the policies of your creditors and bankers.

Declining-balance method: An accelerated method of depreciation in which the book value of an asset at the beginning of the year is multiplied by an appropriate percentage to obtain the depreciation to be taken for that year.

Depreciable base of an asset: The cost of an asset used in the computation of yearly depreciation expense.

Direct expenses: Those expenses that relate directly to your product or service.

Double entry accounting: A system of accounting under which each transaction is recorded twice. This is based on the premise that every transaction has two sides. At least one account must be debited and one account must be credited and the debit and credit totals for each transaction must be equal.

Expenses: The costs of producing revenue through the sale of goods or services.

Financial statements: The periodic reports that summarize the financial affairs of a business.

First in, first out method (FIFO): A method of valuing inventory that assumes that the first items purchased are the first items to be sold. When ending inventory is computed the costs of the latest purchases are used.

Fiscal year: Any 12-month accounting period used by a business.

Fixed assets: Items purchased for use in a business which are depreciable over a fixed period of time determined by the expected useful life of the purchase. Usually includes land, buildings, vehicles and equipment not intended for resale. Land is not depreciable, but is listed as a fixed asset.

Fixed asset log: A record used to keep track of the fixed assets purchased by a business during the current financial year. This record can be used by an accountant to determine depreciation expense to be taken for tax purposes.

Fixed costs: Costs that do not vary in total during a period even though the volume of goods manufactured may be higher or lower than anticipated.

General journal: Used to record all the transactions of a business. Transactions are listed in chronological order and transferred or posted to individual accounts in the general ledger.

General ledger: In double entry accounting, the master reference file for the accounting system. A permanent, classified record is kept for each business account. The forms used for the accounts are on separate sheets in a book or binder and are then referred to as the general ledger.

Gross profit on sales: The difference between net sales and the cost of goods sold.

Gross profit margin: An indicator of the percentage of each sales dollar remaining after a business has paid for its goods. It is computed by dividing the gross profit by the sales.

Horizontal analysis: A percentage analysis of the increases and decreases on the items on comparative financial statements. A horizontal financial statement analysis involves comparison of data for the current period with the same data of a company for previous periods. The percentage of increase or decrease is listed.

Indirect expenses: Operating expenses that are not directly related to the sale of your product or service.

Interest: The price charged or paid for the use of money or credit.

Inventory: The stock of goods that a business has on hand for sale to its customers.

Investment measures: Ratios used to measure an owner's earnings for his or her investment in the company. See "Return-on-investment (ROI)."

Invoice: A bill for the sale of goods or services sent by the seller to the purchaser.

Last in, first out method (LIFO): A method of valuing inventory that assumes that the last items purchased are the first items to be sold. The cost of the ending inventory is computed by using the cost of the earliest purchases.

Liabilities: Amounts owed by a business to its creditors. The debts of a business.

Liquidity: The ability of a company to meet its financial obligations. A liquidity analysis focuses on the balance sheet relationships for current assets and current liabilities.

Long-term liabilities: Liabilities that will not be due for more than a year in the future.

Mileage log: The recording of business miles travelled during an accounting period.

Modified accelerated cost recovery system (MACRS): A method of depreciation or cost recovery used for federal income tax purposes for long-term assets purchased after January 1, 1987. Under MACRS, long-term assets fall automatically into certain classes, and the costs of all assets in a class are charged to expense through a standard formula.

Net income: The amount by which revenue is greater than expenses. On an income statement this usually expressed as both a pre-tax and after-tax figure.

Net loss The amount by which expenses are greater than revenue. On an income statement this figure is usually listed as both a pre-tax and after-tax figure.

Net profit margin: The measure of a business's success with respect to earnings on sales. It is derived by dividing the net profit by sales. A higher margin means the firm is more profitable.

Net sales: Gross sales less returns and allowances and sales discounts.

Net worth: See "Owners' equity."

Note: A written promise with terms for payment of a debt.

Operating expenses: Normal expenses incurred in the running of a business.

Operating profit margin: The ratio representing the pure operations profits, ignoring interest and taxes. It is derived by dividing the income from operations by the sales. The higher the percentage of operating profit margin the better.

Other expenses: Expenses that are not directly connected with the operation of a business. The most common is interest expense.

Other income: Income that is earned from nonoperating sources. The most common is interest income.

Owners' equity: The financial interest of the owner of a business. The total of all owner equity is equal to the business's assets minus its liabilities. The owners' equity represents total investments in the business plus or minus any profits or losses the business has accrued to date.

Partnership: The form of business legal structure that is owned by two or more persons.

Personal financial history: A summary of personal financial information about the owner of a business. The personal financial history is often required by a potential lender or investor.

Petty cash fund: A cash fund from which non-check expenditures are reimbursed.

Physical inventory: The process of counting inventory on hand at the end of an accounting period. The number of units of each item is multiplied by the cost per item resulting in inventory value.

Posting: The process of transferring data from a journal to a ledger.

Prepaid expenses: Expense items that are paid for prior to their use. Some examples are insurance, rent, prepaid inventory purchases, etc.

Principal: The amount shown on the face of a note or a bond. Unpaid principal is the portion of the face amount reamining at any given time.

Profit & loss statement: See "Income statement."

Quarterly budget analysis: A method used to measure actual income and expenditures against projections for the current quarter of the financial year and for the total quarters completed. The difference is usually expressed as the amount and percentage over or under budget.

Quick ratio: A test of liquidity subtracting inventory from current assets and dividing the result by current liabilities. A quick ratio of 1.0 or greater is usually recommended.

Property, plant, and equipment: Assets such as land, buildings, vehicles and equipment that will be used for a number of years in the operation of a business and (with the exception of land) are subject to depreciation.

Ratio analysis: An analysis involving the comparison of two individual items on financial statements. One item is divided by the other and the relationship is expressed as a ratio.

Real property: Land, land improvements, buildings and other structures attached to the land.

Reconciling the bank statement: The process used to bring the bank's records, the accounts, and the business's checkbook into agreement at the end of a banking period.

Retail business: A business that sells goods and services directly to individual consumers.

Retained earnings: Earnings of a corporation that are kept in the business and not paid out in dividends. This amount represents the accumulated, undistributed profits of the corporation.

Return-on-investment (ROI): The rate of profit an investment will earn. The ROI is equal to the annual net income divided by total assets. The higher the

ROI, the better. Business owners whould should set a target for the ROI and decide what they want their investments to earn.

Revenue: The income that results from the sale of products or services or from the use of investments or property.

Revenue & expense journal: In single entry accounting, the record used to keep track of all checks written by a business and all income received for the sale of goods or services.

Salvage value: The amount that an asset can be sold for at the end of its useful life.

Service business: A business that provides services rather than products to its customers.

Single entry accounting: The term referring to a recordkeeping system which uses only income and expense accounts. Now generally used by many smaller businesses, this system is easier to maintain and understand, extremely effective and 100 percent verifiable.

Sole proprietorship: A legal structure of a business having one person as the owner.

Stockholders: Owners of a corporation whose investment is represented by shares of stock.

Stockholders' equity: The stockholders' shares of stock in a corporation plus any retained earnings.

Straight-line method of depreciation: A method of depreciating assets by allocating an equal amount of depreciation for each year of its useful life.

Sum-of-the-years'-digits method: An accelerated method of depreciation in which a fractional part of the depreciable cost of an asset is charged to expense each year. The denominator of the fraction is the sum of the numbers representing the years of the asset's useful life. The numerator is the number of years remaining in the asset's useful life.

Tangible personal property: Machinery, equipment, furniture and fixtures not attached to the land.

Three-year income projection: A pro forma (projected) income statement showing anticipated revenues and expenses for a business.

Travel record: The record used to keep track of expenses for a business-related trip away from the home business area.

Trial balance: A listing of all the accounts in the general ledger and their balances used to prove the equality of debits and credits in accounts.

Unearned income: Revenue that has been received, but not yet earned.

Variable costs: Expenses that vary in relationship to the volume of activity of a business.

Vertical analysis: A percentage analysis used to show the relationship of the components in a single financial statement. In vertical analysis of an income statement each item on the statement is expressed as a percentage of net sales.

Wholesale business: A business that sells its products to other wholesalers, retailers or volume customers at a discount.

Work in progress: Manufactured products that are only partially completed at the end of the accounting cycle.

Working capital: Current assets minus current liabilities. This is a basic measure of a company's ability to pay its current obligations.

Resources for Small Business

Anatomy of a Business Plan, 1993, Linda Pinson and Jerry Jinnett, Dearborn Financial Publishing. Will enable you to research and write your own business plan. The step-by-step format is designed to take away the mystery and help you to put together a plan that will both satisfy a lender and enable you to analyze your company and implement changes that will ensure success. Software available, see p. 172. (Softcover, 176 pp. $17.95)

Target Marketing for the Small Business, 1993, Linda Pinson and Jerry Jinnett, Upstart Publishing Co., Inc., Dover, NH. A comprehensive guide to marketing your business. This book not only shows you how to reach your customers, it also gives you a wealth of information on how to research that market through the use of library resources, questionnaires, demographics, etc. (Softcover, 176 pp., $19.95)

Steps to Small Business Start-Up, 1993, Linda Pinson and Jerry Jinnett, Upstart Publishing Co., Inc., Dover, NH. A step-by-step guide for starting and succeeding with a small or home-based business. Takes you through the mechanics of business start-up and gives an overview of information on such topics as copyrights, trademarks, legal structures recordkeeping and marketing. (Softcover, 256 pp., $19.95)

Upstart Publishing Company, Inc. These publications on proven management techniques for small businesses are available from Upstart Publishing Company, Inc., 12 Portland St., Dover, NH 03820. For a free current catalog, call (800) 235-8866 outside New Hampshire, or 749-5071 in state.

The Home-Based Entrepreneur, 1993, Linda Pinson and Jerry Jinnett, Upstart Publishing Co., Inc. A step-by-step guide to all the issues surrounding starting a home-based business. Issues such as zoning, labor laws and licensing are discussed and forms are provided to get you on your way. (Softcover, 170 pp. $19.95)

The Woman Entrepreneur, 1992, Linda Pinson and Jerry Jinnett, Upstart Publishing Co, Inc. Thirty-three successful women business owners share their practical ideas for success and their sources for inspiration. (Softcover, 244 pp., $14.00)

The Business Planning Guide, 6th edition, 1992, David H. Bangs, Jr. and Upstart Publishing Company, Inc. A manual that helps you write a business plan and financing proposal tailored to your business, your goals and your resources. Includes worksheets and checklists. (Softcover, 208 pp., $19.95)

The Market Planning Guide, 1990, David H. Bangs, Jr. and Upstart Publishing Company, Inc. A manual to help small-business owners put together a goal-oriented, resource-based marketing plan with action steps, benchmarks and time lines. Includes worksheets and checklists to make implementation and review easier. (Softcover, 160 pp., $19.95)

The Cash Flow Control Guide, 1990, David H. Bangs, Jr. and Upstart Publishing Company, Inc. A manual to help small-business owners solve their number one financial problem. Includes worksheets and checklists. (Softcover, 88 pp., $14.95)

The Personnel Planning Guide, 1988, David H. Bangs, Jr. and Upstart Publishing Company, Inc. A 176-page manual outlining practical, proven personnel management techniques, including hiring, managing, evaluating and compensating personnel. Includes worksheets and checklists. (Softcover, 176 pp., $19.95)

The Start Up Guide: A One-Year Plan for Entrepreneurs, 1989, David H. Bangs, Jr. and Upstart Publishing Company, Inc. This book utilizes the same step-by-step, no-jargon method as The *Business Planning Guide*, to help even those with no business training through the process of beginning a successful business. (Softcover, 160 pp., $19.95)

Managing By the Numbers: Financial Essentials for the Growing Business, 1992, David H. Bangs, Jr. and Upstart Publishing Company, Inc. Straightforward techniques for getting the maximum return with a minimum of detail in your business's financial management. (Softcover, 160 pp., $19.95)

On Your Own: A Women's Guide to Starting Your Own Business, Second edition, 1993, Laurie Zuckerman, Upstart Publishing Company, Inc. *On Your Own* is for women who want hands-on, practical information about starting and running your own business. It deals honestly with issues like finding time for your business when you're also the primary care provider, societal biases against women and credit discrimination. (Softcover, 320 pp., $19.95)

Buy the Right Business—At the Right Price, 1990, Brian Knight and the Associates of Country Business, Inc., Upstart Publishing Company, Inc. Many people who would like to be in business for themselves think strictly of starting a business. In some cases, buying a going concern may be preferable—and just as affordable. (Softcover, 152 pp., $18.95)

Borrowing for Your Business, 1991, George M. Dawson, Upstart Publishing Company, Inc. This is a book for borrowers and about lenders. Includes detailed guidelines on how to select a bank and a banker, how to answer the lender's seven most important questions, how your banker looks at a loan and how to get a loan renewed. (Hardcover, 160 pp., $19.95)

Problem Employees, 1991, Dr. Peter Wylie and Dr. Mardy Grothe, Upstart Publishing Company, Inc. Provides managers and supervisors with a simple, practical and straightforward approach to help all employees, especially problem employees, significantly improve their work performance. (Softcover, 272 pp., $22.95)

Other Available Titles

Marketing Sourcebook for Small Business, 1989, Jeffrey P. Davidson, John Wylie Publishing. A good introductory book for small business owners with excellent definitions of important marketing terms and concepts. (Hardcover, 325 pp., $24.95)

Guerrilla Marketing: Secrets for Making Big Profits from Your Small Business, 1984, J. Conrad Levinson, Houghton-Mifflin. A classic tool kit for small businesses. (Hardcover, 226 pp., $14.95)

Forecasting Sales and Planning Profits: A No Nonsense Guide for Growing a Business, 1986, Kenneth E. Marino, Probus Publishing Co. Concise and easily applied forecasting system based on an analysis of market potential and sale requirements, which helps establish the basis for financial statements in your business plan. Book is currently out of print, check second-hand bookstores for the title.

Periodicals

Small Business Reporter. An excellent series of booklets on small business management published by Bank of America, Department 3120, P.O. Box 37000, San Francisco, CA 94137 (415) 622-2491. Individual copies are $5 each. Ask for a list of current titles—they have about 17 available, including, *Steps to*

Starting a Business, Avoiding Management Pitfalls, Business Financing and *Marketing Small Business.*

In Business. A bimonthly magazine for small businesses, especially those with less than ten employees. The publisher is J. G. Press, P.O. Box 323, Emmaus, PA 18049. Annual subscriptions are $18.

Inc. One of the leading small business magazines. 38 Commercial Wharf, Boston, MA 02110 (617) 248-8000.

D & B Reports. Excellent case studies and updated financial information for small businesses. Dun and Bradstreet, 299 Park Ave., New York, NY 10171 (212) 593-6724.

Small Business Forum: Journal of the Association of Small Business Development Centers. Case studies and analyses of small-business problems gleaned from a nationwide network of small-business development professionals. Includes book reviews. Reprints available. Issued three times a year, $25.00 per year. University of Wisconsin, SBDC, 432 North Wake St., Madison, WI 53706.

Software

Automate Your Business Plan Software, Linda Pinson and Jerry Jinnett, Out of Your Mind . . . and Into the Marketplace, 13381 White Sand Dr., Tustin, CA 92680 (714) 544-0248, Fax (714) 730-1414. An IBM and compatible software program that prints out a finished business plan based on the formats used in *Anatomy of a Business Plan.* The program comes complete with word processor and pre-formatted and pre-formulated spreadsheets. To order call or write to the above address or use the order form on page 198 of this book.

Additional Resources

Small Business Development Centers (SBDCs). Call your state university of the Small Business Administration (SBA) to find the SBDC nearest you. Far and away the best free management program available, SBDCs provide expert assistance and training in every aspect of business management. Don't ignore this resource.

SCORE, or Service Corps of Retired Executives. Sponsored by the U.S. Small Business Administration, provides free counseling and also a series of workshops and seminars for small businesses. Of special interest: SCORE offers a Business Planning Workshop that includes a 30-minute video produced specifically for SCORE by Upstart Publishing and funded by Paychex, Inc. There are over 500 SCORE chapters nationwide. For more information, contact the SBA office nearest you and ask about SCORE.

Small Business Administration (SBA). The SBA offers a number of management assistance programs. If you are assigned a capable Management Assistance Officer, you have an excellent resource. The SBA is worth a visit, if only to leaf through their extensive literature.

Colleges and universities. Most have business courses. Some have SBDCs, others have more specialized programs. Some have small-business expertise—the University of New Hampshire, for example, has two schools that provide direct small-business management assistance.

Keye Productivity Center. Offers business seminars on specific personnel topics for a reasonable fee. Call them at (80) 821-3919 for topics and prices. Their seminar entitled *Hiring and Firing*, is excellent, well-documented and useful. Good handout materials are included. Their address is P.O. Box 23192, Kansas City, MO 64141.

Comprehensive Accounting Corporation. They have over 425 franchised offices providing accounting, bookkeeping and management consulting services to small businesses. For information call, (800) 323-9009, or write 2111 Comprehensive Drive, Aurora, IL 60507.

Center for Entrepreneurial Management. The oldest and largest nonprofit membership association for small-business owners in the world. They maintain an extensive list of books, videotapes, cassettes and other small-business management aids. Their address is: 29 Greene Street, New York, NY 10013, (212) 925-7304.

Libraries. Do not forget to take advantage of the information readily available at your local library.

APPENDIX

III

Worksheets

These blank forms and worksheets are for you to fill out and use.

BEGINNING JOURNAL

Date	1. Check # 2. Cash 3. C/Card	Paid To or Received From	Explanation of Income or Expense	Income		Expense	
Total Income and Expenses							

GENERAL JOURNAL

GENERAL JOURNAL				Page____

DATE	DESCRIPTION OF ENTRY	POST. REF.	DEBIT	CREDIT
199_				

GENERAL LEDGER ACCOUNT

ACCOUNT _____   ACCOUNT NO. _____

DATE	DESCRIPTION OF ENTRY	POST. REF.	DEBIT	CREDIT	BALANCE	DR. CR.
19 __						

REVENUE & EXPENSE JOURNAL

Month: _____ 19___, page ___

—— Customize these headings to match the business ——→

CHECK NO.	DATE	TRANSACTION	REVENUE	EXPENSE								MISC.
		Balance forward----										
		TOTALS										

PETTY CASH RECORD

PETTY CASH - 19___					Page___	
DATE	PAID TO WHOM	EXPENSE ACCOUNT DEBITED	DEPOSIT	AMOUNT OF EXPENSE	BALANCE	
	BALANCE FORWARD					

INVENTORY RECORD
IDENTIFIABLE STOCK

WHOLESALER:_____   Page____

PURCH. DATE	INVENTORY PURCHASED		PURCH. PRICE	DATE SOLD	SALE PRICE	NAME OF BUYER (Optional)
	Stock #	Description				

INVENTORY RECORD
NON-IDENTIFIABLE STOCK

DEPARTMENT/CATEGORY: _____

PRODUCTION OR PURCHASE DATE	INVENTORY PURCHASED OR MANUFACTURED		NUMBER OF UNITS	UNIT COST		VALUE ON DATE OF INVENTORY (Unit Cost X Units on Hand)	
	Stock #	Description				Value	Date

FIXED ASSETS LOG

COMPANY NAME: _____

ASSET PURCHASED	DATE PLACED IN SERVICE	COST OF ASSET	% USED FOR BUSINESS	RECOVERY PERIOD	METHOD OF DEPRECIATION	DEPRECIATION PREVIOUSLY ALLOWED	DATE SOLD	SALE PRICE

ACCOUNTS RECEIVABLE
ACCOUNT RECORD

CUSTOMER: _____

ADDRESS: _____

_____

TEL. NO: _____ ACCOUNT NO._____

INVOICE DATE	INVOICE NO.	INVOICE AMOUNT		TERMS	DATE PAID	AMOUNT PAID		INVOICE BALANCE	

ACCOUNTS PAYABLE
ACCOUNT RECORD

CREDITOR: _____

ADDRESS: _____

_____

TEL. NO: _____   ACCOUNT NO._____

INVOICE DATE	INVOICE NO.	INVOICE AMOUNT	TERMS	DATE PAID	AMOUNT PAID	INVOICE BALANCE

MILEAGE LOG

NAME: _____

DATED: From_____To_____

DATE	CITY OF DESTINATION	NAME OR OTHER DESIGNATION	BUSINESS PURPOSE	NO. OF MILES

		TOTAL MILES THIS SHEET	

ENTERTAINMENT EXPENSE RECORD

NAME: _____

DATED: From_____To_____

DATE	PLACE OF ENTERTAINMENT	BUSINESS PURPOSE	NAME OF PERSON ENTERTAINED	AMOUNT SPENT	

TRAVEL RECORD

TRIP TO: _____ To: _____

Dated From: _____

Business Purpose: _____

No. Days Spent on Business _____

| DATE | LOCATION | EXPENSE PAID TO | MEALS | | | HOTEL | TAXIS, ETC. | AUTOMOBILE | | | MISC. EXP. |
			Breakfast	Lunch	Dinner	Miscell.			Gas	Parking	Tolls	
TOTALS →												

BALANCE SHEET

COMPANY NAME: _____

Date: _____ ___, 19___

ASSETS

Current Assets

Cash $ _____

Petty Cash $ _____

Accounts Receivable $ _____

Inventory $ _____

Short-Term Investments $ _____

Prepaid Expenses $ _____

Long-Term Investments $ _____

Fixed Assets

Land (valued at cost) $ _____

Buildings $ _____
1. Cost _____
2. Less Acc. Depr. _____

Improvements $ _____
1. Cost _____
2. Less Acc. Depr. _____

Equipment $ _____
1. Cost _____
2. Less Acc. Depr. _____

Furniture $ _____
1. Cost _____
2. Less Acc. Depr. _____

Autos/Vehicles $ _____
1. Cost _____
2. Less Acc. Depr. _____

Other Assets
1. $ _____
2. $ _____

TOTAL ASSETS $ _____

LIABILITIES

Current Liabilities

Accounts Payable $ _____

Notes Payable $ _____

Interest Payable $ _____

Taxes Payable
Fed. Inc. Tax $ _____
State Inc. Tax $ _____
Self-Emp. Tax $ _____
Sales Tax Accrual $ _____
Property Tax $ _____

Payroll Accrual $ _____

Long-Term Liabilities
Notes Payable $ _____

TOTAL LIABILITIES $ _____

NET WORTH

Proprietorship $ _____
or
Partnership
(Name's) Equity $ _____
(Name's) Equity $ _____
or
Corporation
Capital Stock $ _____
Surplus Paid In $ _____
Retained Earnings $ _____

TOTAL NET WORTH $ _____

Assets - Liabilities = Net Worth

Total Liabilities and Equity will always be equal to Total Assets

PROFIT & LOSS STATEMENT (INCOME STATEMENT)

Company Name: _____

FOR THE YEAR 19___.	JAN	FEB	MAR	APR	MAY	JUN	JUL	AUG	SEP	OCT	NOV	DEC	YEAR TOTAL
INCOME													
1. NET SALES (Gross less ret. & allow.)													
2. COST OF GOODS SOLD (c. - d.)													
a. Beginning Inventory													
b. Purchases													
c. C.O.G. Available for Sale (a+b)													
d. Less End. Inv. (Dec. 31st)													
3. GROSS PROFIT ON SALES (1. minus 2.)													
EXPENSES													
1. VARIABLE (Selling/Direct Exp.) (a. thru h.)													
a.													
b.													
c.													
d.													
e.													
f.													
g.													
h. Miscell. Selling Exp.													
2. FIXED (Administrative/Indirect) (a. thru h.)													
a.													
b.													
c.													
d.													
e.													
f.													
g.													
h. Miscell. Overhead													
TOTAL OPERATING EXPENSE (Variable+Fixed)													
NET INCOME FROM OPERATIONS (Gross Profit less Operating Expense)													
OTHER INCOME (INTEREST)													
OTHER EXPENSE (INTEREST)													
NET PROFIT (LOSS) BEFORE INCOME TAXES													
TAXES (Federal, Self-Employment, State)													
NET PROFIT (LOSS) AFTER TAXES													

PROFIT & LOSS (INCOME) STATEMENT

COMPANY NAME: _____

For the period beginning _____ and ending _____

INCOME		
1. NET SALES (Gross less ret. & allow.)		
2. COST OF GOODS SOLD (c. minus d.)		
a. Beginning Inventory		
b. Purchases		
c. C.O.G. Available for Sale (a+b)		
d. Less End. Inv. (Dec. 31st)		
3. GROSS PROFIT ON SALES (1 minus 2)		
EXPENSES		
1. VARIABLE (Selling/Direct) (a. thru h.)		
a.		
b.		
c.		
d.		
e.		
f.		
g.		
h. Miscellaneous		
2. FIXED (Administrative/Indirect) (a. thru h.)		
a.		
b.		
c.		
d.		
e.		
f.		
g.		
h. Miscellaneous		
TOTAL OPERATING EXPENSE (1 + 2)		
NET INCOME FROM OPERATIONS (Gross Profit less Total Op. Exp.)		
OTHER INCOME (INTEREST)		
OTHER EXPENSE (INTEREST)		
NET PROFIT (LOSS) BEFORE INCOME TAXES		
TAXES (Federal, Self-Employment, State)		
NET PROFIT (LOSS) AFTER TAXES		

CASH TO BE PAID OUT WORKSHEET
(CASH FLOWING OUT OF THE BUSINESS)

1. START-UP COSTS
   a. Business License $ _____
   b. Corporation Filing   _____
   c. Legal Fees   _____
   d. Other start-up costs:

   _____   _____
   _____   _____
   _____   _____

2. INVENTORY PURCHASES
   Cash out for goods intended for resale   _____

3. VARIABLE EXPENSES (SELLING/DIRECT)
   a. $ _____
   b.   _____
   c.   _____
   d.   _____
   e.   _____
   f.   _____
   g. Miscell. Selling Expense   _____
   TOTAL SELLING EXPENSES   _____

4. FIXED EXPENSES (ADMINISTRATIVE/INDIRECT)
   a. $ _____
   b.   _____
   c.   _____
   d.   _____
   e.   _____
   f.   _____
   Miscell. Admin. Expense   _____
   TOTAL OPERATING EXPENSE   _____

5. ASSETS (LONG-TERM PURCHASES)
   Cash to be paid out in current period   _____

6. LIABILITIES
   Cash outlay for retiring debts, loans
   and/or accounts payable   _____

7. OWNER EQUITY
   Cash to be withdrawn by owner   _____

TOTAL CASH TO BE PAID OUT $ _____

SOURCES OF CASH WORKSHEET

(CASH FLOWING INTO THE BUSINESS)

1. CASH ON HAND $ _____

2. SALES (REVENUES)

Sales Income   _____

Services Income   _____

Deposits on Sales or Services   _____

Collections on Accounts Receivable   _____

3. MISCELLANEOUS INCOME

Interest Income   _____

Payments to be Received on Loans   _____

4. SALE OF LONG-TERM ASSETS   _____

5. LIABILITIES   _____

Loan Funds (To be received during period
from banks, SBA and other lending institutions)

6. EQUITY

Owner Investments (Sole Prop/Partners)   _____

Contributed Capital (Corporation)   _____

Sale of Stock (Corporation)   _____

Venture Capital   _____

TOTAL CASH AVAILABLE: **A.** *Without Sales* $ _____

B. *With Sales* $ _____

PRO FORMA CASH FLOW STATEMENT

Company Name: _____

FOR THE YEAR 19___	TOTAL	JAN	FEB	MAR	APR	MAY	JUN	JUL	AUG	SEP	OCT	NOV	DEC
BEGINNING CASH BALANCE													
CASH RECEIPTS													
a. Sales revenues (Cash sales)													
b. Receivables to be collected													
c. Interest income													
d. Sale of long-term assets													
TOTAL CASH AVAILABLE													
CASH PAYMENTS													
a. Cost of goods to be sold													
1. Purchases													
2. Material													
3. Labor													
b. Variable expenses (Selling, Direct)													
1.													
2.													
3.													
4.													
5.													
6.													
7. Miscellaneous Variable Expenses													
c. Fixed expenses (Administrative, Indirect)													
1.													
2.													
3.													
4.													
5.													
6.													
7. Miscellaneous Fixed Expenses													
d. Interest expense													
e. Federal income tax													
f. Other uses													
g. Payments on long-term assets													
h. Loan payments													
i. Owner draws													
TOTAL CASH PAID OUT													
CASH BALANCE/DEFICIENCY													
LOANS TO BE RECEIVED													
EQUITY DEPOSITS													
ENDING CASH BALANCE													

QUARTERLY BUDGET ANALYSIS

Company Name: _____

For the Quarter Ending _____, 19 ____ *YTD = year-to-date

BUDGET ITEM	BUDGET THIS QUARTER	ACTUAL THIS QUARTER	VARIATION THIS QUARTER	YTD BUDGET	ACTUAL YTD	VARIATION YTD
SALES REVENUES						
Less Cost of Goods						
GROSS PROFIT						
VARIABLE EXPENSES						
1.						
2.						
3.						
4.						
5.						
6.						
7. Miscellaneous						
FIXED EXPENSES						
1.						
2.						
3.						
4.						
5.						
6.						
7. Miscellaneous						
NET INCOME FROM OPERATIONS						
INTEREST INCOME						
INTEREST EXPENSE						
NET PROFIT (LOSS) BEFORE TAXES						
TAXES						
NET PROFIT (LOSS) AFTER TAXES						
NON-INCOME STATEMENT ITEMS						
1. L-Term Asset Repay'ts						
2. Loan Repayments						
3. Owner Draws						

Budget Deviation: 1. Current Quarter = $_____ 2. Year-To-Date= $_____

THREE-YEAR
INCOME PROJECTION

FOR THE YEARS 19____, 19____ AND 19____.	YEAR 1	YEAR 2	YEAR 3
INCOME			
1. NET SALES (Gross less returns & allow.)			
2. COST OF GOODS SOLD (c. minus d.)			
a. Beginning Inventory			
b. Purchases			
c. C.O.G. Available for Sale (a+b)			
d. Less End. Inv. (Dec. 31st)			
3. GROSS PROFIT ON SALES (1 minus 2)			
EXPENSES			
1. VARIABLE (Direct/Selling) (a. thru h.)			
a.			
b.			
c.			
d.			
e.			
f.			
g. Miscellaneous Selling Exp.			
h. Depreciation (Product/Services Assets)			
2. FIXED (Indirect/Administrative) (a. thru h.)			
a.			
b.			
c.			
d.			
e.			
f.			
g. Miscell. Administrative Expense			
h. Depreciation (Office Equipment)			
TOTAL OPERATING EXPENSES (Variable+Fixed)			
NET INCOME FROM OPERATIONS (Gross Profit less Expenses)			
OTHER INCOME (INTEREST)			
OTHER EXPENSE (INTEREST)			
NET PROFIT (LOSS) BEFORE INCOME TAXES			
TAXES (Federal, Self-Employment, State)			
NET PROFIT (LOSS) AFTER TAXES			

BREAK-EVEN ANALYSIS

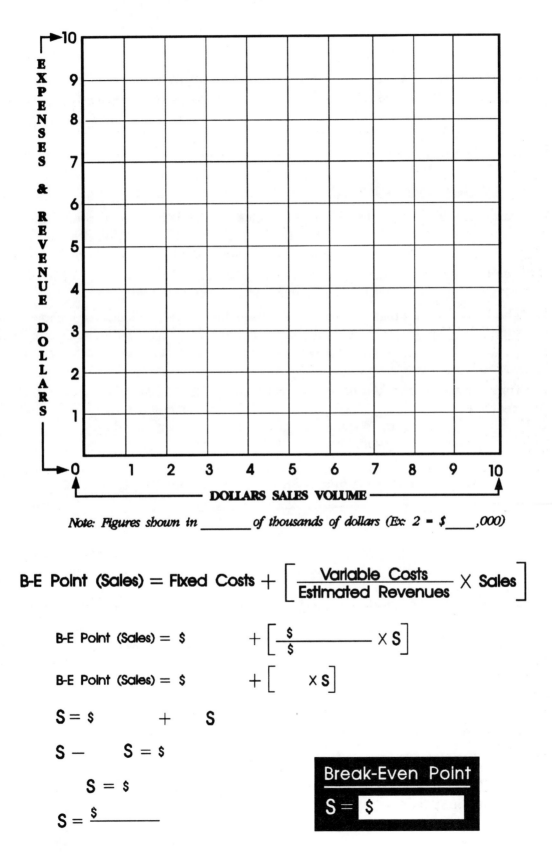

Note: Figures shown in _____ of thousands of dollars (Ex: 2 = $____,000)

B-E Point (Sales) = Fixed Costs + $\left[\dfrac{\text{Variable Costs}}{\text{Estimated Revenues}} \times \text{Sales}\right]$

B-E Point (Sales) = $ + $\left[\dfrac{\$}{\$}\rule{2cm}{0.4pt} \times S\right]$

B-E Point (Sales) = $ + $\left[\ \ \times S\right]$

S = $ +   S

S −   S = $

S = $

S = $\dfrac{\$}{\rule{2cm}{0.4pt}}$

Break-Even Point

S = $

AUTOMATE YOUR BUSINESS PLAN

Companion Software to
"Anatomy of a Business Plan"

Technical Requirements:

- IBM PC, AT, or 100% compatible computer
- No Hard Drive Needed, No Other Software Needed
- 640K of Internal memory
- PCDOS/MSDOS version 2.0 or higher
- Any standard PC compatible printer

THREE PROGRAMS IN ONE

1. "Automate Your Business Plan" will guide you step by step through the business planning process, calculate your spreadsheets, provide a working draft and print out a finished plan that will serve as your business guide and satisfy your lender.

2. The text editor can also be used in the stand-alone mode. It is a full-featured word processor including pull down menus and context sensitive help.

3. The spreadsheet program can also be used for other applications. You can create additional spreadsheets that might be helpful in the operation of your business. While it is not as expansive as larger programs, it is very easy to learn and should serve all your needs.

4. Text created within "Automate Your Business Plan" is standard ASCII text. That means you can readily incorporate business plans created using "Automate Your Business Plan" into documents produced by other word processors such as WordPerfect or Microsoft Word.

5. The companion book, "Anatomy of a Business Plan" is included free with the software. The authors were selected by the SBA in Washington, D.C. to write the new official business plan publication, "How to Write a Business Plan" (to be released soon), based on this book, which has been used extensively in colleges and libraries.

ORDER TODAY
(JUST FILL IN THE ORDER BLANK BELOW)

**AUTOMATE YOUR BUSINESS PLAN
& ANATOMY OF BUSINESS PLAN**
Software & Text Pkg. @ $95.00 _____

**California Residents please
add 7¾% sales tax** _____

Shipping Fees $4.50

Next Day Air Express $21.00 _____

2nd Day Air Express $12.00 _____

Total Amount Due $ _____

Prices Effective March 1993

NAME_____

ADDRESS_____

CITY _____

STATE_____ ZIP_____

TELEPHONE_____

Make Check or Money Order Payable To:

**OUT OF YOUR MIND...
AND INTO THE MARKETPLACE™**
13381 White Sand Drive
Tustin, CA 92680
Telephone: (714) 544-0248

Index

1612